D. H. LAWRENCE: *An Eastern View*

OTHER BOOKS BY CHAMAN NAHAL

The Weird Dance (Short Stories)
A Conversation with J. Krishnamurti

D. H. LAWRENCE:
An Eastern View

Chaman Nahal

"Lawrence was a Yogi who had missed his way and come into a European body to work out his difficulties."
—Sri Aurobindo

South Brunswick and New York: A. S. Barnes and Company
London: Thomas Yoseloff Ltd

A. S. Barnes and Co., Inc.
Cranbury, New Jersey 08512

Thomas Yoseloff Ltd
108 New Bond Street
London W1Y OQX, England

ISBN 0-498-07720-9
Printed in the United States of America

For

ROBERT H. PARRY

(in praise of Wales)
Caraf ei morfa a'i mynyddedd
A'i chaer ger ei choed a'i chain diredd,
A dolydd ei dwfr a'i dyffrynnedd.
— Hywel ab Owain Gwynedd
d.1170

Contents

8   D. H. Lawrence: An Eastern View

Foreword

I have enjoyed reading Dr. Chaman Nahal's book, because of his quick-witted, warm-hearted and highly intelligent approach to D. H. Lawrence. Dr. Nahal has a wide knowledge of the whole range of English literature, especially of the modern period; he also knows a great deal about the literature and culture of his own country. The book is particularly interesting because of the thoughtful and stimulating comparisons which Dr. Nahal draws between various aspects of Eastern and Western thought. It certainly throws light on aspects of Lawrence that have been dismissed by most Western critics as heretical.

Worthing, U. K.   Vivian de Sola Pinto
1969

Preface

It has taken me about ten years to complete this study and see it safely in the hands of my publisher. In its initial form the work was done at Nottingham, U.K., during a two-year stay, from 1959 to 1961, sponsored by the British Council, to which body I shall be ever grateful for the financial and moral support it gave me in those critical years. Later it was continued at Delhi, my home university, and finally at Princeton University, where I have been a visiting teacher since 1967.

During this long time, I have had the benefit of advice from several friends at different stages. But the finest encouragement all along came from Robert H. Parry, whom I first met in a formal capacity as an officer of the British Council, but who later gave me his friendship and whose family home in North Wales has since become a second home for me. In the Nottingham years, the manuscript was carefully read over by Professor Vivian de Sola Pinto, who made innumerable useful suggestions. It is sad that Professor Pinto died last year and was unable to see the book in print. But both Professor Pinto and his wife, Mrs. Irène de Sola Pinto, have been a source of much strength to me over the years. The typescript in its final stages was read by my friend Nirad C. Chaudhuri, the Indian writer, whose challenging criticism helped me see a good many things in a fresh perspective. Sections of the book were also seen by my colleague at Princeton, Professor A. Walton Litz, who made several stimulating comments on the subject of the book. To these persons I remain much indebted.

Others who were not directly associated with the preparation but helped me with the vaster process of life during the same period, and thus were instrumental in their own way in getting the book completed, include R. S. Azad, Carlos H. Baker, P. E. Dustoor, V. V. John, Frank Moraes, M. Mujeeb, Felisa Nunez, S. C. V. Stetner, and Eleanore Weed. Such expression of appreciation to friends unconnected with the work in question is not usually recorded, but I do not see how the business of doing serious work and living one's life can really be separated.

My special thanks go to my two lovely daughters, Ajanta and Anita Nahal, who dutifully checked the text of each quotation in the book and compared it with the original. The index was prepared by my wife, Sudarshna Nahal, who also corrected the proofs with me, and to whom my gratitude is profound and many-sided.

The proofs were also read for me by Dorothy and Datus C. Smith, Jr., knowing whom has been one of the great privileges of our stay in Princeton. Datus Smith has been a remarkable publisher as the former Director of Princeton University Press, and he and his wife are highly receptive to different cultures. Datus Smith in particular has shown a lively interest in the book for quite some time, and I think its publication will give him as much satisfaction as it gives me.

A final acknowledgment must be made to libraries, without whose help no scholarly project can ever be undertaken. In this context I should like to mention Delhi University Library; Nottingham University Library; City Library, Nottingham; St. Deiniol's Library, Hawarden, Wales; The British Museum; Sri Aurobindo Study Circle, London; and Firestone Library, Princeton, where I received invaluable assistance. Permission to examine and to quote from the unpublished papers of the late William Hopkin was given to me by Mrs. Olive L. Hopkin when

I was in Nottingham and I am grateful to her for the courtesy.

A word about the make-up of the chapters. Each large chapter is divided into two parts. The first proposes a line of reasoning, based on my assessment of what Lawrence thought and what he was trying to do in his art. The second applies that line of reasoning to Lawrence's creative works and offers a reading of them.

I have not appended a bibliography, as the practice has become somewhat superfluous. Compiling a bibliography of a major author is a subject in itself these days, and there seems little point in duplicating in critical works materials that exist in easily accessible forms elsewhere. I have given only a list of books to which I have actually made a reference in my study. For biographical details on Lawrence the reader is referred to the three volumes of Edward Nehls' *D. H. Lawrence: A Composite Biography* and for bibliographical information to *A Bibliography of D. H. Lawrence* compiled by Warren Roberts. This standard "Soho Bibliography" was published in 1963. Of the new books that have appeared since, details can be seen in the annual bibliographies issued by the *PMLA*, which continue to be the primary source of most new listings. Another valuable guide to new work on Lawrence is *The D. H. Lawrence Review*, a journal ably edited by James C. Cowan of the University of Arkansas.

Princeton, N. J.   Chaman Nahal
1970

Acknowledgments

Acknowledgment is made with thanks by the author to:
Arya Book Depot, New Delhi, for permission to quote
from my book *A Conversation with J. Krishnamurti.*

Sri Aurobindo Ashram, Pondicherry, India, for permission to quote from the works of Sri Aurobindo.

The Estate of the late Mrs. Frieda Lawrence Ravagli;
Laurence Pollinger, Ltd.; and Messrs. William Heinemann, Ltd., London; for permission to quote from the
copyrighted works of D. H. Lawrence.

Harper and Row, New York, and Victor Gollancz, Ltd.,
London, for permission to quote from J. Krishnamurti's
The First and Last Freedom, Commentaries on Living
and *Commentaries on Living, Second Series.*

Alfred A. Knopf, Inc., New York, for permission to quote
from the copyrighted works of D. H. Lawrence.

Quest, Bombay, for permission to reprint my article "Lawrence and *Lady Chatterley's Lover:* the Chronicle of 'Battered Warriors.' "

The University Library, Nottingham, for permission to
quote from the manuscript material on D. H. Lawrence
in its possession.

The Viking Press, Inc., New York, for permission to quote
from the following works of D. H. Lawrence: *Sons and
Lovers,* Copyright 1913 by Thomas Seltzer, Inc.; *The
Rainbow,* Copyright 1915 by David Herbert Lawrence,
renewed 1943 by Frieda Lawrence; *Women in Love,* Copyright 1920, 1922 by David Herbert Lawrence, renewed
1948, 1950 by Frieda Lawrence; *Aaron's Rod,* Copyright
1922 by Thomas Seltzer, Inc., renewed 1950 by Frieda
Lawrence; *Kangaroo,* Copyright 1923 by Thomas Seltzer,

D. H. LAWRENCE: *An Eastern View*

1

An Eastern View

D. H. Lawrence was all his life attracted by India, particularly by Hindu philosophy. It is true that occasionally we have from him statements like this one made in 1916:

> I become more and more surprised to see how far higher, in reality, our European civilisation stands than the East, Indian and Persian, ever dreamed of. And one is glad to *realise* how these Hindus are horribly decadent and reverting to all sorts of barbarism in all sorts of ugly ways. We feel surer on our feet, then. But this fraud of looking up to them —this wretched worship-of-Tagore attitude—is disgusting. 'Better fifty years of Europe' even as she is. Buddha-worship is completely decadent and foul nowadays: and it *was* always only half civilised. *Tant pour l'Asie:* it is ridiculous to look to the East for inspiration.[1]

Or, there is this, in 1922:

> No, the East doesn't get me at all. Its boneless suavity, and the thick, choky feel of tropical forest, and the metallic sense of palms and the horrid noises of the birds and creatures, who hammer and clang and rattle and cackle and explode all the livelong day, and run little machines all the livelong night; and the scents that make me feel sick, the perpetual nauseous overtone of cocoanut and cocoanut fibre and oil, the sort of tropical sweetness which to me suggests an undertang of blood, hot blood, and thin sweat; the undertaste of blood and sweat in the nauseous tropical fruits; the nasty faces and the yellow robes of the Buddhist monks, the little vulgar dens of the temples: all this makes up Ceylon to me, and all this I cannot bear.[2]

But these passages are not representative of his views. The former comment was prompted by Manucci's *History of the Mogul Dynasty in India*—a record of life at a Muslim court, it describes the Hindus in an unfavorable manner—which he had just read, and the latter by the impressions that he had hastily gathered in the course of a month spent in Ceylon. When much later he had himself gone through the philosophical thought of the country, his considered opinion in 1925 was: "That seems to me the true psychology, how shallow and groping it makes Western psychology seem."[3]

In this book, however, I do not intend to bring out Lawrence's admiration for Hindu thought. Earl Brewster's *D. H. Lawrence, Reminiscences and Correspondence* is full of references to this effect, and William York Tindall in *D. H. Lawrence and Susan His Cow* lists in detail the books of Hinduism that Lawrence had read and the number of times mention of India or Indian characters is made in his works (see particularly pp. 148–53). In spite of all that Brewster and Tindall say, my idea, on the contrary, is that Lawrence's acquaintance with the real (Scriptural) Hindu thought was very meager. He was perhaps familiar with some of the Vedic hyms, as the following letter to Brewster shows: "I was disappointed in 'D. G.' I am never very fond of abstract poetry, not even Blake. And the theme of this I prefer in the old hymns and Vedas, in the original, when it had a quivering which is gone here. . . . One can't put the mystery of Oriental philosophy . . . in a rather brief, rhyming poem."[4] But it is doubtful whether he ever read the Upanishads, the closing sections of the Vedas, which epitomize the depth of Hindu thought, or that he ever made a serious study of the Vedic hymns in a consolidated form. He has left a careful record of most of the books that he went through in the course of his life and the Vedas and the Upanishads are never listed by him by title anywhere. He definitely wanted to go to India, but his desire never materialized. Whatever knowledge of Hinduism he came to acquire was through volumes on Hinduism, not directly through the Scriptures.

So it is not suggested here that Lawrence was influenced by Hinduism to any considerable extent. He was a product of the Christian tradition and though, in the course of his long fight with Christianity, he rose above its conventional teachings and put forward views radically opposed to it, he continued to belong to the heritage of his own civilization. The object of this work is something different. It is to bring out the deep affinities, irrespective of what Lawrence might or might not have known of Hinduism, that exist between Lawrence's approach to life and the approach to life as signified in the Vedas. While attempting to do this, it is my premise, of course, that Lawrence's art can be appreciated better, can be understood and assimilated better, if it is analyzed through a parallel body of thought having an outlook similar to his own, through a body of thought in which his views and concepts will be accepted as genuine and reliable and not classified as "heretical." For a critic brought up in the Christian faith can only end up with a final "but" while assessing Lawrence's work, in which—if the critic is a Christian—he must offer some sort of compromise to adjust Lawrence against Christianity. Lawrence had rejected Christianity and did not change his position throughout his creative career. In the following chapters we discuss at length the grounds on which he did so. But it must be seen here that when an artist of such a fundamentally non-Christian outlook on life is evaluated by a critic belonging to that faith, the critic in the end must either reject Christianity or reject Lawrence (see discussion later). As I said in a paper read before the Nottingham Mechanics Institution in 1960, "If D. H. Lawrence is accepted, Christianity has to be modified"; and this is something no Christian critic can accept. And as far as my reading goes, there appears to be no specific non-Christian attempt to assess Lawrence's work till this date.

What is therefore aimed at here is a discussion of Lawrence's creative output as judged by, or as compared with, the Vedic view of life in India. Let me hasten to add that Hinduism is a religion about five thousand years old. During the course of this long history a number of new developments took place in the main body of the religion, which to some extent changed the various details in the new schools that sprang up. We shall not take those developments into account, but shall confine ourselves to the Vedas alone. On the basis of the affinities as seen there, we shall then analyze Lawrence's work.

The first remarkable feature of Hindu philosophy that we should begin with is that it thinks of man as one of the living forms of life, and measures him and philosophizes about him *not* in isolation but in relation to the other forms of life and in relation to the rest of the universe. In the early Vedic hymns as collected in the *Rig Veda*, there are songs in praise of almost every phenomenon of nature—hymns addressed to the dawn, to the sun, to the waters, to air, to fire, to speech, to night, and so on. And one notices that almost all these songs are songs of praise and wonder, songs of awe.

To give an illustration of the spirit of these hymns, here is one of them in full: the hymn entitled "The Song of Creation."

> Then was not non-existent nor existent: there was
>   no realm of air, no sky beyond it.
> What covered in, and where? and what gave shelter?
>   Was water there, unfathomed depth of water?
>
> Death was not then, nor was there aught immortal: no
>   sign was there, the day's and night's divider.
> That one thing, breathless, breathed by its own nature:
>   apart from it was nothing whatsoever.

Darkness there was: at first concealed in darkness, this
  All was indiscriminated chaos.
All that existed then was void and formless: by the
  great power of warmth was born that unit.

Thereafter rose desire in the beginning, Desire, the
  primal seed and germ of spirit.
Sages who searched with their heart's thought discovered
  the existent's kinship in the non-existent.

Transversely was their severing line extended: what was
  above it then, and what below it?
There were begetters, there were mighty forces, free
  action here and energy up yonder.

Who verily knows and who can here declare it, whence it
  was born and whence comes this creation?
The gods are later than this world's production. Who
  knows, then, whence it first came into being?

He, the first origin of this creation, whether he formed
  it all or did not form it,
Whose eye controls this world in highest heaven, he
  verily knows it, or perhaps he knows not.[5]

The inquiring and the daring, vitality of these early
seers of Hindu thought is clearly noticeable from the
last two stanzas of this hymn, where we see that the mind
refuses to acknowledge any absolute values. It is a rational
and yet faith-filled outlook that these hymns portray; a
particular object or phenomenon is looked at, its beauty
and power are described, and yet no attempt is made to
solve its mystery; the mystery is rather accepted as a
symbol of its own separate entity, with its own life and
relevance. In addition, in almost all these hymns, invoca-
tions are made that these powers of nature may accept man
as one of them—as a member into a much bigger family—
and be kind to him and further his well-being, Thus this
invocation to *Agni* (Fire) :

> Ruler of sacrifices, guard of law eternal, radiant one,
> Increasing in thine own abode.

Be to us easy of approach, even as a father to his son;
Agni, be with us for our weal.[6]

And to *Surya* (The Sun):

His bright rays bear him up aloft, the god who knoweth
all that lives,
Surya, that all may look on him.

The constellations pass away, like thieves, together
with their beams,
Before the all-beholding Sun.

His herald rays are seen afar refulgent o'er the world
of men,
Like flames of fire that burn and blaze.

Swift and all beautiful art thou, O *Surya*, maker of
the light,
Illuming all the radiant realm.[7]

To Dawn:

The fair, the bright is come with her white offspring;
to her the dark one hath resigned her dwelling.
Akin, immortal, following each other, changing their
colours, both the heavens move onward.

Singing the praises of refulgent mornings with his hymn's
web, the priest, the poet, rises.
Shine then today, rich maid, on him who lauds thee,
shine down on us the gift of life and offspring.[8]

To the Waters:

Forth from the middle of the flood the Waters—their
chief the sea—flow cleansing, never sleeping.
Indra, the bull, the thunderer, dug their channels;
here let these Waters, goddesses, protect me.

Waters which come from heaven, or those that wander
dug from the earth, or flowing free by nature,
Bright, purifying, speeding to the ocean; here let
those Waters, goddesses, protect me.[9]

To Night:

> With all her eyes the goddess Night looks forth
>   approaching many a spot;
> She hath put all her glories on.
>
> Immortal, she hath filled the waste, the goddess
>   hath filled height and depth:
> She conquers darkness with her light.[10]

And to *Vayu* (Air):

> Travelling on the paths of air's mid-region, no
>   single day doth he take rest or slumber.
> Holy and earliest-born, friend of the waters,
>   where did he spring and from what region came he?
>
> Germ of the world, the deities' vital spirit, this
>   god moves ever as his will inclines him.
> His voice is heard, his shape is ever viewless. Let
>   us adore this Wind with our oblation.[11]

There are also hymns addressed to the various gods by name: to Varuna (king of the air and of the sea), to Indra (god of thunder), to Vishnu (god of the heavens), and to many others. It was necessary to quote passages from some of them to explain our term of reference here: man's intimate relationship with the rest of the universe. For it should be clear from the extracts cited that there was no tragedy of the divided soul for the early Hindu mind, and that the Vedic thinkers saw the presence of the divine in everything.

This then is the first great affinity that we find between Lawrence and the Vedic thought: reverence for life— reverence not for man alone, but for all life, man being only a part of it. The importance of this concept is discussed in the next chapter, where it is explained how Lawrence in his creative work conceived of a like love for the actual process of living. But the following from his essay "Aristocracy" is illustrative of how he marks man in his proper place in the vast universe in which he lives, and how to him this alone—acceptance of this attitude—can enable man to breathe to the utmost the life force in and around him:

Man is great according as his relation to the living universe is vast and vital.

Men are related to men: including women: and this, of course, is very important. But one would think it were everything. One would think, to read modern books, that the life of any tuppenny bank clerk was more important than sun, moon, and stars; and to read the pert drivel of the critics, one would be led to imagine that every three-farthing whipper-snapper who lifts up his voice in approval or censure were the thrice-greatest Hermes speaking in judgment out of the mysteries.

This is the democratic age of cheap clap-trap, and it sits in jackdaw judgment on all greatness.

And this is the result of making, in our own conceit, man the measure of the universe. Don't you be taken in. The universe, so vast and profound, measures man up very accurately, for the yelping mongrel with his tail between his legs, that he is. And the great sun, and the moon, with a smile will soon start dropping the mongrel down the vast refuse-pit of oblivion. Oh, the universe has a terrible hole in the middle of it, an oubliette for all of you, whipper-snappering mongrels.

Man, of course, being measure of the universe, is measured only against man. Has, of course, vital relationship only with his own cheap little species. Hence the cheap little twaddler he has become.

In the great ages, man had vital relation with man, with woman: and beyond that, with the cow, the lion, the bull, the cat, the eagle, the beetle, the serpent. And beyond these, with narcissus and anemone, mistletoe and oak-tree, myrtle, olive, and lotus. And beyond these with humus and slanting water, cloud-towers and rainbow and the sweeping sun-limbs. And beyond that, with sun, and moon, the living night and the living day.[12]

Lawrence believed that when a man lived in harmony with the rest of nature, he extracted something from it and made himself a more powerful man (Wordsworth and Lawrence are very close to each other in this). His emphasis on the word "power" (as developed in novels like *Aaron's Rod, Kangaroo,* and *The Plumed Serpent*) has been sadly abused by some of his readers to imply autocracy, or bullying authority of one person over the other. What Lawrence had in mind when he talked of power was openness to the rest of the known life, and openness equally to the unknown. He himself defines the word in "Blessed are the Powerful." Before doing so, he states: "It isn't bossing or bullying, hiring a manservant or Salvationising your social inferior, issuing loud orders and getting your own way, doing your opponent down. That isn't power."[13] And then the definition comes: "Power is *pouvoir*: to be able to."[14] And the ability to do or accomplish a thing comes to man in direct proportion to his respect for the unknown mystery as seen in every particle of the universe. As Lawrence explains a little later in the same essay:

> However smart we be, however rich and clever or loving or charitable or spiritual or impeccable, it doesn't help us at all. The real power comes in to us from beyond. Life enters us from behind, where we are sightless, and from below, where we do not understand.

> And unless we yield to the beyond, and take our power and might and honour and glory from the unseen, from the unknown, we shall continue empty.[15]

This leads to a very important conclusion, which should be set down now. Where Reality ever is, where every moment is supposed to be a direct representation of the Eternal, where whatever one sees or hears or touches is taken in some measure to be a manifestation of the supreme Life force—where such an approach to life exists, there can be no question then of any "particularity" in the revelation of the Unknown. Almost all religions of the world except Hinduism build their faith on a "particular" revelation at a "particular" time in the history of the world. In Hinduism, however, the particular particularity may be very meaningful in its own particular time, but beyond that the religion leaves itself free to recognize and accept other particularities in other times. As a matter of fact, any "particularity" as such has no value in Hindu thought; it is mentioned only to be afterward negated; the reality is as it is—from moment to moment.

The Vedic religion thus is not merely an affirmation of a few chosen moments of life; it is an affirmation of life in its continuity. As M. Hiriyanna points out: "There is no thought in these Mantras of the physical universe or any aspect of it being unreal."[16] The hymns of the *Rig Veda* and many passages of the Upanishads bear witness to this doctrine. Here, for instance, is the invocation to *Isa Upanishad*: "The invisible is the Whole, the visible too is the Whole. From the Whole, the visible universe of infinite extension has come out. The Whole remains the same, even though the infinite universe has come out of it." Or let us take the following verse from *Taittiriya Upanishad*: "He, the Atman, desired: May I become many; let Me procreate Myself. He meditated over Himself. Having meditated, He projected all this—whatever there is here. Having brought it forth, verily, He entered into it; having entered it, He became both the Being and the Beyond. He became the defined and undefined, the founded and the foundation-less, the conscious and unconscious, the real and the unreal; whatever else there is—yea, He became the entire Reality. For that reason the sages declare that all this is Real."[17] The drift of both these extracts, as may be seen, is to impress upon the reader that the same basic reality that exists in the non-observable unknown also exists in the observable known.

The subsequent chapters of this volume show how passionately Lawrence was devoted to the Spirit of Life as revealed from moment to moment; and how lack of reverence for physical life in his own religion, and how the stress laid in it on the "particularity" of Christ, in exclusion to, and in denial of, the holiness of the other endless moments of life, turned him away from Christianity. In his thought, it is not the Christ that matters. It is man's openness to the living moment that is of importance; man's openness to other forms of life, man's openness to the stars and the moon and the seasons, and most of all man's openness to that spring of all life-giving energy, the sun. In *Taittiriya Upanishad* it is stated that the highest form of bliss that a man can achieve on the face of this earth is nothing more than the bliss, or is the form of bliss, that is constantly coming out of the sun—"And this Bliss which is in the human being and in the yonder Sun are the same."[18] In a similar mood Lawrence states in his essay "Aristocracy": "With the sun he has his final and ultimate relationship, beyond man or woman, or anything human or created. And in this final relation is he most intensely alive, surpassing."[19] Lawrence calls such a man—a man living in harmony with the rest of the universe—an "aristocrat"; the Upanishads too call him an aristocrat, a man who has *vidya*. He is a man who, according to both Lawrence and the Upanishads, would have truly come to himself.

In "The Risen Lord," Lawrence borrows the Christian symbol of the risen Jesus to denote any many risen to the joy of living (as opposed to the conventional meaning, which takes it to be the actual coming back to life of the historical Christ), and in an imaginary dialogue between such an "aristocrat" and the modern Devil, Mammon, he condemns Mammon in the following terms:

> . . . only life is lovely, and you, Mammon, prevent life. I love to see a squirrel peep round a tree; and left to you, Mammon, there will soon be no squirrels to peep. I love to hear a man singing a song to himself, and if it is an old, improper song, about the fun between lads and girls, I like it all the better. But you, beastly mealy-mouthed Mammon, you would arrest any lad that sings a gay song. I love the movement of life, and the beauty of life, O Mammon, since I am risen, I love the beauty of life intensely; columbine flowers, for example, the way they dangle, or the delicate way a young girl sits and wonders, or the rage with which a man turns and kicks a fool dog that suddenly attacks him —beautiful that, the swift fierce turn and lunge of a kick, then the quivering pause for the next attack; or even the slightly silly glow that comes over some men as they are getting tipsy—it still is a glow, beautiful; or the swift look a woman fetches me, when she would really like me to go off with her, but she is troubled; or the real compassion I saw a woman express for a man who slipped and wrenched his foot: life, the beauty, the beauty of life![20]

The passage takes us a little further into Lawrence's conception of "relatedness." We observe from this that the relationship between an individual and the universe that Lawrence has in mind is not of an idealistic, super-spiritual nature, loaded with such objectives as piety, or goodness, or kindness, and the like. He was not against these sentiments. But along with these, he felt there were other emotions locked in the human heart, emotions of a totally different nature, like anger and passion; and these sentiments were as genuine to the human soul as the other ones. In addition, he saw that there was a certain passion, the passion of sex—the passion on which the day-to-day continuation of the human race and the other living organisms depended—that was virtually excluded from the doctrines of most religions. This being irrational and contrary to the scheme of things as seen in nature, we find that in Lawrence's view of interrelationship, a living organism's sexual relationship with a member of the opposite sex of its own species forms a major link which must be appreciated and accepted.

Here is the second affinity that we find between Lawrence and Hinduism. For Hinduism, among all religions, stands alone in giving sex a conspicuous place, indeed a venerable place, in its teachings. It is not the highest place, for sex is not considered there as the end of life, as indeed it is not considered the end in Lawrence. The end of life is the Self, as indeed, again, it is with Lawrence. But sex, fulfillment of sex, is looked upon in Hinduism as an essential requisite for the enlightenment and health of the spirit.

This part of man's life is designated in Hinduism by the word *kama*. S. Radhakrishnan, explaining that *kama* relates to the emotional life of man, writes: "If man is denied his emotional life, he becomes a prey to repressive introspection and lives under a continual strain of moral torture."[21] As early as the Vedas, we notice that, whereas most of the hymns are addressed to male deities, goddesses like Usha and Saraswati are also mentioned and worshiped. In the period immediately following the Vedas, the Puranic period, three deities arose in Hindu thought, Brahma, Vishnu, and Shiva, the last of whom, Shiva, was the personification of *Shakti,* which means power—power of destruction *and* of regeneration (sexual power). In that capacity Shiva is worshiped to this day. In temples dedicated to him, the idol is a stone Lingam, a phallus, placed in a round base, and thousands upon thousands of Hindus pay homage to it (the phallus, the Lingam, signifies the divine sex act, which maintains the universe in a state of perpetuity). Lawrence was himself aware of the existence of this Hindu god and the rituals associated with his name, for he told Earl Brewster once: "I have always worshipped Shiva."[22]

Not only has sex been honored and accepted as a natural part of life throughout Hindu thought; saints and learned men in the past devoted a lifetime of study to the subject and wrote monumental treatises on it. Legends mention many works in this connection, but the most important of those that have survived and come down to posterity are Vatsyayana's *Kama Sutra,* Koka Pandit's *Rati Rahisya,* and Kalyanmalla's *Ananga Ranga.* All three speak in detail on the subject of sex, without the slightest trace of inhibition. It is true that in these days asceticism has come to be a salient feature of Hinduism, dating back to the rise of Buddhism, a religion based on extreme abstinence, many rigid codes of which the later Hindu schools incorporated into their own systems. But in the Hindu Scriptures, renunciation is considered an act of denial and the emphasis is on *living,* rather than on renouncing life. In the Vedas the instruction is so much in favor of life that a widow, when her husband is dead and cremated, is asked to get up and go to the living, to marry again, and to forget the man who is no more (see *Rig Veda,* X, xviii, 8). The power, the regenerative vitality of Shiva to which I have referred above, is, as a matter of fact, so much honored that Shiva is considered to be the founder and inspirer of all forms of Indian arts as well—particularly Indian music (where Shiva is spoken of as *Natraja,* the king of dancers) and Indian drama (almost all the plays of Kalidasa were dedicated to Shiva). And this power is always the power of *kama,* of emotions, of feelings, of sensations, of fervor, of verve, and of rhythm.

A man acknowledging these urges of the body was no doubt a Risen man, according to Lawrence. As he records in "The Risen Lord": "If Jesus rose as a full man, in full flesh and soul, then he rose to take a woman to Himself, to live with her, and to know the tenderness and blossoming of the twoness with her; He who had been hitherto so limited to His oneness, or His universality, which is the same thing. If Jesus rose in the full flesh, He rose to know the tenderness of a woman, and the great pleasure of her, and to have children by her."[23]

Statements like these Christianity would scarcely approve of; hence the difficulty in "accepting" Lawrence among the Christians. In Hinduism this would pass as absolutely reasonable.

However, the end of all Lawrence's work is the Self, and it is there that the affinity between Hinduism and D. H. Lawrence is most marked and conspicuous. As Hindu thought progresses from the Vedic hymns to the Upanishads, we find that it becomes more contemplative, more meditative; it becomes more philosophical. The Upanishads are many in number—about two hundred, but the subject discussed in each is the same: the Self (*Atman*). Even in the Vedic hymns, it is clearly expressed that all reality is the same. It now comes to be specifically formulated that the reality within man (*Atman*) and the reality outside (*Brahman*) are one and the same, and that there is no Authority, or God, as a unit apart from the *Atman* and the *Brahman* taken together.

The effect of such a development is first, the concentration by the Upanishads of all spiritual authority within man, and second, the firm assertion that this spiritual authority can be comprehended only through intuition. Writing on the approach of the Upanishads, Sri Aurobindo says in *The Life Divine*:

> For, if we examine carefully, we shall find that Intuition is our first teacher. Intuition always stands veiled behind our mental operations. Intuition brings to man those brilliant messages from the Unknown which are the beginning of his higher knowledge. Reason only comes in afterwards to see what profit it can have of the shining harvest. Intuition

gives us that idea of something behind and beyond all that we know and seem to be which pursues man always in contradiction of his lower reason and all his normal experience and impels him to formulate that formless perception in the more positive ideas of God, Immortality, Heaven and the rest by which we strive to express it to the mind. For Intuition is as strong as Nature herself from whose very soul it has sprung and cares nothing for the contradictions of reason or the denials of experience. It knows what is because it is, because itself it is of that and has come from that, and will not yield it to the judgment of what merely becomes and appears.[24]

And he adds:

It is by an error that scholars sometimes speak of great debates or discussions in the Upanishad. Wherever there is the appearance of a controversy, it is not by discussion, by dialectics or the use of logical reasoning that it proceeds, but by a comparison of intuitions and experiences in which the less luminous gives place to the more luminous, the narrower, faultier or less essential to the more comprehensive, more perfect, more essential. The question asked by one thinker of another is "What dost thou know?", not "What dost thou think?" nor "To what conclusion has thy reasoning arrived?" Nowhere in the Upanishads do we find any trace of logical reasoning urged in support of the truths of Vedanta. Intuition, the sages seem to have held, must be corrected by a more perfect intuition; logical reasoning cannot be its judge.[25]

Both passages are self-explanatory. This is the form the Upanishads adopt to understand the nature of existence, to understand the Self. They are an assertion of the inability, of the fundamental limitations, of human knowledge, which can never extend itself to the extent of knowing the unknowable. But, though the unknowable is beyond human reason, the human heart is constantly in touch with it.

This study thus seeks to appreciate Lawrence's creative

work in its three main aspects: (1) the Joy that is implicit in existence all the time in its totality; (2) the physical being as an essential part of the spiritual, hence the value of sex, love, and marriage in human life; and (3) the realization of Self. Other allied issues, as they appear in Hinduism and are found in Christianity, are discussed where relevant. This book, however, is a study of Lawrence and not of Hinduism and therefore only those features of Hinduism are pointed out where the affinity is most prominent. Discussion of these should make the meaning of Lawrence clearer, but essentially the book remains a review of Lawrence's creative achievement.

In one of the less well known of his essays, entitled "Life," Lawrence wrote in 1918:

This is the law. We shall never know what is the beginning. We shall never know how it comes to pass that we have form and being. But we may always know how through the doorways of the spirit and the body enters the vivid unknown, which is made known in us. Who comes, who is that we hear outside in the night? Who knocks, who knocks again? Who is that that unlatches the painful door?

Then behold, there is something new in our midst. We blink our eyes, we cannot see. We lift the lamp of previous understanding, we illuminate the stranger with the light of our established knowledge. Then at last we accept the newcomer, he is enrolled amongst us.

So is our life. How do we become new? How is it we change and develop? Whence comes the newness, the further being, into us? What is added unto us, and how does it come to pass?

There is an arrival in us from the unknown, from the primal unknown whence all creation issues. Did we call for this arrival, did we summon the new being, did we command the new creation of ourselves, the new fulfilment? We did not, it is not of us. We are not created of ourselves. But from the unknown, from the great darkness of the outside that which is strange and new arrives on our threshold, enters and takes place in us. Not of ourselves, it is not of ourselves, but of the unknown which is the outside.

This is the first and greatest truth of our being and of our existence. How do we come to pass? We do not come to pass of ourselves. Who can say, Of myself I will bring forth newness? Not of myself, but of the unknown which has ingress into me.

And how has the unknown ingress into me? The unknown has ingress into me because, whilst I live, I am never sealed and set apart; I am but a flame, conducting unknown to unknown, through the bright transition of creation. I do but conduct the unknown of my beginning to the unknown of my end, through the transfiguration of perfect being. What is the unknown of the beginning and what is the unknown of the end? That I can never answer, save that in my completeness of being the two unknowns are consummated in a oneness, a rose of perfect explanation.

The unknown of my beginning has ingress into me through the spirit. My spirit is troubled, it is uneasy. Far off it hears the approach of footsteps through the night. Who is coming? Ah, let the newcomer arrive, let the newcomer arrive. In my spirit I am lonely and inert. I wait for the newcomer. My spirit aches with misery, dread of the newcomer. But also there is the tension of expectancy. I expect a visit, I expect a newcomer. For oh, I am conceited and unrefreshed, I am alone and barren. Yet still is my spirit alert and chuckling with subtle expectancy, awaiting the visit. It will come to pass. The stranger will come.[26]

The value of this passage grows as we proceed with the detailed appreciation of Lawrence's genius.

2
Delight of Creation

I

1. LAWRENCE AND TRADITION

In order to assess the range, the depth, and the quality of Lawrence's imaginative field, we should first briefly go over the ground, already covered by several other critics, of Lawrence and tradition. That D. H. Lawrence was a great artist came to be recognized by even his most hostile critic, the late T. S. Eliot, of whom Colin Wilson said "in a letter to me in 1956, he dismissed my view that Shaw could be considered the most important writer of the twentieth century, and suggested that Lawrence might be a better choice."[1] And yet the suspicion persists that Eliot would hardly allow Lawrence the benefit of tradition that he himself is supposed to enjoy. In his statement for the Lady Chatterly Trial of 1960—a statement prepared on behalf of the defense, but not delivered—Eliot made a courageous but only a qualified retraction of what he had said about Lawrence in *After Strange Gods*. He admitted in that statement that "some" of his remarks about Lawrence in his book were too sweeping and that "certain" of his opinions he no longer upheld, but he neither specified which remarks were sweeping nor which he might be prepared to withdraw.[2] The gist of his argument in *After Strange Gods*, therefore, remains unaltered. My contention, however, is that the difference between

37

T. S. Eliot and Lawrence is not in Lawrence's having no tradition but in his having a tradition of a different kind from Eliot's. An artist without tradition is a contradiction in terms; the stuff that his material is made of is directly derived by him from his national legacy. The vehemence with which Eliot condemned Lawrence on this score is thus worth close scrutiny. For out of tradition Lawrence rose, and in that tradition lies the special myth of life that attracted him.

Tradition for Eliot meant an artist's having "the historical sense"; and the historical sense, as stated in "Tradition and Individual Talent," means that the literature of his own country and the entire literature of Europe from Homer onward "has a simultaneous existence and composes a simultaneous order."[3] But a truly classical awareness of the past—if one insists on having the historical sense—should not confine itself to the domain of one race or one set of identical races alone; it should also include a knowledge and awareness of other cultures and races. In fairness to Eliot, it must be stated that he later widened the scope of his definition, when he accepted that the cultures of different people do influence each other and that there should be a "reciprocity" between them.[4] But in spite of all this, when Eliot spoke of tradition and culture, he essentially meant, for his purposes, the Christian culture. He was quite categorical when he said that "the culture of Europe, such as it is, is a Christian culture."[5]

Now, so far as Christian tradition is concerned, eminent scholars like F. R. Leavis and V. de Sola Pinto have shown that Lawrence had as full and rich a share of this cultural heritage as anyone else. Pinto asserts, "Lawrence was *not* an ignorant man, as T. S. Eliot has called him, and he was not a crude, wild 'genius,' but he came from a tradition and a cultural background which are not understood by many people like Mr. Eliot who come to

England from abroad, and spend their lives among the gentlemanly upper middle class of London and the South of England, the world of the *Times* and *Punch* and the London clubs."[6] Pinto goes on to explain that living tradition comes more through a direct contact with the soil, the intimate firsthand consciousness of it through experience; and Lawrence was a man of the soil. This did not exclude knowledge and learning in Lawrence's life. A glance at his record in the various educational institutions he attended and the number of works he read privately with Jessie Chambers show how good a student he was. As Pinto remarks, "I wonder how many upper middle class 'gentlemanly' households in the England of that time contained young people who could have matched the long list of books in English, French and Latin (besides translations from the Greek and Russian) which E. T. records as having been read by her and Lawrence in those years."[7] What has to be seen is that Lawrence had all this, but he did not stop here in his "historical sense"; he went further. Knowledge was absorbed by him with an openness of mind that enabled him to accept the cultural tradition to which he was born—the cultural tradition of Europe, of England, of the Midlands—and yet he was free and not limited by it.

Tradition, one should presume, is either a matter of inheritance—a cultural legacy from the past passed on to posterity—or of intellect, something to be deliberately acquired through a prolonged mental and physical effort. T. S. Eliot makes his position clear on this, when he says, "It cannot be inherited, and if you want it you must obtain it by great labour."[8] In another mood in *After Strange Gods*, Eliot does grant that tradition is unconscious assimilation, but by associating it at the same time with orthodoxy, "which calls for the exercise of all our conscious intelligence," he retains the academic nature of the concept. This is a crucial statement, for it is completely wrong and it makes it possible for us to see why Eliot misunderstands Lawrence. The *Shorter Oxford Dictionary* gives many meanings of the word, but almost all of them insist that tradition refers to a heritage acquired through the spoken word rather than the written one, as, for example, "transmission of statements, beliefs, rules, customs, or the like, esp. by word of mouth, or by practice without writing down." Obviously, therefore, tradition is not to be confused with scholarship or an effort of the intellect, and when T. S. Eliot advocates a knowledge of Greek and Latin as essential and preliminary to an understanding of European culture, desirable though it is, a mere knowledge of Greek and Latin is *not* either tradition *or* European culture. The man of letters has his importance in that he pictures the life of his nation in its multifarious glory with a sublimity of language given to a few; he is certainly instrumental in heightening the meaning of the living tradition through the medium of his art; if he has anything significant to contribute, he leaves an impact on the consciousness of his age. But he does not "pass on" anything as such to posterity, that process being determined by a complicated set of day-to-day social details and customs. Though he may continue to be read by the generations to come, the future men and women would frequent his pages not necessarily to learn a culture or tradition but to see and enjoy the great artist he was. It would be folly to presume that we read Homer to "acquire" Greek tradition, or that a study of Shakespeare or Milton or T. S. Eliot, for that matter, will enable one to imbibe English tradition. Tradition is something of day-to-day usage found in the common majority; it would be passed on even if there were no artists to write about it and one would inherit it even if he were ignorant of the great literary figures of the past.

We are not denying here the value of academic knowledge; far from it. In order to be a great artist, a familiarity with the artists of the past would, perhaps, be of utmost importance. What is suggested is the incorrect usage of T. S. Eliot in speaking of Lawrence's having no tradition. Millions of Indians do not know a word of Sanskrit; thousands of them have never read a line of the Vedas or the *Ramayana* or the *Mahabharata* even in translation; many of them would not know who the authors of these texts were or what the niceties of their style are; and yet in the whole length and breadth of the vast land of India almost every single Hindu—notwithstanding the many different languages in different parts of the country—has the same common religious tradition. Undoubtedly there will be other customs—economic, political, social—which members of the different social strata will acquire, but that will not be "a common heritage." If Eliot's quarrel with Lawrence is that he came from a different economic background from his own, the argument is understandable. But the type of heresy of which he accuses Lawrence in his bitter monologue *After Strange Gods* is logically false and untrue. No European artist—believer or unbeliever—born in the Christian era could have escaped the influence and power of this faith. And D. H. Lawrence was no exception.

We may legitimately conclude that tradition cannot be wholly acquired through a deliberate or purposeful attempt of the intellect. Tradition is mainly an unconscious assimilation of the past through experience and usage, and it is received, more or less, by every individual living in a certain period of history, the more or less depending on the individual's sensitivity, the openness of his mind and its inherent receptivity, and the living touch in his life of other equally sensitive and receptive individuals. We are not aware of the private influences in the life of T. S. Eliot. Lack of such spiritual forces in his life may account for his fearful dryness (see the different tone in him after his happy second marriage; in particular see the romantic dedication to *The Elderly Statesman*[9]), but we know that Lawrence received in all its strength the Christian dogma through his mother and his early membership in the Congregational Church, and Christian love through Jessie Chambers. In fact the whole range of his creative output shows that he was a man who wrote with an acute consciousness of the Christian tradition, and that he could not have expressed himself the way he did—could never have written a story like *The Man Who Died* —but for the dominant pull this tradition had exercised on him.

But to be influenced by a tradition and to be bound by a tradition are two different things. When one accepts a tradition with mental slavery (quite often, erroneously, confused by people with "faith"), with an unequivocal acceptance that the past was always right and the true and the glorious could never be better revealed than through the medium of the past, that is limiting oneself, binding oneself to a tradition. For implicit acceptance of a dogma or a tradition (or a faith or belief or usage) immediately subordinates the reality of the thing to the dogma or belief in practice. Reality is a philosophical concept and cannot be limited to one exclusive line of approach; the moment we try to so limit it, we split it into the Christian reality, or the Muslim reality, or the Buddhist reality, and it straightway loses its universality. In such an approach, one moves from the "known" to the "known"; one starts with certain accepted propositions of a certain religion—a few accepted ideas about God and soul and universe—and from that *fixed* starting point argues or reasons about the subsidiary problems. The mind, the intellect, merely keeps revolving around an approved hypothesis, a principle to which, for one reason or the other, allegiance has been pledged (to the exclusion of other principles and feelings). This intellectual process then continues from generation to generation, each generation taking up the mental spinning of the past and propagating it. There is no scope for a breath of fresh air; a map of a person's emotional life is presented to him and he is expected to follow the map faithfully—that is, blindly. As is clear, there can be no joy of discovery in this process. It is an absolutely closed circle and, like Fabre's ants, one must run on the beaten path.

The factor to be recognized is the crippling influence of "conditioning" on man. D. H. Lawrence has a richer and longer tradition than T. S. Eliot, for he is not limited in his thinking by one particular line of reasoning. It is not implied that he knew of every other tradition and culture, since that standard would be humanly impossible to achieve. He merely takes himself back to a period of history when the different cultures, being simpler and more elemental, may have been more identical and universal.

In a series of lectures delivered at McGill University, Montreal, in 1954, S. Radhakrishnan said:

> Greece, Palestine and Rome were greatly influenced by the East. Greece drew nourishment from the cultures of Asia Minor and Egypt. The spiritual ferment that brought forth the Judaean-Christian conception of God and man owed a great deal to the religious insights of the East which permeated the Jewish world in the centuries before Jesus. Christianity wove into the pattern the threads of earlier beliefs, the cult of Mithra and the reforms of Mani.[10]

The idea is that Europe has had no exclusive cultural pattern that could not be traced to an earlier civilization. The recent discoveries of anthropologists and archaeologists also prove that. After all, in a progressively moving chain of tradition, one could stretch the links as far backward and sideways as possible. Christianity is only one of the links in the chain, and decidedly not the first one. Eliot essentially stops at this link and refuses to take equal cognizance of earlier thought. As a reviewer in *The Times Literary Supplement* (March 4, 1960) once stated pertinently, Eliot himself suffers from "a failure of historical imagination." But Lawrence, though brought up in an atmosphere where the Bible was "poured into the childish consciousness day in day out, year in, year out,"[11] and though, as Jessie Chambers tells us, he himself contemplated becoming a priest at one time, had a more searching mind.

It was only in the year 1915—an eventful year in Lawrence's life, with the publication and subsequent suppression of *The Rainbow*, the birth of the journal *Signature*, and friendship with Bertrand Russell—that Lawrence finally renounced orthodox Christianity (though he is on record as saying that he turned away from it at the age of twenty-one), and felt that he saw the answers to what he had been looking for in earlier periods of man's existence. Instead of ignoring Christianity, or being ignorant of it, he had been hitherto too much preoccupied with it. He wrote to Russell, "I have been wrong, much too Christian, in my philosophy."[12] Again: "I am rid of all my Christian religiosity. It was only a muddiness."[13] But he found it otherwise with the earlier cultures.

It would perhaps be more fruitful to approach Lawrence through anthropology rather than religion. It is not fully recognized how well-read he was in this subject. He was familiar with the works of scientists like Charles Darwin and T. H. Huxley. This might have diverted him to Tylor and Harrison and Frazer, in the last of whom he was particularly interested. Writing to Bertrand Russell on December 8, 1915, he says: "I have been reading Frazer's Golden Bough and Totemism and Exogamy. Now I am convinced of what I believed when I was about twenty —that there is another seat of consciousness than the brain and the nerve system: there is a blood-consciousness which exists in us independently of the ordinary mental consciousness."[14] It is a fairly long letter, in which Lawrence discusses further the significance of blood-consciousness and the far-reaching impact this consciousness can have on human life. All that he means by the term is that there is an implicit awareness of things in us (as a cat is aware of its master in the dark, Lawrence says in one of his essays), and that there are channels other than the mind and the nervous system which may influence life and shape it. He insists, at the end of the letter: "It is *very* important: the whole of our future life depends on it."

Formalized religions, he believed—whether the religion be Christianity or Islam or Hinduism—interfered with the basic intelligence of the individual and imposed a barrier to true living. For he saw each formal religion as an expression of egoism; of the "mind"; of what he also called the self-aware-of-itself. "Now the self-aware-of-itself has *always* the quality of egoism. The spirit is always egoistic. The greatest spiritual commands are *all* forms of egoism, usually inverted egoism, for deliberate humility, we are all well aware, is a rabid form of egoism. The Sermon on the Mount is a long string of utterances from the self-aware-of-itself, the spirit, and all of them are rabid aphorisms of egoism, back-handed egoism"[15] (Lawrence's emphasis).

But through anthropology Lawrence reached an earlier and more fundamental state of man. What he found there suited his temperament—"If only we would realise that, until perverted by the mind, the human body preserves itself continually in a delicate balance of sanity!"[16] It was by working within such a basic tradition that Lawrence produced most of his creative work.

2. SIN AND DELIGHT

With the understanding that reality ever is, Lawrence conceives of the special myth of life that permeates all his work. And that is, that the universe is the result not of Sin but of Delight. If there is any major difference at all to be seen between Lawrence's approach to life and Eliot's, it is that in Lawrence the Christian concept of Original Sin has no meaning (as it has no meaning in Hinduism). Lawrence considers creation as nothing but Delight. It is a question of the whole fundamental outlook: whether what is going on around us, the endless play of universal propagation, started because of God's anger, Adam having disobeyed him, or as a self-explicit phenomenon of God's delight, a fountain of spontaneous joy. For Lawrence, it most certainly is not the former view; it is the latter.

It is a vision of "sinless" enjoyment of nature that is at the core of the artist in Lawrence. Though he does not specifically talk of Original Sin, the doctrine has colored most Christian thinking till today and Lawrence was concerned with it. His friend Frederick Carter remarks, "Beyond all, what he desired most to know was the history—the real true myth—of the descent of man into this life's bondage of the spirit. Why did he come from heaven? What had he left? Towards what did he purpose journeying? Such answers as were given by the Neo-Platonists he took to beg the question, a juggling with words, telling of nothing sufficiently significant!"[17]

Now, what do we mean by "Original Sin"? There are two parts of the Biblical myth that deserve attention. First, it refers to a state of grace that man has lost. And second, it suggests the reason why man fell from that exalted position and became wicked. According to the biblical story, the loss came about when man disobeyed

God in eating the fruit of the tree of knowledge of good and evil. The difficulty arises in the interpretation of these words, in deciding on the exact nature of man's offence. Opinion on the issue is divided, but tradition seems to hold that the knowledge of good and evil pertains to sexual desire. This alone can explain the hostile attitude to sex that has persisted in the history of Christianity. To quote Norman Powell Williams, a distinguished scholar in the field: "It is worth while noting that, in the very beginnings of the idea of Original Sin, there emerges a tendency which has profoundly influenced the course of Christian speculation on the subject, more particularly in its Augustinian phase: and that is the tendency to regard the flaw or weakness inherent in the structure of human personality as caused by, or at least closely connected with, what is known in the language of technical theology as 'concupiscence.' "[18] In her publication *Three Traditions of Moral Thought,* Dorothea Krook gives a detailed analysis of the Christian approach to the issue of sex and, starting from St. Augustine and tracing the orthodox thought to Canon Jacques Leclercq in our own time, she states that for the Church sexual love has never been considered redemptive in itself.[19] So there appears to be more than a merely casual connection between sexual desire and Original Sin.

The best observations on the subject, however, could be offered by the Jews, since it is in their scripture, the Old Testament, that the story is related. And what one gathers from *The Zohar,* the massive rabbinical commentary on the Pentateuch, is that the Jews thought of Original Sin as pertaining to the knowledge of sex. The Jews of the Old Testament period were a healthy, highly sexed race; but they seem to have held the view that man became aware of sex only when he had disobeyed God. We see for ourselves that the Universe created by the biblical God is a curiously sexless universe. In the great labor of

God, we hear of many names of animals and fowls, which God creates, but no mention is ever made of a female of a species (except in Genesis 1:27, where it does not fit in with the pattern of the rest). To be sure the command is there, "Be fruitful and multiply," but the impression left is that the said multiplication is to be through a process not involving the sexual element—through division, perhaps, or fragmentation. Even when man is created, the impression is that the first man was made up of man and woman both, a sort of asexual or bisexual unit, complete in himself, and one is left to wonder how he had to multiply and with what or with whom. If God had created along with him, as a matter of routine, the female as well, as is stated in Genesis 1:27, why should God have felt the necessity of creating Eve afterwards, as an event of special significance?

The Jews were quick to notice this, and we have Rabbi Simeon ben Yohai in *The Zohar* commenting on it, saying that the word Adam "embraces the upper and the lower in virtue of its three letters, *aleph, daleth,* and *mim* final. When these three letters descended below, together in their complete form, the name Adam was found to comprise male and female. . . . Observe that Adam came last of all, it being fitting that he should find the world complete on his appearance."[20] According to this, Adam was complete in himself and the presence of a woman as a separate entity was not considered essential, either for his existence or for the continuation of his species. (The explanation is later repeated in *The Zohar,* " 'Let us make man': the word *adam* (man) implies male and female, created wholly through the supernal and holy Wisdom."[21] And again: "*The Man*: as we have explained, male and female, together and not separated, so as to turn face to face."[22]) It is only later that God thinks of creating a woman in her own right, to keep company with Adam and to help him. But even then there is no hint of any sexual relationship between them. For one thing, we observe that there is no sign of any children born to them yet; they just continue to live as they are (in ignorance). It is only after they have tasted of the tree of knowledge of good and evil that Eve conceives and gives birth to Cain and Abel, the implication being that previously Adam and Eve were not aware of the sexual urge. We read in *The Zohar* that the seduction of Eve by the Serpent and later on of Adam by Eve, means that Eve, becoming aware of the new urge, had sexual connection with both of them. It is recorded there: "When they begat children, the first-born was the son of the (serpent's) slime. For two beings had intercourse with Eve, and she conceived from both and bore two children. Each followed one of the male parents, and their spirits parted, one to this side and one to the other, and similarly their characters."[23]

It is doubtful whether the sentences attributed to Rabbi Simeon, the second-century Jewish philosopher, are genuine or whether he was the author of *The Zohar*. But it is generally accepted that *The Zohar* is a work of great value and that it contains most of the early Jewish folklore and opinion. The comments contained therein should therefore be taken by us as representative of the mind of those people. In the Eastern Church, it is held even now that man was complete at the time of creation, and there was no sex-play in the first creation of God; sex-play was the result of the Fall: "Man is divided into two sexes, male and female, a division which becomes definitive after sin, in the state of fallen human nature";[24] for, "It was the divinely appointed function of the first man, according to St. Maximus, to unite in himself the whole of created being."[25]

It is thus in many Western Churches as well. I quote below Article IX of the Anglican Church (the Church to which T. S. Eliot belonged), which throws light on the subject and describes the accepted sense in which the doctrine is viewed there:

> Original Sin standeth not in the following of Adam (as the Pelagians do vainly talk), but it is the fault and corruption of the nature (vitium et depravatio naturae) of every man, that naturally is engendered of the offspring of Adam, whereby man is far gone from original righteousness, and is of his own nature inclined to evil, so that the flesh lusteth always contrary to the spirit, and therefore, in every person born in this world, it deserveth God's wrath and damnation. And this infection of nature doth remain, yea, in them that are regenerated; whereby the lust of the flesh, called in Greek φρονημα σαρκός, which some do expound the wisdom, some sensuality, some the affection, some the desire of the flesh, is not subject to the law of God. And although there is no condemnation for those that believe and are baptized; yet the Apostle doth confess, that concupiscence and lust hath of itself the nature of sin.

Probably all the Christian churches are not of the same view, but the difference is only one of degree. In all of them concupiscence is linked with the Fall, even if there be divergent opinion on whether in itself it is sin or not.

Well, once that is acknowledged, it certainly subordinates sexual desire in man to a low position. Not only that, as the other verses of Genesis show, it fixes the origin of the present universe in a holocaust of curses and accusations and a list of punishments: God's curse on man, God's curse on woman, God's curse on the serpent. God sees in the beginning that his creation is "good"; but the good about it ends when the progeny, the race of Adam starts, and instead we are left with the "sweat of thy face."

And it is this part of the story that Lawrence apparently felt most dissatisfied with. He believed that Adam and Eve had sexual relations even before the Fall (see his remarks in *Fantasia of the Unconscious,* p. 76, and in his essay "Hawthorne and The Scarlet Letter" in *Studies in Classic American Literature,* pp. 86-87). But he could never accept that the beginning of the universe meant a "fall," a state of deterioration; he felt it was a state of improvement, if anything, on the earlier state. As Carter explains Lawrence's stand on the subject: "He wanted a document from antiquity to tell of this, a tale long cherished in the heart of man. Not a tale of fall—a failure—but as a glorious exploit and an escape from the less to the more and the better."[26]

We have dwelt on the subject at some length, as there is a body of thought, a systematic, important body of opinion that holds a completely different view of creation. As "The Song of Creation" quoted earlier from the *Rig Veda* has it, all our ideas of creation are, after all, a guess; none of us witnessed the moment of creation and no records of the event have survived. It appears somewhat artless for Archbishop Usher to have fixed 4004 B.C. as the time of creation, for mankind had existed for millenniums prior to that date. In most of these ages men wrestled, according to their understanding, with the idea of creation. I refer now to the account given in the Indian scriptures.

The Vedas, it should be explained, do not have exact equivalents of several words in common use in the vocabulary in the West. This gives a wholly different meaning to the picture of the cosmos that is painted there. For instance, the word "God," in the sense that it is used in the West, is totally missing there. This word invariably brings to mind a vision of an extra-cosmic creator. In the Vedic vocabulary the word used is "Brahman," which means everything that exists and that does not exist. Thus while one is busy reading of the nature of Brahman in the Vedas, one is constantly kept conscious of the fact that this God (to use a familiar term) that we are trying to understand *includes* us as well. Brahman is this; Brahman is that: the reader knows that the discussion is not about a body distinct and separate from him; the discussion is about whatever is, about everything. Similarly the word "soul" does not exist in the Vedas; this word, again, marks a division between the creator and the created world. We have instead the expression "Atman" (insufficiently rendered into English as Self), which is just another word for Brahman; the two terms are interchangeable. Last, for our purpose, the expression "sin" does not exist in the Vedas. There is reference—repeated reference—to "pleasure" and "pain," but they are merely aspects of Brahman and not the by-product or result of any sin.

The Vedas comprise a vast body of literature and it is not possible to quote from all their references to creation. But the essentials are as follows: nothing exists, or has ever existed, or will exist, except Brahman. In point of fact, as Swami Sharvananda points out in his notes to *Aitareya Upanishad,* I, 1, "According to the Veda there is no such thing as first creation."[27] The expression "in the beginning" (*Agre* in Sanskrit) only implies the beginning of a new cycle. What was there before that cycle, or before the cycle prior to that cycle, the Vedas say no one can know—except that Brahman was always there. At times, to get round this business of using words to describe something of which man can never have any precise knowledge, the creation is summarized in the Vedas by the use of the symbol *Om*—which is not a word but only a sound, a mystic sound, according to Hindu philosophy. "All this world is the syllable *Om*. Its further explanation is this: the past, the present, the future—everything is just *Om*. And whatever transcends the three divisions of time—that, too is just *Om*."[28] (Lawrence, incidentally, was fascinated by the sound of *Om*. Speaking of the definition of the word "God," he states in "On Being Religious": "Of course, nobody can define it. And a word nobody can define isn't a word at all. It's just a noise and a shape, like pop! or Ra or Om."[29] In *Fantasia of the Unconscious* he makes use of this symbol to explain his views on the "First Cause" of the universe: "But it is tiring to go to any more tea parties with the Origin, or the Cause, or even the Lord. Let us pronounce the mystic Om, from the pit of the stomach, and proceed."[30] Immediately afterwards, he adds, "There's not a shadow of doubt about it, the First Cause is just unknowable to us, and we'd be sorry if it wasn't. Whether it's God or the Atom. All I say is Om!"[31]) In any case, in the passages where explicit reference to creation is made in the Vedas, it is stated that at a certain stage Brahman had the "desire" (*kama*) to create the present universe. In the joy of that desire, in its delight, he therefore threw out forms and the world was born. In the same delight the universe—that is, Brahman—still continues.

This is a brief summary of lengthy arguments and discussions. How much (what percentage) of Brahman came to be "bound" in the form of living beings, and how much of him is unbound, the Hindus say man cannot know; all that man can know is that he is a part of Brahman. But the emphasis, let us notice, is invariably on the delight. At one place in the Upanishads, the delight of creation is stressed to such an extent as to assert that the Creator, before the act of creation, was without any joy and he created the universe to experience delight:

> He, verily, had no delight. Therefore he who is alone has no delight. He desired a second. He became as large as a woman and a man in close embrace. He caused that self to fall into two parts. From that arose husband and wife.[32]

We must note the sexual imagery that keeps coming up in these descriptions. As earlier stated, it is all a hypothesis, but it clearly shows how the early Hindu mind worked. If we turn to "The Song of Creation" in the *Rig Veda*, we find that *kama*, desire, is referred to there as "the primal seed of germ and spirit." And this cosmic desire of the creator, this *kama*, is endless. Continuing

our story from *Brhadaranyaka Upanishad,* after the husband and the wife have been created as the result of the
cosmic desire, the wife feels a little appalled that the
Creator should sleep with her, having produced her from
his own self. She therefore changes her form and disappears. But the desire, the *kama,* of the Creator will not
leave her alone. The Creator seeks her out and in whatever
shape or form she may be, he assumes a similar shape and
still unites with her.

> She thought, "How can he unite with me after having
> produced me from himself? Well, let me hide myself." She
> becomes a cow, the other becomes a bull and thus was united
> with her and from that cows were born. The one became
> a mare, the other a stallion. The one became a she-ass, the
> other a he-ass and was united with her; and from that one
> hoofed animals were born. The one became a she-goat, the
> other a he-goat, the one became a ewe, the other became a
> ram and was united with her and from that goats and sheep
> were born. . . .[33]

There is no need to discuss the relative values of the
biblical and the Vedic approach to the subject of creation.
The noteworthy thing is that whereas the one looks upon
creation as the result of God's punishment, the other considers it an expression of God's limitless delight. We should
pay particular attention to this fact, for I believe that it
is within the supreme myth of Creation as Delight that
Lawrence casts all his work. The test of a great artist lies
not in his "message," in the communication of facts, but
in his reaction, his response—the texture and the feel of
his response—to the facts of life, and D. H. Lawrence
registers the same response commendably consistently
throughout his work. It is the response of an artist spell-
bound by the great myth of creation. It is the response to
an extra-biblical, extra-religious, anthropological myth of
life. Lawrence was in sympathy with the myth, and so his
response records the joy he felt as an artist in the inherent
and implicit beauty of the created world.

II

1. *THE WHITE PEACOCK*

In light of the above, we shall now examine Lawrence's very first novel, *The White Peacock*—a novel that has been described by even such an admirer of Lawrence as F. R. Leavis as "painfully callow." It is unfortunate that this book should have received such scant treatment so far. Apart from Graham Hough, no one has ever attempted a systematic study of it. It certainly is amateurish; to sum up its faults with Leavis, "there is a great deal of the literary and conventional in the style and the treatment," about it. That Lawrence himself was aware of the weakness of the novel appears in his letters to Blanche Jennings, to whom he had submitted the first version of the novel to ask her opinion. Those letters are now included in Harry T. Moore's edition of Lawrence's letters, but excerpts from them were first published in an article in *A Review of English Literature* entitled "D. H. Lawrence and Blanche Jennings," which also gives an interesting account of the hitherto unknown friendship between the two. On occasion Lawrence would write to her, "I shrink from the thought of any one reading that work —if I were not vain and poor I should like to put it in the fire."[34] On other occasions, he would be more cheerful: "In Laetitia [*The White Peacock* was called *Laetitia* in the earlier version] there is, I would declare in the teeth of all the jabbering critics in the world, some beautiful writing—there are some exquisite passages, such as I shall not write again."[35] But the most systematic criticism of the novel appears in the following letter, dated November 11, 1908:

It bores me mightily in parts. You can none of you find

one essence of its failure: it is that I have dragged in conversations to explain matters that two lines of ordinary prose would have accomplished far better; I must cut out many pages of talk, and replace them with a few paragraphs of plain description or narrative; secondly, one is cloyed with metaphoric fancy; thirdly, folk talk about themes too much; —slight incidents—such as the sugar in Eugenie—should display character, not fine speeches; fourthly, I don't believe Lettie ever did break her engagement with Leslie—she married him. The construction—changeable and erratic as it is— is defensible; there are some fine, swift bits, e.g. the latter half of the party; there are some strong scenes, e.g.—the churchyard scene with Annable, the motor accident, and, for a moment, Leslie's appeal to Lettie when he comes to her sick, also the death of the father; there is some rare suggestiveness—the burial of the keeper, the idiot girl 'Christmass'. The father scene is not superfluous. I will defend my construction throughout.

The characters are often weak—the men—George and Leslie specially. Lettie herself is not bad. The rest are undeveloped. What the whole thing needs is that the essential should be differentiated from the non-essential. I will have another go at it this winter. . . .[36]

The final version of the novel has several alterations in the plot and improvements in style and technique, to judge by Lawrence's criticism in the above-mentioned letter and the novel as it stands now. But one has to agree with Leavis; it continues to be "conventional."

Yet, a great deal of "Lawrence" is still there in the book. Dug "in incoherent bits from the underground of my consciousness," and spread over four years of work and five or six drafts, it represents some of Lawrence's basic responses to life. And from the first page till the last it is vibrant with at least one thing: the joy and the music of the created world.

It is relevant to stress here that early in life Lawrence seems to have developed a curious conception of good and evil. William Hopkin has left among his papers the details

of a talk he had with Lawrence on the subject when Lawrence was very young:

> I should think Lawrence would be about 16-17 when, as
> we were alone one day, he said: "I am not surprised that
> you kick against a lot of the Bible. I do not like Command-
> ments of any sort and why certain Commandments should
> be considered the last word in the ordering of human con-
> duct I fail to see. Life is not static, and neither is conduct
> or morality, so called. All these things spring up in various
> ways, and for various reasons, and they have a life, and like
> the trees eventually fade away, to be followed by newer
> concepts in place of the dead and useless ones. There is a
> principle of evil—"
> Here I interrupted him by asking: "What is the principle
> of evil, and where was its origin?"
> He replied rather hastily, "Origin be damned. The prin-
> ciple of evil is simply resistance to the life principle. Not
> merely *a* principle, but you and every other intelligent per-
> son must feel, if you do any thinking, that what we call life
> is a mystery, and a sacred one too. If you do not feel this
> there is something wrong with you."
> Later in the day several young people came in, and at
> supper I brought up the subject again. Lawrence repeated
> in a general way what he had said to me earlier, and one
> girl, Cooper I think, said, "I think I see what you mean,
> Bert."
> He replied sharply—"Seeing is not a damned bit of use.
> Seeing is from the head. Unless you feel it right deep down
> inside you it remains a theory and has no substance. Get on
> with your supper!"[37]

It is apparent from this narration that Lawrence was
gifted with a perceptive intelligence of an uncommon
quality. Years later he wrote in the same vein: "There is
only one sin in life, and that is the sin against life, the
sin of causing inner emptiness and boredom of the
spirit."[38] Pronouncements such as these, it should be seen,
do not deny the presence of evil—presence of pain and
misery; nor do these pronouncements justify the presence

of evil. He told Brewster: "Both exist. There is good and there is evil. There is no higher plane where evil is justified."[39] The assertion is that life, by its very nature, constitutes what passes for "good" and, at the same time, what passes for "evil"; and in the utter acceptance of both of them, the transcendent feeling experienced by the individual is the feeling of release, the feeling of joy. As Lawrence says in "The Crown": "It is not easy to achieve immortality, to win a consummate being. It is supremely difficult. It means undaunted suffering and undaunted enjoyment, both. And when a man has reached his ultimate of enjoyment and his ultimate of suffering, *both*, then he knows the two eternities, then he is made absolute, like the iris, created out of the two. Then he is immortal."[40]

It cannot be denied that the problem of evil is something with which most of us are ever occupied. Why should there be evil in a world created by a kind and loving God? St. Augustine posed the question relevantly centuries back, without suggesting an answer. The fact is that there can be no answer to it if the issue is tackled in its present form. If there is a creator—a God, *apart* from the universe, away and separate from it, its master and its administrator—and if pain and evil and suffering exist in the world, then most surely this God has to bear the blame for it and relinquish his claim to being an all-loving and all-kind God. As Sri Aurobindo says:

> If we say that pain is a trial and an ordeal, we do not solve the moral problem, we arrive at an immoral or non-moral God,—an excellent world-mechanist perhaps, a cunning psychologist, but not a God of Good and of Love whom we can worship, only a God of Might to whose law we must submit or whose caprice we may hope to propitiate. For one who invents torture as a means of test or ordeal, stands convicted either of deliberate cruelty or of moral insensibility and, if a moral being at all, is inferior to the highest instinct of his own creatures.[41]

But if we dismiss the concept of an extra-cosmic creator, the problem either vanishes or acquires a different proportion. For we see that words like "pain" or "suffering" or "good" or "evil" are extremely relative expressions, their significance depending on certain meanings that we have habitually attached to them, generally determined by the material or physical harm suffered by one individual to the profit of another or others. But where the different individuals are considered as units of the same cosmic reality, the pain and suffering of one individual and the relative painless existence of the other become merely different aspects of the same reality. In brief, when the unit is ignored and only the whole is taken, we notice, as Sri Aurobindo declares, that "the sum of the pleasure of existence far exceeds the sum of the pain of existence—appearances and individual cases to the contrary notwithstanding—and that the active or passive, surface or underlying pleasure of existence is the normal state of nature. . . ."[42]

In *The White Peacock,* it is a picture of "the sum of the pleasure of existence" that Lawrence paints. For Lawrence a personal God, or a Godhead, has no appeal. Commenting on Benjamin Franklin's devotion to a Godhead, he said: "As for his Godhead, his Providence, He is Head of nothing except a vast heavenly store that keeps every imaginable line of goods, from victrolas to cat-o-nine tails."[43] There is a universal spirit which dominates each one of us, and that alone is God. Time and again the biblical phraseology appears in Lawrence's texts, so deeply was he rooted in the Bible, but with a totally different meaning.

Man doth not live by bread alone, to absorb it and to evacuate it.

What is the breath of life? My dear, it is the strange current of interchange that flows between men and men, and men and women, and men and things. A constant current

of interflow, a constant vibrating interchange. That is the
breath of life.[44]

It is not a breath of life breathed into a heap of clay by
an "outside" authority, a "separate" breath in each one
of us, but "the strange current of interchange," the same
in each one of us, in men and things. It is the "constant
current of interflow, a constant vibrating interchange."
It is the breath of life that keeps things in existence, that
keeps the universe going.

The White Peacock is cast in such a setting; it is a portrait of the universal health and vitality, a song in praise
of the beauty of the world. It offers a panoramic view of
the seasons—of summer, autumn, winter and spring—and
within this large framework we have man, and the animals,
and the plants, all fitted in in a homogeneous whole. It is
not merely what Lawrence described as the "spirit of
place." "Every continent has its own great spirit of place.
. . . Different places on the face of the earth have different vital effluence, different vibration, different chemical
exhalation, different polarity with different stars: call it
what you like. But the spirit of place is a great reality."[45]
Yes, we know this and there is nothing new about it. One
of the characteristics of any great artist is that he catches
something of the spirit of place of his age (his country,
his times) in his work. Lawrence, as a genius, could certainly register the spirit of a place, but it is not the graphic
representation of that moment that fascinates the reader.
It is the intrinsic delight of the individual living in that
moment regardless of what the spirit of the place may be
—cold or hot, wet or dry; regardless of whether there be
sorrow or pleasure, gain or loss, affliction or success. It is
this that attracts one to Lawrence. The sprouting of new
life goes on right in the center of the vast paraphernalia
of a particular place, and this sprouting is always a source
of joy. It is here that one finds his greatness.

The delight in diversity—the invariable self-releasing perpetuity, irrespective of moral, social, and ethical demands and limitations—is the theme of most of Lawrence's work, and though afterwards he was to develop it to almost a creed, in *The White Peacock* we find it displayed at its simplest best. There is a constant music of life in the book which never ceases. A dignity and grandeur is attached even to the movements of animals and birds: the rats sit and "wipe" their sharp faces and "stroke" their whiskers, a crow "folds" himself up "in black resignation to the detestable weather," the lapwings are shown "crying, crying" (see how the repetition of the word makes the lapwing more real), a cow "coughs noisily," a terrier "roars," a kitten is moody enough to get "tired." Not only that, almost every other observable object is described as a heaving mass of living personality: the leaves "chatter," the corn "stands drowsily," the oat sheaves "whisper" to each other as they stand "embracing," the wild raspberries "nod," the clouds tumble and sweep by like "companies of angels," the window-panes "shiver," winter "gathers" her limbs as she "drifts with saddened garments northward," the hills have "breasts" and they "heave," water has "blue eyes" which shut and open, the full moon looks "like a woman with child." It is an extreme example of myth-making, where the universe is conceived of as innumerable shapes and images, all of them the various links and parts of the great impersonal life force behind them, the force itself having no shape of its own, except as the shape emerging out of the multiplicity of shapes otherwise seen.

And the point is that the flow of life always goes on. No matter what may happen to cases in isolation, the sum total of life is an expression of gushing delight. Lawrence himself refers to it in *The White Peacock* at one place as "the roaring passion of life,"[46] and at another as "the triumphant tilt of the joy of life."[47]

To give a sufficiently explicit illustration, let us take the scene of Annable's burial, the scene that, according to Lawrence's letter to Blanche Jennings, has "some rare suggestiveness". It is an important scene and has already been commented upon by a few critics. Richard Aldington includes it in full in his anthology of Lawrence's prose, called *The Spirit of Place*, and Graham Hough quotes a part of it in *The Dark Sun*. But neither of them does justice to its glory. Annable is dead; he is about to be buried; but the cosmos is vibrant as ever, thronging not merely with life (which both Aldington and Hough notice), but with life-which-is-bliss-in-itself. It may sound blasphemous to talk of the joy of life when someone is dead. But that is how it is; we cannot but recognize the "is-ness" of things—things as they are, regardless of how we would like them to be. And if we have our eyes open, we see that in nature there is no mourning; there are no dirges sung for the dead; there are only songs for the living.

It was a magnificent morning in early spring when I watched among the trees to see the procession come down the hillside. The upper air was woven with the music of the larks, and my whole world thrilled with the conception of summer. The young pale wind-flowers had arisen by the wood-gale, and under the hazels, when perchance the hot sun pushed his way, new little suns dawned, and blazed with real light. There was a certain thrill and quickening everywhere, as a woman must feel when she has conceived. A sallow tree in a favoured spot looked like a pale gold cloud of summer dawn; nearer it had poised a golden, fairy busby on every twig, and was voiced with a hum of bees, like any sacred golden bush, uttering its gladness in the thrilling murmur of bees, and in warm scent. Birds called and flashed on every hand; they made off exultant with streaming strands of grass, or wisps of fleece, plunging into the dark spaces of the wood, and out again into the blue.

A lad moved across the field from the farm below with a dog trotting behind him,—a dog, no, a fussy, black-legged lamb trotting along on its toes, with its tail swinging behind.

They were going to the mothers on the common, who moved like little grey clouds among the dark gorse.

I cannot help forgetting, and sharing the spink's triumph, when he flashes past with a fleece from a bramble bush. It will cover the bedded moss, it will weave among the soft red cow-hair beautifully. It is a prize, it is an ecstasy to have captured it at the right moment, and the nest is nearly ready.

Ah, but the thrush is scornful, ringing out his voice from the hedge! He sets his breast against the mud, and models it warm for the turquoise eggs—blue, blue, bluest of eggs, which cluster so close and round against the breast, which round up beneath the breast, nestling content. You should see the bright ecstasy in the eyes of a nesting thrush, because of the rounded caress of the eggs against her breast!

What a hurry the jenny wren makes—hoping I shall not see her dart into the low bush. I have a delight in watching them against their shy little wills. But they have all risen with a rush of wings, and are gone, the birds. The air is brushed with agitation. There is no lark in the sky, not one; the heaven is clear of wings or twinkling dot—

Till the heralds come—till the heralds wave like shadows in the bright air, crying, lamenting, fretting forever. Rising and falling and circling round and round, the slow-waving peewits cry and complain, and lift their broad wings in sorrow. They stoop suddenly to the ground, the lapwings, then in another throb of anguish and protest, they swing up again, offering a glistening white breast to the sunlight, to deny it in black shadow, then a glisten of green, and all the time crying and crying in despair.

The pheasants are frightened into cover, they run and dart through the hedge. The cold cock must fly in his haste, spread himself on his streaming plumes, and sail into the wood's security.

There is a cry in answer to the peewits, echoing louder and stronger the lamentation of the lapwings, a wail which hushes the birds. The men come over the brow of the hill, slowly, with the old squire walking tall and straight in front; six bowed men bearing the coffin on their shoulders, treading heavily and cautiously, under the great weight of the glistening white coffin; six men following behind, ill at ease, waiting their turn for the burden. You can see the red handkerchiefs knotted round their throats, and their shirt-fronts blue and white between the open waistcoats. The coffin is of new unpolished wood, gleaming and glistening in the sunlight; the men who carry it remember all their lives after the smell of new, warm elm-wood.[48]

"A certain thrill and quickness everywhere" are the key words here. The Indians describe this as *ananda*. They refer to God as *Sachchidananda*, which means Existence-Consciousness-Bliss. Everything that exists exists in delight. In *The Dark Sun*, Graham Hough observes with his usual astuteness: "Coming on the heels of the game-keeper's horrible death, it suggests that the life of man is in itself a small thing: it is only an expression of a force that is everywhere, quick, tender and strong."[49] Here Hough to a considerable extent catches the spirit of what Lawrence is trying to do. But in the very next sentence he reverts to the conventional line of reasoning when he continues, "How to share in it without denying the claims of the specifically human situation—that is the eternal problem of man's existence." Obviously Hough, like the other Western intellectuals, feels that the force of life or reality, even if it be universal, is somewhat different in man from what it is in the other creatures. For otherwise, the question of sharing in it "without denying the claims of the specifically human situation" would not arise; the two do not contradict each other; they complement. Hough is further wrong in his conclusions, when he adds that it was a question that was to concern Lawrence for the rest of his days. The question surely is posed only by Hough; for Lawrence, there was no such problem or dilemma. He, on the contrary, advocated that the "specifically human situations" were purely man made, and if only man could simplify his wants and needs and live closer to the life of the cosmos, he would be a far happier man. A little later in his analysis, Hough talks of Annable's death as a kind of punishment meted out to him, "either by nature itself or by other men," for Annable does not distinguish between the life of nature and life of man and lives by *mana* "in its crudest and least differentiated form."[50] All these observations show that it is somewhat difficult for Western thinkers to comprehend oneness or wholeness of reality—not a fixed, static oneness or wholeness, but ever-changing, ever-remodifying completeness. Even though Hough grasps the essence of Lawrence's approach, his mind is, as one may discern, still revolving in terms of taskmasters and punishments, between "this" and "that," between *mana*,—the reality, being in pure form and in crude form,—and similar catchwords, which betray an inherent division between the creator and the created world, with the creator taken as one unit and everything else as the other. A better way to take in what Lawrence is saying is to forget this dividing line and, having done that, to move with him in the totality that he has in his consciousness.

And in this totality health, beauty, and sanity dominate. This scene—or the rest of of the novel—does not in any way suggest that the life of a man is essentially a small thing, as Hough put it in *The Dark Sun*. It certainly is a small thing, once one is dead. The point is that it is a great thing when one is alive. And therefore it behooves man to live his life to the full, so long he *has* the force of life in him. The universe is a bowl of joy for the living, and those who are more alive than others theirs is the kingdom and the glory. The throwback to nature which Lawrence effects is to give an illustration of how life moves on in the cosmos: painlessly, slowly, silently—always moving onward. And if man ignores the cosmos, does not take his proper place in it, he is only denying himself a large flood of happiness that would otherwise be his.

The novel opens with the love of Lettie for George. But Lettie later gets engaged to Leslie and not to George, which development in the plot enforces the main feature of my argument: the joy the living present offers, regardless of what one might or might not want. There is ample evidence in the story of the fact that in Lawrence's mind if a person is unhappy the fault is entirely his, as he just does not know how to extract the maximum force from the stream of life; he is too timid, as George is here.

There is a touching, if somewhat sentimental, scene which brings this out quite effectively. As the time of Lettie's and Leslie's wedding draws near, George and Lettie meet one day and go out into the wood. They are both extremely sad, George particularly:

> Once a horse had left a hoofprint in the soft meadow; now the larks had rounded, softened the cup, and had laid there three dark-brown eggs. Lettie sat down and leaned over the nest; he leaned above her. The wind running over the flower heads, peeped in at the little brown buds, and bounded off again gladly. The big clouds sent messages to them down the shadows, and ran in raindrops to touch them.[51]

The image of the hoofprint and the eggs in it and George and Lettie leaning over is particularly captivating. It symbolizes the past and the future life enshrined in the present. It bespeaks the endless continuity. George and Lettie are unfortunately not to marry and be happy together, but what is to be seen here is that the ocean of life tumbles on all around them with the same unceasing force and vigor, nevertheless.

> The wood was high and warm. Along the ridings the forget-me-nots were knee deep, stretching, glimmering into the distance like the Milky Way through the night. They left the tall, flower-tangled paths to go in among the blue-bells, breaking through the close-pressed flowers and ferns till they came to an oak which had fallen across the hazels, where they sat half screened. The hyacinths drooped magnificently with an overweight of purple, or they stood pale and erect, like unripe ears of purple corn. Heavy bees swung down in a blunder of extravagance among the purple

flowers. They were intoxicated even with the sight of so much blue. The sound of their hearty, wanton humming came clear upon the solemn boom of the wind overhead. The sight of their clinging, clambering riot gave satisfaction to the soul. A rosy campion flower caught the sun and shone out. An elm sent down a shower of flesh-tinted sheaths upon them.[52]

George makes a half-hearted appeal to claim Lettie, but she knows better:

"No, my dear, no. The threads of my life were untwined; they drifted about like floating threads of gossamer; and you didn't put out your hand to take them and twist them up into the chord with yours. Now another has caught them up, and the chord of my life is being twisted, and I cannot wrench it free and untwine it again—I can't."[53]

That in a way clinches the issue, so far as George and Lettie are concerned. The life was there, but they did not claim it. George particularly is too slow, and this appals Lettie. Notice the contempt in her voice when, a little before her marriage, she meets him in the last hope that he may still be bold enough to claim her, but George just stands there dumb and shy. In the end he says "good night" and departs:

"Really," she said bitterly, when we were going up the garden path. "You think rather quiet folks have a lot in them, but it's only stupidity—They are mostly fools."[54]

But what now? She cannot have the man she wants, but will the misfortune totally deaden the life in her? The answer is that it is up to her—to deny life, or reject it. In *The White Peacock* Lawrence expresses an attitude which he does not register so forcefully in his later novels; that is, that the pleasure of being alive is greater than any other pleasure in life. To be alive is better than to be dead and extinct. Love is a great thing; it beautifies one's outlook, but healthy life is even greater than love—it has a charm of its own. In "D. H. Lawrence and the Art of Nihilism" (*The Kenyon Review* 20, no. 4, Autumn 1958) Kingsley Widmer talks of the "icy mountain image" in Lawrence and the persistent flight into annihilation in his books. There are other critics as well who have spoken of the element of hatred in Lawrence, the instinct for destruction, for death. There is undoubtedly some bitterness in the tone of his later novels (traceable to his own unhappy experiences), but one fails to see in him any symbolic icy mountains, or negativeness and nihilism. On the other hand, we find him the most profound and vigorous exponent of positive existence. Certainly there is death; there is death in the life of each one of us; there is death every day. We are constantly dying to something or the other—old ideas, old hopes, old friendships—and it is only sensible to recognize this. But, at the same time, there is the constant rebirth; a constant resurrection, as well, in the life of every observable thing and person. In fact, one of the reasons we do not experience the joy of new birth is that we do not know how to die—how to let the things that are dying in our lives recede into the past and vanish. We wish to hold on to the skeleton of our hopes—some idea, some love that we picked up and found pleasing, which later on, for some reason, came to an end—we cry, we fret, we fume, we pray, we beg that the same should continue. And even when we know that we cannot have it any longer, we project a mental picture of that past and keep nursing those outdated memories in our heart. And this is eternal death, for we are living only in the company of the dead. But to accept the death of the dying things is the height of wisdom. Once we do so, we have recognized the fact of it and the dead memory is behind us; we have finished with it. And then the "self" is ready for the "new."

In Lettie we discover this ability to appreciate the new.

In many ways, she resembles Tolstoy's Natasha of *War and Peace*. Like Natasha, she is sprightly and breezy and there is a lot of animal vigor in her. Springs of energy hidden in her and prompting her, she is ever ready to go ahead and find out what life is offering her. It would have been most joyous if she and George had got married. But life must be as it is, and, since they are not to marry, she takes up the threads of her broken life, unwinds them, and lets them grow in other directions. For grow they must; the joy of living cannot be extinguished.

And this is how we find Lettie, a few months after her marriage to Leslie:

> She had developed strangely in six months. She seemed to have discovered the wonderful charm of her womanhood. As she leaned forward with her arm outstretched to the lamp, as she delicately adjusted the wicks with mysterious fingers, she seemed to be moving in some alluring figure of a dance, her hair like a nimbus clouding the light, her bosom lit with wonder. The soft outstretching of her hand was like the whispering of strange words into the blood. . . .[55]

Even the silent, slow George is awakened out of his stupor, for he has meanwhile got married to Meg. Love or no love, she is willing to surrender herself to him without any reservations, to give herself completely to him, physically. The result is that for George, too, all of a sudden a strange and bewildering world is let open:

> She was such a treat, so soft and warm, and so amusing. He was always laughing at her quaint crude notions, and at her queer little turns of speech. She talked to him with a little language, she sat on his knee and twisted his mustache, finding small unreal fault with his features for the delight of dwelling upon them. He was, he said, incredibly happy. Really he couldn't believe it. Meg was, ah! she was a treat.[56]

Thus we see that, regardless of isolated episodes of

sorrow and unhappiness, the gush, the heaviness, the force
of life continues in pure and flawless delight. This force
is extremely well presented in the final end of these two
characters, George and Lettie. Years pass, old memories
fade away, new ones arrive—and both of them have children by now, he by Meg, she by Leslie. It is at this stage
that one discerns the two opposing tendencies, "for" life
and "against" life, which are finally typified in Lettie and
George respectively. Lettie gets so absorbed with the new
that she forgets the old. "The easy, light tickling of the
baby's blood" near her, her own baby, is a fountain of
spring, and she keeps herself open to remain aware of
this newness. And she is saved. Resurrection is the saving
grace, but not the mythical resurrection of a certain historical figure in the past; it is the endless resurrection in
the cosmos. George, however, fails to bring about in himself any resurrection. After the initial experiences of joy
with Meg, he returns to his dead past with Lettie and
elects to live within that; he cannot forget Lettie. Consequently the eyes of his soul are shut and he is henceforth
doomed. He takes to drinking and becomes abusive; even
the sight of his own children, just delivered, does not
mean anything to him:

> " 'Blast 'em then!' he said. He stood there looking like
> a devil. Sybil dear, I did not know our George could look
> like that. I thought he could only look like a faithful dog
> or a wounded stag. But he looked fiendish. He stood watch-
> ing the poor little twins, scowling at them, till at last the
> little red one began to whine a bit. . . . George scowled
> blacker than ever, and went out, lurching against the wash-
> stand and making the pots rattle till my heart jumped in
> my throat."[57]

This is from Alice's letter to Cyril, describing George's
downfall. The chapters toward the end of the book, where
George's extinction is completed, are rather touching.

But though we feel sorry for him, we also feel that the fault somehow is his own. The laws of the cosmos are independent of ethical or moral obligations. There is a time of life for each one of us, but as soon as we fail in the vital breath, either in due course, or prematurely through our own folly, we are silently but firmly eliminated by these cosmic principles from among the living. George is such a "condemned man." He has alienated himself from others and has become foreign to the joy of living. As described by Lawrence, he is "like a tree that is falling, going soft and pale and rotten, clammy with small fungi." And there is no saving him.

And yet—ah! the yet of life—inside the house and outside (George is spending a few days with his sister Emily, at her place), there is a "flow of thick sweet sunshine." Emily is married by this time and is expecting a baby. She has grown to be a full-blooded, large, healthy female, "stately now with the stateliness of a strong woman six months gone with child." We see her in the kitchen, preparing the midday meal. Her brown arms are covered with the white flour; she has just this very minute brushed her forehead with her arm, pasted accidently some flour on the tip of her nose, and made herself even more beautiful. The men are busy with the wheat harvest outside and at last they come in to have their dinner. They eat largely and with zest. There is a healthy display of wit among the men, a coquettish remark or so between Emily and her husband, and finally they each have a glass of wine. And then the men vigorously troop out, for there is more work waiting for them.

George has been sitting with them at the meal, but he is spectral, not belonging to them. Cyril grasps his arm and takes him out to watch the men in the fields. He is deeply touched by his misery but knows there is no hope for him. George is too far gone among the dead.

In the stackyard, the summer's splendid monuments of wheat and grass were reared in gold and grey. The wheat was littered brightly round the rising stack. The loaded wagon clanked slowly up the incline, drew near, and rode like a ship at anchor against the scotches, brushing the stack with a crisp, sharp sound. Tom climbed the ladder and stood a moment there against the sky, amid the brightness and fragrance of the gold corn, and waved his arm to his wife who was passing in the shadow of the building. Then Arthur began to lift the sheaves to the stack, and the two men worked in an exquisite, subtle rhythm, their white sleeves and their dark heads gleaming, moving against the mild sky and the corn. The silence was broken only by the occasional lurch of the body of the wagon, as the teamer stepped to the front, or again to the rear of the load. Occasionally I could catch the blue glitter of the prongs of the forks. Tom, now lifted high above the small wagon load, called to his brother some question about the stack. The sound of his voice was strong and mellow.

I turned to George, who also was watching, and said: "You ought to be like that."[58]

From this simple view of the cosmos Lawrence's work springs, and the feeling of the "interdependability" of things never leaves him. There is an undercurrent of force and life everywhere in the cosmos, and it is up to man to keep himself open to this flow. For the vitality in nature aids the vitality in man. The closer to nature man is, the greater the vitality in him, the greater the life force, the greater the life-furthering procreative power; the farther away from nature (industrialized communities), the less the vitality, the less the power. Lawrence takes an ordinary thing from nature, a vigorous, strong pine tree, and for him even that tree is a huge storehouse of vital existence ("a strong-willed, powerful thing-in-itself, reaching up and reaching down"). He assumes, without the slightest hesitation, "It gives out life, as I give out life. Our two lives meet and cross one another, unknowingly: the tree's life penetrates my life, and my life the tree's. We cannot live near one another, as we do, without affecting one another."[59] And he goes on:

> Is it truer to life to insulate oneself entirely from the influence of the tree's life, and to walk about in an inanimate forest of standing lumber, marketable in St. Louis, Mo.? Or is it truer to life to know, with a pantheistic sensuality, that the tree has its own life, its own assertive existence, its own living relatedness to me: that my life is added to, or militated against, by the tree's life? Which is really true? Which is truer, to live among the living, or to run on wheels?[60]

The same life force exists in every object of nature and every other living creature as well, and that is why the world of nature is ever resplendent with a perpetual glow of beauty. That is why the hills look haunting, the lakes fathomless and deep and mysterious; that is why the trees and plants have a magic language of their own and can nod their heads in an inscrutable manner; that is why the animals glisten with a seductive lure, and go on glistening. In the case of man, however, the monstrous habit of his of demanding this alone or that alone brings a cleavage in the wholeness of his existence. The result is that in the cosmic interflow he has neither anything to give nor anything to receive. And he is cast out by life. But those who know how to experience this "sharing" continue to receive life's benevolence.

This, in a nutshell, is the theme of *The White Peacock*. It is a magnificent view of the cosmos that emerges from such an approach to life—as if the traditional Tibetan "Third Eye" were opened in one's forehead and one saw new colors in a hitherto drab and restricted existence. It should be repeated: it is a concept of the origin and day-to-day running of the universe in which the idea of sin has no place. This is the main import of the present chapter. The universe, in its giant heaving and pulsating of life, is, in all essentials, a sinless organism. In other words, ethics and morality, as we know of them, are absent from the cosmos, which has its own maxims. It requires great insight and courage to face the truth of it; for it removes man from the "central" place he wishes to occupy in the universe, and it is rather hard for him to accept this. In fact, in many ways, judged by the ethical laws evolved by man, the rest of the universe may even appear unethical. For our ethical laws are evolved only to serve our ends, and these ends can often be conflicting with the needs of the rest of life in the cosmos. As the Indian thinker puts it, "We have to recognise, if we thus view the whole, not limiting ourselves to the human difficulty and the human standpoint, that we do not live in an ethical world."[61] This is from Sri Aurobindo, whose two chapters (XI and XII) on "Delight of Existence," in *The Life Divine* are particularly recommended to those who may like to read further in the subject. Sri Aurobindo adds:

> The attempt of human thought to force an ethical meaning into the whole of Nature is one of those acts of wilful and obstinate self-confusion, one of those pathetic attempts of the human being to read himself, his limited habitual human self into all things and judge them from the standpoint he has personally evolved, which most effectively prevent him from arriving at real knowledge and complete sight. Material Nature is not ethical; the law which governs it is a coordination of fixed habits which take no cognisance of good and evil, but only of force that creates, force that arranges and preserves, force that disturbs and destroys impartially, non-ethically, according to the secret Will in it, according to the mute satisfaction of that Will in its own self-formations and self-dissolutions.[62]

It is important to realize this, for only then can one understand the delight involved in the process of creation. The emphasis here is not on the purity of all things, or their piety, or their saintliness; things are as they are. As Lawrence comments: "This Nature-sweet-and-pure business is only another effect of intellectualizing. Just an attempt to make all nature succumb to a few laws of the human mind. The sweet-and-pure sort of laws."[63] A little later he adds: "You can idealize or intellectualize. Or, on the contrary, you can let the dark soul in you see for yourself."[64] For it is certainly a bit naïve to imagine that nature is always kind to man, or even kind in itself—that its effect on man is always beneficial. There are storms, hurricanes, earthquakes, and other natural phenomena, which are positively harmful to man. On the other hand, it would be equally naïve to presume that nature is always unkind to man. Nature is as it is, never deliberately kind and never deliberately unkind; man takes his own place in this vastness, giving and receiving, determined by the one sole law of life: the law of self-preservation and self-propagation. And in this scheme of things, the concept of sin is obviously nonexistent.

This ability to catch the intrinsic joy of each living organism, caught in a moment in time, is to my mind one of the greatest qualities of Lawrence as an artist. He asserts forcefully:

Life, the ever-present, knows no finality, no finished crystallization. The perfect rose is only a running flame, emerging and flowing off, and never in any sense at rest, static, finished. Herein lies its transcendent loveliness. The whole tide of all life and all time suddenly heaves, and appears before us as an apparition, a revelation. We look at the very white quick of nascent creation. A water-lily heaves herself from the flood, looks around, gleams, and is gone. We have seen the incarnation, the quick of the ever-swirling flood. We have seen the invisible. We have seen, we have touched, we have partaken of the very substance of creative change, creative mutation. If you tell me about the lotus, tell me of nothing changeless or eternal. Tell me of the mystery of

the inexhaustible, forever-unfolding creative spark. Tell me
of the incarnate disclosure of the flux, mutation in blossom,
laughter and decay perfectly open in their transit, nude in
their movement before us.[65]

One could add more illustrations from Lawrence's creative
work to describe his range as a supreme artist of the delight
of living, and a discussion of some of his other novels will
later reinforce this. But in his short stories, like "The
Horse-Dealer's Daughter," "Sun," *Love Among the Hay-
stacks*, or *The Virgin and the Gipsy*, or in some of his
poems in *Look! We Have Come Through!*, *Birds, Beasts
and Flowers*, *Pansies*, and *More Pansies*, the instantaneous
joy of living is even more sharply registered. In the novels
the horizon is much wider, and moral and ethical problems
must be satisfactorily handled to go with the action of the
moment. In the shorter pieces, Lawrence is not obliged
to work out the implications of an action. It is the undis-
turbed joy, the calm thrill, the power of the moment
alone that he is after there.

2. *LAWRENCE AND THE
"FATHER-SPARK"*

This chapter will close with a consideration of the
impact of Lawrence's father, Arthur John Lawrence, on
D. H. Lawrence (and, by derivation, the impact of the
working-class community in general). Critics have observed how Lawrence's mother molded his personality
and the power she wielded over him. But Lawrence's
creative work is a testimonial not to the memory of his
mother but to the memory of his father. The tall, ruddy,
physically vital man dominates his books and appears and
reappears, time and again, in almost every story and every
article that Lawrence wrote. Gipsies, gamekeepers, miners;
men from the soil; men of potency and strength and

power; men living a natural religion rather than one enforced on them; men with a reverence for the life of creation; men with sharp instincts; men slumberously awake, heavy with the pull of their bodies; it is men such as these (and women such as these, for that matter) for whom Lawrence shows respect. And they are all obviously the product of the imprint that Arthur Lawrence left on his son's imagination.

What are the things for which Lawrence is most noted? His tenderness; his love for the nonhuman as well as human world; his infinite joy in the passing moment; his keen sensitivity to the truly alive. And these traits, we notice now, were the very traits of Lawrence senior. In autobiographical sketches such as "Rex" and "Adolf," we have delicate descriptions of this man who was ridiculed and bullied in his own house, and we see that he was far more compassionate than his wife, far more kind. In "Rex" we find the following observations of D. H. Lawrence about his mother: "My mother detested animals about the house"; "she could not bear the mix up of human with animal life." And, referring to her constant habit of sarcasm, even with her own children, "she must have wasted some twenty years or more of irony on our incurable naïvete"; and, referring to her pride, "I think now, my mother scorned us for our lack of pride. We were a little *infra-dig*, we children." In "Adolf," when the father brings home an orphan rabbit, we have: "my mother's voice of condemnation," "clouds of my mother's anger," and "my mother reminded him of other little wild animals he had brought, which had sulked and refused to live, and brought storms of tears and trouble in our house of lunatics." On the other hand, this is what we hear about the father:

He loved the open morning, the crystal and the space, after a night down pit. He watched every bird, every stir in the trembling grass, answered the whinnying of the pewits and tweeted to the wrens. If he could, he also would have whinnied and tweeted and whistled in a native language that was not human. He liked non-human things best.[66]

The diversity of outlook on life of these two human beings comes out fairly clearly in the passage below.

. . . She was too fastidious. My father, however, would take on a real dog's voice, talking to the puppy: a funny, high, sing-song falsetto which he seemed to produce at the top of his head. " 'S a pretty little dog! 's a pretty little doggy!—ay!—yes!—he is, yes!—Wag thy strunt, then! Wag thy strunt, Rexie!—Ha-ha! Nay, tha munna—" This last as the puppy, wild with excitement at the strange falsetto voice, licked my father's nostrils and bit my father's nose with his sharp little teeth.

" 'E makes blood come," said my father.

"Serves you right for being so silly with him," said my mother. It was odd to see her as she watched the man, my father, crouching and talking to the little dog and laughing strangely when the little creature bit his nose and tousled his beard. . . .[67]

Even a cursory study of Lydia Beardsall's character shows that she was a highly ambitious woman, who could only be happy if she completely dominated the occasion or the individual concerned. Somehow the carefree, relaxed personality of her husband eluded her grasp. As it was, she was unhappy for having married into a family beneath her standard. But she would have been perfectly contented if Arthur John had submitted himself to her and allowed her to make a "gentleman" of him. This would have given her the superficial elation of domination, the elation of a tyrant, for which she was always looking, and would have reconciled her to him. But it was something that the free and uninhibited miner never allowed her to do. And it was this that bred resentment in her, the selfishness of the impotent to abuse and debase the other. Night after night she poured out tales of horror about him to his children, and made him foreign to them.

Years later, when the overpowering influence of the terrible will of their mother had abated, his children themselves realized how much they had wronged him. In 1932, Ada Clarke, his daughter, said, "I wonder if there would have been quite so much misery in our childhood if mother had just been a little more tolerant."[68] The man was driven to drink in his misery and even then he would feel honestly guilty and sorry whenever he stayed out late. He was still willing to be saved, but the mother's nagging gradually "turned him from his slightly fuddled and pleasantly apologetic mood into a brutal and coarse beast."[69] And all for what? Because he, the man, would not sell his soul to her, the woman.

Let us have a closer look at the pen portraits left by his children. D. H. Lawrence describes him, in the auto-biographical *Sons and Lovers*, as "well set-up, erect, and very smart. He had wavy black hair that shone again, and a vigorous black beard that had never been shaved. His cheeks were ruddy, and his red, moist mouth was noticeable because he laughed so often and so heartily. He had that rare thing, a rich, ringing laugh";[70] and again as "soft, non-intellectual, warm, a kind of gambolling."[71] Ada Clarke has a similar version:

> I can remember my father as a handsome man of medium height with black wavy hair, dark brown beard and moustache. He boasted that a razor had never touched his face. He had dark flashing eyes and a ruddy complexion. His voice was very melodious, and for some years he was in the choir at Brinsley church. My mother, who had never visited a mining village, met him at a party in Nottingham, and was attracted by his graceful dancing, his musical voice, his gallant manner and his over-flowing humour and good spirits.[72]

And this healthy man, brimming with a peculiarly ex-

citing if somewhat vulgar humor, was confronted in matri-
mony with a woman with tight lips and a rigid face, with
an arrogant mind and a bitter tongue. She looks fearful
the way her daughter describes her, even though she is
called ladylike: "How ladylike we thought she looked
when dressed for chapel in her black costume, and black
silk blouse, little black bonnet decorated with black and
white ospreys (she never wore a hat), and an elegant
black and white feather boa round her neck."[73] It is
surprising that none of her children says that she ever
"smiled," or "laughed," or "sang," or "danced," or
"shouted with joy" at the beauty of nature, though Lawrence admits that she had a real sense of humor.[74] It was
as if the visible universe did not exist for her, as if her
whole world consisted of a mentally distorted, egoistical
picture of what *should* be. The two of them, John Arthur
Lawrence and Lydia Beardsall, were certainly poles apart.

In fact, D. H. Lawrence seems to have admired his
father so much that, unconsciously, he made him the hero
of most of his stories. Even in *The White Peacock*, written
in the immediate vicinity of the mother's influence, although there is an attempt as Graham Hough has noticed,
to obliterate the connection with the father (an attempt
because the mother had forced the children to think as
if they had no father), the father emerges, and emerges
forcefully. For Annable is like the father. Annable's lusty,
full-throated voice and his bawdy, care-free humor—his
whole personality—are based on Arthur John Lawrence's
attitude to life, if that simple man could be said to have
had an "attitude." When Annable first comes upon George
and others in the wood and talks roughly to them, and
is told to be respectful in the presence of ladies, his answer
is—"Very sorry, Sir! You can't tell a lady from a woman
at this distance at dusk." When asked, "Have you been
a groom?" he replies, "No groom but a bridegroom, Sir,
and then I think I'd rather groom a horse than a lady,

for I got well bit—if you will excuse me, Sir." Talking
about his children, later, he says, "Aren't they a lovely
little litter?—aren't they a pretty bag o' ferrets?—natural
as weasels—that's what I said they should be—bred up
like a bunch of young foxes, to run as they would." And
again, about the children, "I watch my brats—I let 'em
grow. They're beauties, they are—sound as a young ash
pole, every one. They shan't learn to dirty themselves
wi' smirking deviltry—not if I can help it. They can be
like birds, or weasels, or vipers, or squirrels, so long as
they ain't human rot, that's what I say."

In every line that this man speaks there are echoes of
Arthur John Lawrence. How much intrinsic pride and
love for the family there is in these expressions, particularly deep love for the children. Arthur John Lawrence
had a similar love for his children. Ada Clarke remarks

> When we were all very young he mended our boots and
> shoes, and was never more happy than when seated tailor-
> wise on the rug, with the hobbing iron, hammering away
> and singing at the top of his voice. If the pans and kettles
> leaked he could always mend them, and when the eight-day
> clock was out of order we loved to watch him take it to pieces,
> carefully putting the screws and spare parts in saucers, and
> boiling the works in a big saucepan to clean them thor-
> oughly.[75]

A little later, she adds, decisively: "He was so proud of
us all."[76]

It is doubtful if the mother, Lydia Beardsall, loved any
of the children. She loved only herself, and attached herself first to this child and then to that, depending on where
she could have a better chance of seeing her ideas being
kept alive. She first selected Ernest, the second son; it
was he who was her favorite first. After his death she attached herself to David. But one fails to see any kindness,
or compassion, in this attachment. It was just drive, a

clutch of vice. The two sketches "Rex" and "Adolf,"
quoted from earlier, are replete with instances which show
how much the children, in their early days, turned to the
father for a moment of help rather than to the mother,
and how much more of a common bond there was between
them and him than between them and her. They are
always crying "father this!" and "father that!" and he is
always solacing them, comforting them. They are worried
that the little rabbit he has just brought home might die:
"It won' die, father, will it? Why will it? It won't." Back
comes the comforting reply, "I s'd think not." The next
day they discover that the rabbit, though weak, is still
alive. And they all shout: "Father!" " 'Father!' My father
was arrested at the door, 'Father, the rabbit's alive.' 'Back
your life it is,' said my father." Finally, when the rabbit
has to be released into the wild, it is the father who keeps
them in touch with it by bringing them news about it:
"My father kept an eye open for him. He declared that
several times passing the coppice in the early morning, he
had seen Adolf peeping through the nettle-stalks. He had
called him, in an odd, high-voiced, cajoling fashion. But
Adolf had not responded." Similarly, when the dog Rex
disappears, we hear the father's consoling voice: "Never
mind, my duckie, I s'll look for him in the morning." And
sure enough, in this search, he walks miles the next morning. My reading of similar passages conveys the picture of
a man inexhaustibly tender, merciful at heart, loud and
vociferous but also sensitive to others' suffering, independent in spirit and daring and bold, and ever willing to
live dangerously in anticipation of the new.

True, Lawrence loved his mother, as most children do.
If he was over-attached to her, that too, according to the
psychologists, is a normal feature of all male children. As
a matter of fact, she *was* a positive influence in shaping
the life of Lawrence, and this cannot be ignored; but for
her insistence that he should read and educate himself,

he might well have been a drunken miner somewhere. But with his deep-rooted aversion to dogmatism, he could never have appreciated her rigidity and fixity. He was bound to her, but with resentment in his heart. In a way she was as hard as the Church, and the temperament of Lawrence mutinied against such hardness. Owing to filial piety, he was probably unwilling to admit the fact even to himself. But as years passed, he must have realized all this with overwhelming clarity. For only a decade after her death, we find him confessing, in 1922, to Achsah Brewster, that "he had not done justice to his father in *Sons and Lovers* and felt like rewriting it."[77]

There is a moving account of this disclosure by Achsah Brewster. To give it in her words (it follows after the sentence mentioned above) :

When children they had accepted the dictum of their mother that their father was a drunkard, therefore was contemptible, but that as Lawrence had grown older he had come to see him in a different light; *to see his unquenchable fire and relish for living.* Now he blamed his mother for her self-righteousness, her invulnerable Christian virtue within which she was entrenched. She had brought down terrible scenes of vituperation upon their heads from which she might have protected them. She would gather the children in a row and they would sit quaking, waiting for their father to return while she would picture his shortcomings blacker and blacker to their childish horror. At last the father would come in softly, taking off his shoes, hoping to escape unnoticed to bed, but that was never allowed him. She would burst out upon him, reviling him for a drunken sot, a good-for-nothing father. She would turn to the whimpering children and ask them if they were not disgusted with such a father. He would look at the row of frightened children, and say: "Never mind, my duckies, you needna be afraid of me. I'll do ye na harm."[78] (emphasis mine)

It is a very tragic and heartrending narration. How much suffering there is—and loneliness—in the last remark! That Arthur John Lawrence could survive through it, and after his wife's death could still say to those who advised him to remarry, "I've had one good woman—the finest woman in the world, and I don't want another,"[79] is a measure of his courage and good sense, illiterate though he was. It is obvious that he would have proved a better example, a better parent, to his children, if he had been left unmolested. He had more fortitude, more patience and more tolerance than the other parent. Not only that, judged by his intrinsic qualities, he possessed that rare something of which his wife had no share at all, "his unquenchable fire and relish for living."

During the last years of his life Lawrence made before many other persons confessions like the one above to Mrs. Brewster. In 1926, Barbara Weekley Barr, Frieda's daughter, noticed how he had "swung in sympathy" toward his father, "away from his mother": "Sometimes he talked of his childhood, proudly saying that there had been more life and richness in it than in any middleclass child's home."[80] Rhys Davies visited him in the winter of 1928, and he records:

> An interesting admission he made to me was that he had come to respect his father much more than when he wrote *Sons and Lovers*. He grieved having painted him in such a bitterly hostile way in that book. He could see now that his father had possessed a great deal of the old gay male spirit of England, pre-puritan, he was natural and unruined deep in himself. And Lawrence, by implication, criticized his mother who had so savagely absorbed him, the son. Frieda told me, in answer to my opinion that *Sons and Lovers* was Lawrence's finest book, "No, it's an evil book, because of that woman in it, his mother."[81]

In a wise but sharply critical essay, "That Women Know Best," Lawrence describes the disputes that he used to watch as a child. He states there how his mother would refuse to recognize the authority of the father in the house, alleging that she was better informed about life than he. Lawrence makes this an occasion to generalize that all women think they know "best." But at the end of the essay he states:

Alas, after many years the truth comes out: they don't know. The courage is largely bravado. Even my mother, when she was older, realised that she didn't know. She had stood like a lighthouse for so many years. But when we put it to her: Are you sure you're showing the real way of life? she had to admit, she wasn't quite sure. The lighthouse wavered its beams and went out. It wasn't really sure of itself. It didn't absolutely know right from wrong.[82]

The following lines from Frieda Lawrence's letter to V. de S. Pinto, in 1953, give further idea of how deep Lawrence's feelings were about his parents. Frieda writes: "Much later when he came across *Sons and Lovers* again, he said: 'Did I write this? I would be much fairer to my father now as now I know how devastating was my mother's love!' "[83] Taking the story as it stands, Karl Menninger in *Love Against Hate* cites *Sons and Lovers* as a "classic" example more of hatred than love for the mother. He states: "By a pretence of attachment to her such a boy can conceal his hostility to her, eliminate the necessity of any fear of her, and avoid the consequences of attempting to express his masculinity in a normal way."[84]

In *Fantasia of the Unconscious,* Lawrence critically evaluates the mark of a father in the character and mental make-up of a child. He calls it the "father-spark" in a man: "this unquenched father-spark within you sends forth vibrations and dark currents of vital activity all the time; connecting direct with your father. You will never be able to get away from it while you live."[85] As he explains, a little later:

Because the mother-child relation is more plausible and

flagrant, is that any reason for supposing it deeper, more vital, more intrinsic? Not a bit. Because if the large parent mother-germ still lives and acts vividly and mysteriously in the great fused nucleus of your solar plexus, does the smaller, brilliant male-spark that derived from your father act any less vividly? By no means. It is different—it is less ostensible. It may be even in magnitude smaller. But it may be even more vivid, even more intrinsic. So beware how you deny the father-quick of yourself. You may be denying the most intrinsic quick of all.[86]

In the regret that he felt about his own attitude to his father, clearly it was not only the realization of the fact that he had ignored the "father-spark" in himself, but a recognition of its inherent superiority and force over what he had inherited from his mother.

Perhaps without meaning to, Lawrence transfers something of his home atmosphere—the merciless vituperation against the father by the mother—to the life of the later George in *The White Peacock*. The cause of George's sorrow is a different one; so is his end. Arthur John Lawrence, even in the worst moments of his misery, still keeps that reverence for life; George does not. But we are referring to the actual impact of the scenes between George and Meg. They have the same atmosphere: Meg bullying George, without showing any sympathy to him.

> "You couldn't imagine what it's like, Cyril," she said. "It's like having Satan in the house with you, or a black tiger glowering at you. I'm sure nobody knows what I've suffered with him—"
> The children stood with large, awful eyes and paling lips, listening.[87]

It might as well be the voice of Lydia Beardsall condemning Arthur John Lawrence, and the children might as well be the Lawrence children. It is a trifle amusing that the mother could not read the copy of *The White Peacock*, which the devoted son had specifically got ready

for her and rushed to her; otherwise she would have ex-
ulted in her "favourite" Bert, so faithfully picturing the
horror of a wronged wife. She would not have seen—as
Lawrence did not either, but we do—that even in this
presentation, it is the father who wins the sympathy of
the reader and not the mother. The resemblance between
the fictitious and the actual comes out more sharply in the
scene where Meg and her grown-up daughter chaff poor
George, the daughter exactly copying her mother in the
haggling (see pp. 475-78).

The love that Lawrence professed for his mother hardly
appears in that form in his creative writing, except in the
group of poems addressed to her. On the contrary, in one
of his short stories, we have scathing criticism of a monstrous mother, who completely swallows up the lives of
her two sons and persists in not letting them lead an existence of their own.

This story, "The Lovely Lady," is a revealing auto-
biographical miniature. Pauline Attenborough has two
sons, named Henry and Robert. When the story opens,
Henry is already dead. Robert is attached to his cousin,
Cecilia, but is afraid of showing his love for her as his
mother does not approve of it; she wants to keep Robert
wholly to herself. Cecilia would often visit them, but the
mother resents it. It is only when they are alone, the two
of them, the mother and the son, that she feels happy.
We are told that Robert "paid all his attention to his
mother, drawn to her as a humble flower to the sun." And
when they are alone—"And then! Oh, then, the lovely
glowing intimacy of the evening, between mother and son,
when they deciphered manuscripts and discussed points,
Pauline with that eagerness of a girl, for which she was
famous." Cecilia is dismayed at this unhealthy attachment
and resents it: "What would he be when his mother is
dead—in a dozen more years? He would just be a shell,
the shell of a man who had never lived."

The assessment of the mother is presented to us through Cecilia, and now follows a long passage in which Lawrence's own relationship with Jessie Chambers and his mother comes out fairly well:

> The strange unspoken sympathy of the young with one another, when they are overshadowed by the old, was one of the bonds between Robert and Ciss. But another bond, which Ciss did not know how to draw tight, was the bond of passion. Poor Robert was by nature a passionate man. His silence and his agonized, though hidden, shyness were both the result of a secret physical passionateness. And how Pauline could play on this! Ah, Ciss was not blind to the eyes which he fixed on his mother, eyes fascinated yet humiliated, full of shame. He was ashamed that he was not a man. *And he did not love his mother. He was fascinated by her. Completely fascinated. And for the rest, paralysed in a life-long confusion.*[88] (emphasis mine)

The last lines are self-expressive. There was no real love in the attachment Lawrence had for his mother. But to continue with "The Lovely Lady," from casual sentences picked up by Cecilia when Pauline is talking aloud to herself, Cecilia gathers that the mother had similarly interfered and ruined the love of her elder son, Henry, for a girl called Claudia, and finally driven him to death in his despair. Cecilia's comments are: *"What a devil* of a woman!"* (Lawrence's emphasis).

> Ciss knew the facts from her own father. And lately, she had been thinking that Pauline was going to kill Robert as she had killed Henry. It was clear murder: a mother murdering her sensitive sons, who were fascinated by her: the Circe![89]

Apart from minor changes, it is evident that Lawrence's own story is being repeated here. We are told that Robert became his mother's darling only after the death of the elder brother. "Ciss believed that Aunt Pauline had loved her big, handsome, brilliant first-born much more than she loved Robert, and that his death had been a terrible blow and chagrin to her. Poor Robert had been only ten years old when Henry died. Since then he had been the substitute." When Cecilia asks Robert to sit with her for a while in the garden, his terrified reply is: "What about mother?" When Cecilia looks too upset, Robert assures her: "I suppose I shall rebel one day." All these essential remarks remind us of the emotional tension between Lawrence and his mother. Fortunately, by 1927 when this story was written, Lawrence had seen his love for his mother in its true perspective. He actually classifies the story as a "murder" story, and it was first published in *The Black Cap, New Stories of Murder and Mystery*, compiled by Cynthia Asquith.[90] Through a clever artistic device, Pauline is foiled and Cecilia and Robert are presumably to marry. But my interest lies in the ultimate pronouncement of Lawrence on his mother, as presented in the following dialogue:

> "Do you think your mother ever loved anybody?" Ciss asked him tentatively, rather wistfully, one evening.
> He looked at her fixedly.
> "Herself!" he said at last.
> "She didn't even *love* herself," said Ciss. "It was something else—what was it?" She lifted a troubled, utterly puzzled face to him.
> "Power!" he said curtly.
> "But what power?" she asked. "I don't understand."
> "Power to feed on other lives," he said bitterly. "She was beautiful, and she fed on life. She has fed on me as she fed on Henry. She put a sucker into one's soul and sucked up one's essential life."[91]

This is terrible judgment by a son. But what follows is even more terrible. Cecilia asks him: "And don't you forgive her?" And his conclusive reply is: "No."

In "The Lovely Lady," Lawrence travels far from the simpering child who, in the year 1910, doted on his mother uncritically and undiscerningly and, feeling sorry

for her in her illness, could write to a friend, Rachel Annand Taylor, "I've never had but one parent."[92] But,
even in those years, his account clearly reflects the intimate
nature of his father, which, at heart, he admired. For, in
another letter to the same friend, we have: "I will tell you.
My mother was a clever, ironical delicately moulded
woman of good, old burgher descent. She married below
her. My father was dark, ruddy, with a fine laugh. He is
a coal miner. He was one of the sanguine temperament,
warm & hearty, but unstable; he lacked principle, as my
mother would have said. He deceived her & lied to her.
She despised him—he drank."[93] Clearly it is the tutored
voice speaking—tutored by the relentless mother—when
he goes on in the same letter, "Their married life has
been one carnal, bloody fight. I was born hating my
father: as early as ever I can remember, I shivered with
horror when he touched me. He was very bad before I
was born."

But it was the same son who, in 1928, finally admitted
that "his father and X [Norman Douglas], were the only
people he had known who always followed joy. Nothing
else but the joy of life had concerned them."[94]

And this "joy of life"—inherited by him from his father—penetrates every single piece of creative exercise of
D. H. Lawrence. It appears and reappears every time a
man and a woman come together; it rears its head up, fills
the whole being, and makes it thrill when a woman conceives (notice the exquisite dance by Anna Brangwen,
in *The Rainbow*, in the nude, while she has the child in
her womb) ; it shows itself in the roar of the moving
waters, in the might of the rain, in the full and brilliant
moon, in the budding flowers; it shows itself in dance and
song and music; it shows itself in everything that *is*.

In appreciation of the delight of creation, we take our
first step in understanding Lawrence. This is the basic
myth in which he fixes his characters and works out their

destinies. How far he succeeds in doing so is discussed in the subsequent chapters. But the joy of life, the dance of life, the delight of life—in the absolute bliss of just being alive, devoid of sin as such, devoid of a taskmaster God, complete in itself; that is our main term of reference for appreciating Lawrence's work. In the unfinished novel, *The Flying Fish,* his character Gethin Day confronts us with a challenge, lucidly and forcefully. He has had bad news from home; he himself is ill; everything, apparently, looks sad and gloomy. He is on his way to England in a ship, crossing the mighty ocean. And as he sits brooding on the deck, he looks at the huge fish, flying in the ocean:

> Gethin Day watched spell-bound, minute after minute, an hour, two hours, and still it was the same, the ship speeding, cutting the water, and the strong-bodied fish heading in perfect balance of speed underneath, mingling among themselves in some strange single laughter of multiple consciousness, giving off the joy of life, sheer joy of life, togetherness in pure complete motion, many lusty-bodied fish enjoying one laugh of life, sheer togetherness, perfect as passion. They gave off into the water their marvellous joy of life, such as the man had never met before. And it left him wonderstruck.[95]

This joy is infectious. It immediately is communicated to Gethin Day.

> There as he leaned over the bowsprit he was mesmerised by one thing only, by joy, by joy of life, fish speeding in water with playful joy. No wonder Ocean was still mysterious, when such red hearts beat in it! No wonder man, with his tragedy, was a pale and sickly thing in comparison! What civilisation will bring us to such a pitch of swift laughing togetherness as these fish have reached?[96]

The answer is that no "outside" authority, no civilization as such can show the way. The way is there already, and it is for each individual to make the choice: to accept life, or to reject it.

3

Love and Marriage

I

1. MARRIAGE AND CENTRALIZED SEXUALITY

It is necessary now to take note in detail of Lawrence's views on sex, as the greatest harm to his reputation has been done by people who misunderstand him, or understand him imperfectly, in his pronouncements on the subject. He himself did not recognize this for years—why many of his contemporaries, or the public in general, did not give him his due as an artist. It was only after *Lady Chatterley's Lover* was published in 1928 that it struck him that perhaps his average reader mistook the meaning of the word he had used so innocently all his life. We have his surprise and his confession:

> So that at last I begin to see the point of my critics' abuse of my exalting of sex. They only know one form of sex: in fact, to them there *is* only one form of sex: the nervous, personal, disintegrative sort, the "white" sex. And this, of course, is something to be flowery and false about, but nothing to be very hopeful about. I quite agree. And I quite agree, we can have no hope of the regeneration of England from such sort of sex.[1]

He sees the falsity of the whole situation and comments a little later: "the current sort of sex is just what I *don't* mean and *don't* want."[2]

92

What does he mean by sex, then? He elaborates on it in *Apropos*, and in essays like "Love," "Sex Versus Loveliness," and "Nobody Loves Me," but the following quotation from "We Need One Another" (where he discusses the natural necessity of man-woman togetherness) explains his stand more pointedly. In the first place, of course, as discussed in the last chapter, sex is another name for him for the inherent life force, the inherent beauty in every living being. But it also means something else. He writes in "We Need One Another":

> And what is sex, after all, but the symbol of relation of man to woman, woman to man? And the relation of man to woman is wide as all life. It consists in infinite different flows between the two beings, different, even apparently contrary. Chastity is part of the flow between man and woman, as to physical passion. And beyond these, an infinite range of subtle communication which we know nothing about.[3]

He adds a page or so afterwards:

> The relationship is a life-long change and a life-long travelling. And that is sex. At periods, sex-desire itself departs completely. Yet the great flow of the relationship goes on all the same, undying, and this is the flow of living sex, the relation between man and woman, that lasts a life-time, and of which sex-desire is only one vivid, most vivid, manifestation.[4]

We observe from this that "sex" for Lawrence is actually another name for the flow of feelings, any genuine feelings, between the individuals of opposite sexes. Aptly enough, just as Lawrence calls God the *living* God, and Church the *living* Church in his work, he calls sex the *living* sex. Considered as such, we realize how broad a meaning the word had for him and how wide an emotional range it spanned. Thus when he said in *Apropos*, "I want men and women to be able to think sex, fully, completely, honestly, and cleanly,"[5] it was a cleansing of the whole social set-up that he had in mind and not merely of things relating to the sexual act.

But this by itself is not enough. The grandeur of Lawrence as an artist lies in his enunciation of what I propose to term the concept of centralized sexuality (and what Lawrence describes as "conjunction"). Sex is beautiful in itself; but it is even more beautiful if its intensity and flow are concentrated and focused toward a particular object, or rather between two particular objects. Thus, as may be seen in the passage quoted above, the purest form of centralized sexuality conceives of a relationship between *one* man and *one* woman—the same man and the same woman, holding on to the magic for each other all their life. Years will come and go, their needs and their personalities will change, their love for each other will ebb and alternate, and for the all-embracing many-sided vision of reality to be, it surely has to be a lifetime of togetherness for them to understand each other, to "get" each other, to know what it means to be a woman, to know what it means to be a man, to know the "otherness" of a woman, the otherness of a man, to have distinction, to have uniqueness of being alive in the flesh.

And since sex to Lawrence was holy and sacred, centralized sexuality, or marriage (the social institution based on centralized sexuality), was even more holy, was religious. He was a great advocate of marriage, in art as well as in private life. Referring to the forthcoming wedding of Catherine Carswell, he wrote to her: "Your life will run on a stable pivot then, and you will be much happier."[6] Even in his idea of *Rananim,* the ideal community he wished to establish, he had no place for unattached, single men and women, and Catherine Carswell remarks how assiduously he used to plan matches for those who were still unmarried.[7] Writing to her in another letter, he once said:

It is those who are married who should live the life of contemplation together. In the world, there is the long day of destruction to go by. But let those who are single, man torn from woman, woman from man, men all together, women all together, separate violent and deathly fragments, each returning and adhering to its own kind, the body of life torn in two, let these finish the day of destruction, and those who have united go into the wilderness to know a new heaven and a new earth.[8]

So marriage for him was positively sacramental, permanent and binding; and if he comes at all close to conventional religions anywhere, rebel as he otherwise was, it is in his respect for this edifying institution of mankind.

Throughout the following analysis we will see a close parallel between the language of Lawrence and that of conventional religions; yet there is a world of difference in the approach. The best introduction to Lawrence's stand on the subject is contained in that remarkable long essay, *Apropos of Lady Chatterley's Lover.* It is unfortunate that Mark Spilka in *The Love Ethic of D. H. Lawrence* does not pay any serious attention to this essay, for what better summary could one have of Lawrence's "love" ethic than the one he himself has left? On love, on sex, on marriage, *Apropos* is the most reliable report of Lawrence the critic on Lawrence the artist. It is unnecessary to repeat all that is said there, but, briefly, marriage for Lawrence is rooted in genuine love and genuine love is rooted in genuine sex. This is what the conventional religions say too, and Christian theologians have already begun to praise Lawrence for his opinions. A bishop and several other Church dignitaries gave evidence on his behalf at the Lady Chatterley Trial in London. As early as 1937, Father Vann in *Morals Makyth Man* based a large section of his chapter "Christian Marriage" on what Lawrence says in *Apropos,* and prefaced his discussion with the comment, "We do well to remind ourselves of

Lawrence's scalding indictment of 'counterfeit love.' "[9] Thus the Church has done more than merely recognize; it has already started quoting him as one of the authorities on the subject.

But the difference lies in the fact that whereas conventional religions try to impose morality of marriage out of fear—fear of God—Lawrence asserts that that morality is implicit in the very nature of existence. The law of Consummate Marriage, he wrote in a review article, is "that every living thing seeks, individually and collectively."[10] According to Lawrence collective seeking is as much a law of nature, is as much a thing-in-itself, as its counterpart. Hence the morality of marriage, the behavior of "collective seeking," is not to be dictated; it is to be watched and observed in life, and is an understanding arrived at.

The most significant observation that Lawrence makes in this connection is that collective seeking involves absolute concentration of sexuality, absolute limitation, or what we have called absolute "centralization." Centralized sexuality demands that a man's sex should not be wasted; it demands sexual faithfulness. "There is something more important than love!" in life, Lawrence told his American friend, Mabel Luhan. And when she defiantly asked him what it was, his grim answer was: "Fidelity!"[11] His own life stands as a unique illustration of this fact, and as Catherine Carswell remarks, "From first to last Lawrence was for fidelity in marriage."[12] He saw it as a basic principle of things-in-themselves, of all things, that without centralization intensity could not be. The joy of the living moment, of the "now," the intensity of it, that he describes in his work is because of this centralization. To quote from *Apropos*, the scripture of sexual morality: "The instinct of fidelity is perhaps the deepest instinct in the great complex we call sex. Where there is real sex there is the underlying passion for fidelity."[13]

Love and Marriage 97

We see, thus, that on grounds of sheer common sense Lawrence comes to establish a very vital canon of marriage. Marriage must rest on fidelity; not out of fear of God, or conventional morality, but because that is how it is, by the nature of its reality. He was so convinced of the truth of it that he believed even mental infidelity, even mental unfaithfulness, interfered with the joy of centralized sexuality. We find him lamenting in one of his poems

> From all the mental poetry
> of deliberate love-making,
> from all the false felicity
> of deliberately taking
> the body of another unto mine,
> O God deliver me![14]

This is very close to what Jesus says in respect of adultery in the mind; except that according to Lawrence if one does commit such adultery, he will not be sinning against a maker-God but depriving himself of the joy of the living moment with his own chosen partner, hence depriving himself of the joy of the Self. And this will be doing a grievous wrong to one's "being," a wrong to the flowering of the being.

It will not be an exaggeration to say that in his interpretation of marriage, Lawrence rises to heights unsurpassed by many other novelists, living or dead. The superstructure, the edifice of all his novels is built on his veneration for the state of holiness that married sex ushers. I am deliberately avoiding the word "love," for marriage in Lawrence does not rest on love; marriage is centralized sexuality, and it does not, as such, rest on anything. But it is in marriage alone, in its centralized form only, that he conceives of man as being strong enough, being brave enough, to face the mysteries of sex—the divine power that dominates the universe. In his essay "The Novel," he speaks of the flame of sex as a striped tiger, and, again, as a king cobra, which would brook no dallying, no trifling with, and asks: "You will play with sex, will you! You will tickle yourself with sex as with an ice-cold drink from a soda-fountain! You will pet your best girl, will you, and spoon with her, and titillate yourself and her, and do as you like with your sex?"[15] And he goes on: "Wait! Only wait till the flame you have dribbled on flies back at you, later! Only wait!"[16]

2. REGENERATED MAN AND REGENERATED WOMAN

As mentioned before, Lawrence was at one with the established religions in his respect for the sanctity and abidingness of marriage. Whether in the West or in the East, all developed faiths look upon it as sacramental. But —and this is an important point—for Lawrence it was not *every* marriage that was holy. The Christian Church, as well as the Vedic religion in India, both regard any union that comes into being as final, as endless. In so doing, they shift the sanctity of the union to the formality of the marriage, to the ceremony. For Lawrence on the other hand, for the finality and the sanctity to be binding it must be the right type of marriage when it comes into being. The sacramental part does not lie in the ritual of marriage, the sacramental part depends on the validity of the initial desire to marry. As he says, "It is not a question of: Marry the woman and have done with it."[17] It is a far more grave and serious question; it is a question of a conjunction to be formed and no conjunction is binding unless it comes from the very innermost desires of the being.

We must agree that it is bit difficult to get at these innermost desires. The type of marriage Lawrence talks about is so very, very deep, its tentacles so abysmal and profound, that its acceptance involves overhauling of all human values. For in both the East and in the West, marriage is a school based on the idea of "security." Nothing haunts man more in life than the fear of insecurity. The State, Property, Marriage are so constructed as to make the individual feel secure, to give him a guarantee for the future to come. (See Lawrence's letter on the subject to Dorothy Brett—"Thanks for the Marriage book—what a feeble lot of compromises! It's no good talking about it: marriage, like homes, will last while our social system lasts, because it's the thing that holds our system together. But our system will collapse, and then marriage will be different—probably more tribal, men and women being a good deal apart, as in the old *pueblo* system, no little homes. It all works back to individual property, even marriage is an arrangement for the holding of property together, a bore!") [18] Even religion is, in Lawrence's view, used as a means toward this end: security, security in the life to come. The type of social security we look forward to in marriage differs in the East and the West. In the East, where most marriages these days are arranged, the unit of family, children, and a home, is considered a more potent stake for the security of the individual, hence instead of the man and the woman alone, other members of the two families also get together, and come to the conclusion that the prospective man and woman will be compatible. In the West, because of the intellectual emancipation of the individual from the somewhat pedestrian ties of the family, it is the mental security that a man and a woman seek in marriage, and when two persons having like acquired tastes come together, with like reading habits, like eating habits, like leisure habits, they acquire a warm glow for each other, likeness grows, and they agree to give marriage a chance. But genuine love in both cases, in the East as well as in the West, is nonexistent. The type of likeness and fondness that men and women have for each other in the West before marriage, men and women in the East too come to acquire after marriage: it is a likeness based on *the habit of intimacy*. The real basis of their coming together remains "security"—security of the ego, in one form or the other.

For Lawrence, however, a relationship between a man and a woman is a thing complete in itself and should not come into being on any other consideration than the basic desire of the Self for the relationship itself. To quote from his "Morality and the Novel," "It is the *relation itself* which is the quick and the central clue to life, not the man, nor the woman, nor the children that result from the relationship, as a contingency."[19] To take another of his essays, ". . . Love was Once a Little Boy," we read there: "But each calculates the sacrifice. And man and woman alike, each saves his individual ego, her individual ego, intact, as far as possible, in the scrimmage of love. Most of our talk about love is cant, and bunk. The treasure of treasures to man and woman today is his own, or her own ego. And this ego, each hopes it will flourish like a salamander in the flame of love and passion."[20] Lawrence passionately believed in the love between a man and a woman, but it was not the type of love that had a planned goal in view—the fulfillment of the desires of the ego. Desires of the ego bind one to a rigid routine of expectations, and love can exist only in freedom. In his penetrating essay on the subject, "Love," he solemnly pronounces: "There is a goal, but the goal is neither love nor death. It is a goal neither infinite nor eternal. It is the realm of calm delight, it is the other-kingdom of bliss."[21]

How then are two persons to come together? How is a marriage to be formed? Who gives the signal for the centralized sexuality to come into being between the two of them? The signal of course is given by the Unknown, because in Lawrence it is the voice of the unknown alone that is creative, that never misleads. Associations based on measured rules and regulations crumble and fall away, like so many houses of cards, but promptings of the unknown are always final. His essay on "Love" ends with this profound paragraph:

> There is that which we cannot love, because it surpasses either love or hate. There is the unknown and the unknowable which propounds all creation. This we cannot love, we can only accept it as a term of our own limitation and ratification. We can only know that from the unknown, profound desires enter in upon us, and that the fulfilling of these desires is the fulfilling of creation. We know that the rose comes to blossom. We know that we are incipient with blossom. It is our business to go as we are impelled, with faith and pure spontaneous morality, knowing that the rose blossoms, and taking that knowledge for sufficient.[22]

"It is our business to go as we are impelled, with faith and pure spontaneous morality, knowing that the rose blossoms, and taking that knowledge for sufficient"—*that* is the clue to a real marriage, according to Lawrence: it is the coming together of a man and woman in the complete silence of their mind, complete silence of their ego. In the next chapter we elaborate on Lawrence's belief in intuition as the link which unites man with the unknown, in all walks of life. Centralized sexuality is perhaps the most significant of all these walks, and here again, only intuition can help—intuition which keeps the individual in readiness for the urge from the unknown. The unknown is always moral, the unknown has always a meaning in its messages; who will have the blasphemy to accuse it of being otherwise? But to be in tune with the unknown, the mind must be free of the known. The unknown is the living moment emerging from nowhere, every second of it, making itself manifest in thousands upon thousands of unimaginable forms and ways. And when the mind is free of the store of impressions of the yesterdays, or free of imaginary myths of the tomorrows to come, when the mind is passive and yet alert, in a state of receptivity to the new, the unknown comes and fills it up.

Unfortunately, as stated earlier, most people approach love and marriage with a ready-made concept of love; not with genuine feelings but with imitated and imagined feelings. To quote from *Apropos*: "All love today is counterfeit. It is a stereotyped thing. All the young know just how they ought to feel and how they ought to behave, in love. And they feel and they behave like that. And it is counterfeit love."[23] Lawrence was understanding enough to realize that counterfeit and true feelings, both, went into making a man what he was; he never insisted that a person should be, or could be, of one unmixed virtue. What he emphasized was that one should have the inherent capacity to distinguish between the two and to decide what the Self really wanted. To follow it up from *Apropos*:

> Now the real tragedy is here: that we are none of us all of a piece, none of us *all* counterfeit, or *all* true love. And in many a marriage, in among the counterfeit there flickers a little flame of the true thing, on both sides. The tragedy is, that in an age peculiarly conscious of counterfeit, peculiarly suspicious of substitute and swindle in emotion, particularly sexual emotion, the rage and mistrust against the counterfeit element is likely to overwhelm and extinguish the small, true flame of real loving communion, which might have made two lives happy.[24]

The "might have" depends, however, on a very big "if," on "the small, true flame of real loving communion"; and in many marriages Lawrence believed the flame was nonexistent. For the initial desire to marry, the initial impulse, in most cases, was *not* based on intuition, on the voice of the soul; it was based on the promptings of the ego, the ego, which calculates advantages and disadvantages, computes the similarities and dissimilarities, and after these mathematical calculations comes to a conclusion that may provoke a "stable" marriage, a "safe" marriage, even a "happy" marriage, but certainly not a marriage that surpasses all these categories, is stable and unstable both, safe and unsafe, happy and unhappy at the same time, and is yet enriching, ever more enriching and ever more glorifying for the development of the soul. There is a rather simple and enormously profound line in *Aaron's Rod,* where Lilly says to Aaron: "Always know that what you are doing is the fulfilling of your own soul's impulse."[25] Commenting on this line, Eliseo Vivas in his *D. H. Lawrence, The Failure and the Triumph of Art,* says, "it is an expression of Lawrence's unmitigated, immature, foot-stamping, table-pounding, fretting, pouting, cry-baby, petulant selfishness—a sheer, uncomplicated, unrestrained, colossally arrogant, self-centred selfishness."[26] The extremity of some of the critical statements that are published at times makes one lose one's faith in the very function of criticism! The falseness of this particular comment—in any case, its rashness—is self-evident. It pains one to imagine, however, that Lawrence will perhaps remain foreign to some of us for all ages to come. For what, exactly, is wrong with the statement, "Always know that what you are doing is the fulfilling of your own soul's impulse"? Wherein lies the untruth? The ego, the mind may misguide one, but how could the soul, the unknown mislead and misguide? In *The Ladybird,* Count Dionys tells Basil Daphne: "A man can only be happy following his own inmost need"[27]—again, a repetition of the same principle. There is the edge of irony in the fact that both Aaron and Count Dionys are involved in what would normally be termed as "unethical" situations: Aaron has deserted his wife, and Count Dionys has had an illicit relationship with Basil's wife, Lady Daphne; and for *them* to hear about, or to talk about, soul's impulses might sound somewhat insincere. But the strength of Lawrence's art lies in that he does not make these statements appear as a justification of their actions; it is brought to bear upon the reader, and quite convincingly, that the statements are true, independently of what these men have done. Situations do arise when a man may have to leave his wife and go away; situations do arise where extramarital attachments take place. The artist in Lawrence does not approve or disapprove of these situations; he merely so formulates the tale as to leave the undisputed impression that *this* alone is what could have happened in the circumstances, and tragic though it may be, one can do nothing but accept the stark reality of what is and live by it—the soul's urge—at a particular time, in a particular circumstance.

The brief one-sentence extracts, like the one abstracted by Vivas or the one cited by me, actually do not communicate the depth, often the agony, at all times the courage of conviction which Lawrence has when he repeatedly falls back on the urge of the soul as the only valid light of one's conduct. A longer passage from "The Nightmare" chapter of *Kangaroo* (the chapter where Somers talks of the badgering he has received at the hands of the world), shows more penetratingly the merit of Lawrence's line of argument:

> So he discovered the great secret: to stand alone as his own judge of himself, absolutely. He took his stand absolutely on his own judgment of himself. Then, the mongrel-mouthed world would say and do what it liked. This is the greatest secret of behaviour: to stand alone, and judge oneself from the deeps of one's own soul. And then, to know, to hear what the others say and think: to refer their judgment to the touchstone of one's own soul-judgment. To fear one's own inward soul, and never to fear the outside world, nay, not even one single person, nor even fifty million persons.[28]

Even the very paragraph from which Vivas takes his line,

that very paragraph itself, if read in entirety along with the other paragraphs that follow it, leaves the same unmistakable stamp of the gravity and the responsibility involved when one takes the cue for one's action from one's soul:

"So I'd better sit tight on my soul, till it hatches, had I?"
"Oh yes. If your soul's urge urges you to love, then love. But always know that what you are doing is the fulfilling of your own soul's impulse. It's no good trying to act by prescription: not a bit. And it's no use getting into frenzies. If you've got to go in for love and passion, go in for them. But they aren't the goal. They're a mere means: a life-means, if you will. The only goal is the fulfilling of your own soul's active desire and suggestion. Be passionate as much as ever it is your nature to be passionate, and deeply sensual as far as you can be. Small souls have a small sensuality, deep souls a deep one. But remember, all this time, the responsibility is upon your own head, it all rests with your own lonely soul, the responsibility for your own action."
"I never said it didn't," said Aaron.
"You never said it did. You never accepted. You thought there was something outside, to justify you: God, or a creed, or a prescription. But remember, your soul inside you is your only godhead. It develops your actions within you as a tree develops its own new cells. And the cells push on into buds and boughs and flowers. And these are your passion and your acts and your thoughts and expressions, your developing consciousness. You don't know beforehand, and you can't. You can only stick to your own soul through thick and thin.
"You are your own Tree of Life, roots and limbs and trunk. Somewhere within the wholeness of the tree lies the very self, the quick: its own innate Holy Ghost. And this Holy Ghost puts forth new buds, and pushes past old limits, and shakes off a whole body of dying leaves. And the old limits hate being empassed, and the old leaves hate to fall. But they must, if the tree-soul says so. . . ."[29]

And if love and marriage as well came initially from the same soul, if this urge was patiently waited for until its voice came as the unavoidable fate, then that love and that marriage alone could have come into being between that man and that woman, and hence their union would be above reason and comprehension as such, but would be something unavoidable and final, dictated by the very hands of the Unknown.

Unless this happened, unless love and marriage came like that, in Lawrence's terminology it was not love but only a friction, not marriage but only a mockery. The following speech by Don Ramon in *The Plumed Serpent* illustrates the point just mentioned clearly:

> Remember the marriage is the meeting-ground, and the meeting-ground is the star. If there be no star, no meeting-ground, no true coming together of man with the woman, into a wholeness, there is no marriage. And if there is no marriage, there is nothing but an agitation. If there is no honourable meeting of man with woman and woman with man, there is no good thing come to pass. But if the meeting come to pass, then whosoever betrays the abiding place, which is the meeting-ground, which is that which lives like a star between day and night, between the dark of woman and the dawn of man, between man's night and woman's morning, shall never be forgiven, neither here nor in the hereafter. For man is frail and woman is frail, and none can draw the line which another shall walk. But the star that is between two people and is their meeting-ground shall not be betrayed.[30]

The "star" and the "meeting-ground" are Lawrence's different names for the voice of the beyond. How this voice comes, or when it comes, no one can predict in advance; it cannot be generated at will, it heeds no prayers or supplications. The force, the strength of the argument is that once it *does* come, it is final. It has the quality of clinching an issue; not in a pedagogic, despotic manner, but in a creative manner. It only suggests; but it does so in so productive and convincing a fashion that the individual submissive to it is left with no other choice but to obey and to follow. For in that following is his joy. The grandeur of the individual lies in nothing else except this: in his ability to rise to the highest level of consciousness and creation. There is a duel going on in each one of us, a duel between "the mind" and what Lawrence calls "the being." The mind, through clever reasoning and seemingly effective hypotheses, wants to dominate the being, which in all essentiality is a much more simple phenomenon of nature, run by inherent, natural responses. Most of the time the mind leads the being: our civilization, our inheritance is such that it leaves no scope for the intuitive responses of the being to flourish. When J. Middleton Murry sent Lawrence a copy of his book on Dostoevski, Lawrence criticized it mainly on the ground that Murry had given more prominence to mind than to being while analyzing the Russian author, whereas, he wrote to Murry, "it wasn't the being that must follow the mind, but the mind that must follow the being."[31] The being, again, is the voice of the beyond as manifested in the individual from moment to moment. And the union between a man and a woman was valid and fruitful only if it rested on that voice: "Let your heart stay open, to receive the mysterious inflow of power from the unknown: know that the power comes to you from beyond, it is not generated by your own will: therefore all the time, be watchful, and reverential towards the mysterious coming of power into you."[32]

This then is Lawrence's view of marriage: a connection between a man and a woman who come together in the silence of their mind, to share each other's life. If they have not been tethered to the crippling effects of egoism in their existence (or, if they have been, they have seen the guile of it and got over it), if they have not been chained to rigid and hard "principles" in their day-to-day living, if they have kept themselves "open" to the influx of the new all the time, the moment they meet each other their need for each other will strike them (often in spite of themselves). It might amount to love at first sight, only it would be far, far different from what generally passes for "love at first sight." For it will not be a union based on "love." It will not be a union based on physical attraction, either. It will not be a union based on intellectual affinities. The tragedy of love, or of physical attraction, or of intellectual affinity, is not that love or physical attraction or intellectual affinity do not exist; the tragedy is that with the passage of time what goes for "love" passes, physical charm dwindles, intellectual affinity falls to pieces. Marriage, according to Lawrence, on the other hand is based on the firm faith that all these things may pass away and change, and yet the "conjunction" will hold good. And only men and women who have lived in tune with the unknown can know the moment when the conjunction (and with whom) should be formed. As Middleton Murry states in one of his generous moods toward Lawrence, what Lawrence offers is "a new kind of marriage, between a regenerated man and a regenerated woman."[33]

It is odd that Father Tiverton should say of Lawrence, "He was, of course, in most senses of that absurd word, a romantic."[34] For Lawrence had nothing but ridicule for romantic love. We see that he criticizes Petrarch and Dante for crying *"Laura! Laura! Beatrice! Beatrice!"* and wasting their lives in meaningless yearnings.[35] In another essay, he disdainfully remarks on such a passion: "The dream was the mating of two souls, to the faint chiming of the Seraphim. . . . They dreamed of a marriage with all things gross—meaning especially copulation—left out, and only the pure harmony of equality and intimate companionship remaining."[36] In yet another essay, "Give Her a Pattern," he scathingly criticizes men who for centuries have been insisting on giving their women a "pattern," expecting an idealized pattern of love from them. Though he does not mention in that essay that women equally imagine men in a definite pattern, expect from them a definite type of glorified love, he makes that point clear in the essay "Cocksure Women and Hensure Men" (where he talks of "A really up-to-date woman is a cocksure woman. She doesn't have a doubt nor a qualm. She is the modern type") , and in his creative work, his short stories and his novels. For we notice that his characters—like Rupert Birkin in *Women in Love* and Captain Hepburn in *The Captain's Doll*—are afraid of even uttering the word "love"; afraid of acknowledging the romantic non-sense that normally goes with the use of it. " 'The point about love,' he said, his consciousness quickly adjusting itself, 'is that we hate the word because we have vulgarised it. It ought to be prescribed, tabooed from utterance, for many years, till we get a new, better idea.' "[37] So announces Rupert Birkin to Ursula in *Women in Love*. Lawrence himself told Catherine Carswell that he would like to see the word replaced by some other expression—so badly had it been misused and abused—and suggested the em-ployment of "tenderness" as a substitute in its place. Thus, sentimentalism has absolutely no place in Lawrence's love; it is free of fanaticism or quixoticism. The love con-ceived—if we must use the word "love" at all—is of the most austere type. So is the marriage.

The significance of such a solemn conclusion is deep and profound, for it at once shows the lie of the often ex-pressed view that for Lawrence sex—or the sexual act— was an end in itself. Along with the other urges of the body, Lawrence no doubt gave great importance to the sexual urge; he believed that it was perhaps one of the greatest urges. In *Look! We Have Come Through!*, he referred to this urge as a hunger:

> The hunger for the woman. Alas,
> it is so deep a Moloch, ruthless and strong,
> 'tis like the unutterable name of the dead Lord,
> not to be spoken aloud.[38]

a hunger, "more frightening, more profound / than stomach or throat or even the mind; / redder than death, more clamorous." But he never advocated that the satisfaction of that hunger was the only aim of a person's life. Lawrence does *not* make a "religion" out of sex ("and from it has endeavoured to build up the religion it was in primitive life"—J. Isaacs).[39] Nor does he glorify sexual life at the expense of the full personal life ("D. H. Lawrence is not content to recognize the sacredness of the flesh and the wisdom of the dark powers of the blood, but exalts these at the expense of the full personal life"— Amos N. Wilder).[40] Such statements as Isaacs' and Wilder's to the contrary fall far short of doing justice to Lawrence's perception, or to the scope of his perception. Similarly, Edmund Wilson misreads him when he talks of "the glorification of intercourse for its own sake as you get it in D. H. Lawrence."[41] Nothing could be farther from the truth than such hasty summings-up. For Lawrence strongly held that a sexual union was not to be indulged in unless it came from one's innermost desire of the soul; the attitude he adopts symbolizes restraint rather than licentiousness. He says in "The State of Funk": "If there is one thing I don't like it is cheap and promiscuous sex. If there is one thing I insist on it is that sex is a delicate, vulnerable, vital thing that you mustn't fool with. If there is one thing I deplore it is heartless sex. Sex must be a real flow, a real flow of sympathy, generous and warm, and not a trick thing, or a moment's excitation, or a mere bit of bullying."[42]

The emphasis, it has to be seen, is not so much on indulgence in sex as on its fearless acceptance—fearless acceptance of the urges of the body. The whole myth of human metaphysical thought in the West is built on a denial of these urges. In *Apocalypse*, Lawrence speaks of "the religions of renunciation, which are womanless,"[43] and he is right. Though Lawrence praised the early

Church for its glorification of married love (see *Apropos*, pp. 34-39), he does not state that even the Catholic Church in its imposition of celibacy on its priests comes under a similar charge. In India too, monastic sects like Buddhism, or Jainism, or some of the modern revivalist groups like Rama Krishna Math, are all guilty of unnaturalness in their advocacy of rigid celibacy as a step to acquiring "spiritual" powers. It is against this double fabrication—the unnatural denial of the body and the unnatural glorification of the spirit—that Lawrence in general rebelled. A natural man must have his natural urges, and those natural urges must be satisfied when the urge comes. It was in order to offer scope for this that the Vedic culture in India conceived of four stages in the life of every man: (1) studentship, (2) marriage and family, (3) renunciation and meditation (only after one has gone through the second stage and the children born of the union have grown up and been provided for), and (4) priesthood—passing on of the knowledge acquired to others. All of the Hindu gods were married, and a ceremony in the house—any type of ceremony—could not be performed without the presence of the wife. Almost all teachers of the knowledge of Self in the Upanishads were married, too (Yajnavalkya, the most eminent of them, had two wives). And it was so in the ancient cultures of other countries as well, as witness the lives of Hebrew prophets and the Greek gods.

So what Lawrence aimed at was a fearless acceptance of the urges of the body, so that the health of the psyche remains intact, so that the Self flourishes. We have in *Apropos*, "The mind's terror of the body has probably driven more men mad than ever could be counted."[44] And in "The State of Funk," we read, "The whole trouble with sex is that we daren't speak of it and think of it naturally. We are not secretly sexual villains. We are not secretly sexually depraved. We are just human beings with living sex. We are all right, if we had not this unaccountable and disastrous *fear* of sex."[45] Thus, as should be clear from these passages, Lawrence only insists on an openhearted and frank acceptance of sex, so that in due time the Self may flourish. Indulgence in sexual relationship is of a secondary value, relatively; the important thing is to recognize its need. "A great many men and women today are happiest when they abstain and stay sexually apart, quite clean: and at the same time, when they understand and realize sex more fully,"[46] says Lawrence.

At the end of *St. Mawr*, there is a revealing passage where two of Lawrence's characters, a mother and her daughter—both of them mature and adult individuals who have known almost every type of passion in life—sit together and argue out between themselves the eternal problem: "What *is* Life?" The mother, Mrs. Witt, is cynical and bitter, and somewhat contemptuous of the daughter, whom she regards as a dim-wit and an impractical person. The daughter, Lou, is relaxed and composed, though as contemptuous of the mother, whom she regards as superficial and shallow in her emotive responses. Lou has bought a ranch, away from the stifling hum of the crowded cities and has retired there; she has even, for the time being, given up her husband, in whom she is somehow disappointed. The mother thinks the daughter is wasting her time in that barren place and then ventures to suggest that perhaps she is hoping to have a good time with other men, particularly with Phoenix, the servant. It is that remark of hers which provokes the ensuing conversation, and which is now included here in entirety as an additional illustration of Lawrence's view of true human relationships.

"No, mother, no more of that. If I've got to say it, Phoenix is a servant: he's really placed, as far as I can see. Always the same, playing about in the old back-yard. I can't take those men seriously. I can't fool round with them, or fool myself about them. I can't and I won't fool myself about them. I can't and I won't fool myself any more, mother, especially about men. They don't count. So why should you want them to pay me out?"

For the moment, this silenced Mrs. Witt. Then she said: "Why, *I* don't want it. Why should I! But after all, you've got to live. You've never *lived* yet: not in my opinion."

"Neither, mother, in my opinion, have you," said Lou drily.

And this silenced Mrs. Witt altogether. She had to be silent, or angrily on the defensive. And the latter she wouldn't be. She couldn't, really, in honesty.

"What do you call life?" Lou continued. "Wriggling half naked at a public show, and going off in a taxi to sleep with some half-drunken fool who thinks he's a man because—Oh, mother, I don't even want to think of it. I know you have a lurking idea that *that is life*. Let it be so then. But leave me out. Men in that aspect simply nauseate me: so grovelling and ratty. Life in that aspect simply drains all my life away. I tell you, for all that sort of thing, I'm broken, absolutely broken: if I wasn't broken to start with."

"Well, Louise," said Mrs. Witt after a pause, "I'm convinced that ever since men and women were men and women, people who took things seriously, and had time for it, got their hearts broken. Haven't I had mine broken! It's as sure as having your virginity broken: and it amounts to about as much. It's a beginning rather than an end."

"So it is, mother. It's the beginning of something else, and the end of something that's done with. I *know*, and there's no altering it, that I've got to live differently. It sounds silly, but I don't know how else to put it. I've got to live for something that matters, way, way down in me. And I think sex would matter, to my very soul, if it was really sacred. But cheap sex kills me."

"You have had a fancy for rather cheap men, perhaps."

"Perhaps I have. Perhaps I should always be a fool, where people are concerned. Now I want to leave off that kind of foolery. There's something else, mother, that I want to give myself to. I know it. I know it absolutely. Why should I let myself be shouted down any more?"

Mrs. Witt sat staring at the distance, her face a cynical mask. "What is the something bigger? And *pray*, what is it bigger than?" she asked, in that tone of honied suavity which

was her deadliest poison. "I want to learn. I am out to know.
I'm terribly intrigued by it. Something bigger! Girls in my
generation occasionally entered convents, for *something*
bigger. I always wondered if they found it. They seemed
to me inclined in the imbecile direction, but perhaps that
was because I was *something less—*"

There was a definite pause between the mother and
daughter, a silence that was a pure breach. Then Lou said:

"You know quite well I'm not conventy, mother, whatever else I am—even a bit of an imbecile. But that kind of
religion seems to me the other half of men. Instead of running after them you run away from them, and get the thrill
that way. I don't hate men *because* they're men, as nuns do.
I dislike them because they're not men enough: babies, and
playboys, and poor things showing off all the time, even to
themselves. I don't say I'm any better. I only wish, with all
my soul, that some men *were* bigger and stronger and *deeper*
than I am. . . ."

"How do you know they're not?" asked Mrs. Witt.

"How *do* I know?" said Lou mockingly.

And the pause that was a breach resumed itself. Mrs. Witt
was teasing with a little stick the bewildered black ants
among the fir-needles.

"And no doubt you are right about men," she said at
length. "But at your age, the only sensible thing is to try
and keep up the illusion. After all, as you say, you may be no
better."

"I may be no better. But keeping up the illusion means
fooling myself. And I won't do it. When I see a man who
is even a bit attractive to me—even as much as Phoenix—
I say to myself: *Would you care for him afterwards? Does
he really mean anything to you, except just a sensation?* And
I know he doesn't. No, mother, of this I am convinced: either
my taking a man shall have a meaning and a mystery that
penetrates my very soul, or I will keep to myself. And what
I *know* is, that the time has come for me to keep to myself.
No more messing about."

"Very well, daughter. You will probably spend your life
keeping to yourself."

"Do you think I mind! There's something else for me,
mother. There's something else even that loves me and wants
me. I can't tell you what it is. It's a spirit. And it's here, on
this ranch. It's here, in this landscape. It's something more

real to me than men are, and it soothes me, and it holds me
up. I don't know what it is, definitely. It's something wild,
that will hurt me sometimes and will wear me down sometimes. I know it. But it's something big, bigger than men,
bigger than people, bigger than religion. It's something to
do with wild America. And it's something to do with me.
It's a mission, if you like. I am imbecile enough for that!
But it's my mission to keep myself for the spirit that is wild
and has waited so long here: even waited for such as me.
Now I've come! Now I'm here. Now I am where I want to
be: with the spirit that wants me. And that's how it is. And
neither Rico nor Phoenix nor anybody else really matters to
me. They are in the world's back-yard. And I am here, right
deep in America, where there's a wild spirit wants me, a wild
spirit more than men. And it doesn't want to save me either.
It needs me. It craves for me. And to it, my sex is deep and
sacred, deeper than I am, with a deep nature aware deep
down of my sex. It saves me from cheapness, mother. And
even you could never do that for me."

Mrs. Witt rose to her feet and stood looking far, far away
at the turquoise ridge of mountains half sunk under the
horizon.

"How much did you say you paid for Las Chivas?" she
asked.

"Twelve hundred dollars," said Lou, surprised.

"Then I call it cheap, considering all there is to it: even
the name."[47] (Lawrence's emphasis)

3. THE PHALLIC CAPTAIN

There is one issue related to love and marriage that
needs further investigation, and here again Lawrence
displays a clarity of thought and understanding unsurpassed by many other writers. It is somewhat annoying to
see that a man of his sharp faculties should be (or should
have been) spoken of as "muddle-headed,"[48] or "impatient and impulsive."[49] As F. R. Leavis asserts in *D. H.
Lawrence, Novelist*, intelligence was perhaps the greatest
asset Lawrence possessed as a writer: "I myself have always
felt bound to insist—though it should, I can't help think-

ing, be obvious—that genius in Lawrence was, among other things, supreme intelligence."[50] (In a letter to *The Times Literary Supplement*, December 11, 1959, Leavis reiterates his stand: "My preoccupation in writing about Lawrence has always been to express my sense of him as a great original genius—one of the greatest of creative writers and a *supreme intelligence*.") Leavis goes on in his book to say that to him Lawrence's intelligence seems of even more importance than his "insights," for it was through his intelligence that he related his insights. We see that even in the brief section that follows, Lawrence's "intelligence" and "insights" are once again amply revealed; the answer to the problem that he arrives at is the only healthy one possible.

We are referring to the respective positions of the husband and the wife in a family, during the long life of marriage. It is a problem that almost every married man or married woman has to face. Lawrence himself had to face it in his own marriage with Frieda, and though at certain times his union came very near to a collapse, it nevertheless lasted for all his life without shaking his faith, even if Frieda's was shaken.

It should be noted that henceforth, when marriage is spoken of, what is meant is marriage as conceived by Lawrence: a man and a woman coming together through intuition. Now, if we may again notice Lawrence's law of Consummate Marriage, he says there: "Every living thing seeks, individually and collectively." As can be seen, though this emphasizes what is called above centralized sexuality, it also implies that even when centralized sexuality comes to be, even when marriage is formed—when the collective seeking begins its life—the individual seeking does not stop. For either total submission of one partner to the other (what Lawrence in certain places calls "merger") or total insistence on "individuality" by the partners in a marriage means death according to him.

For both these concepts determine in advance what sort of a relationship between the man and the woman there will be; both impose a predetermined design on the relationship. On the other hand, Lawrence would say that the magnificence of marriage rests in the willingness of the two partners to accept the endless change in each other as they grow from day to day. To quote from him: "There is, however, the third thing, which is neither sacrifice nor fight to death: when each seeks only the true relatedness to the other. Each must be true to himself, herself, his own manhood, her own womanhood, and let the relationship work out of itself."[51] The man in a marriage is one unit, the wife the other; and the third unit is this "relatedness." All these units are constantly changing, affected and influenced by countless cosmic forces which can never be rationally apprehended and accounted for; and the stability of a marriage rests not in fixing its course beforehand but in intrinsically accepting the principle of change.

But, accepting the principle of change, accepting the principle of separate identities of the man and the woman, it was Lawrence's profound faith that if a marriage was to be a marriage of bliss, the man in the house should be "the lord and master" (his words) and the woman should submit to him. In one of the chapters in *Kangaroo*, the very chapter that Vivas describes as pure corn: "it is pure corn," and as such it heads the list of "all the many expressions of bad taste that Lawrence has left us,"[52] the chapter entitled "Harriet and Lovat at Sea in Marriage," Lawrence elaborates on it at length. Vivas is welcome to his opinion, to consider Lawrence's reasoning as bad taste there, but so far as another reader is concerned, the examination indicates that Lawrence was not only capable of arriving at intelligent conclusions, but was also capable of being bold and forthright in self-criticism.

The chapter opens with this:

When a sincere man marries a wife, he has one or two courses open to him, which he can pursue with that wife. He can propose to himself to be (a) the lord and master who is honoured and obeyed, (b) the perfect lover, (c) the true friend and companion.[53]

Lawrence then takes up each one of these courses, one by one, and through painful attempts shows how, but for the first one, the others are unrelated to reality. The "perfect" love never exists, it is a contradiction in terms; love is of a multiple nature, both perfect and imperfect, and "whole love between man and woman is sacred and profane together."[54] In such a case, soon after the marriage there is disillusionment, and then the crash. "The perfect-lover marriage ends usually in a quite ghastly anti-climax, divorce and horrors and the basest vituperation."[55] As for the "true friend and companion," it is not bad if the object of marriage is merely for the man and the woman somehow to pass through life together and *nothing else*; if the aim is merely to go through the routine of life at a lower level—to eat, and to drink, and to reproduce, and perish:

> Well, they are grey waters, and the perfect companion-
> ship usually resolves, subtly, and always under the perfect
> love flag, into a very nearly perfect limited liability com-
> pany, the bark steering nicely according to profit and loss,
> and usually "getting on" fabulously. The Golden Vanity.
> If this perfect love flag is a vanity, the perfect-companion-
> ship management is certainly Golden. I would recommend
> perfect-companionship to all those married couples who
> truly and sincerely want *to get on*.[56]

The "bark" spoken of in the passage is the Ship of Marriage, which all married persons have to take. Lawrence, it may be noticed, looks upon all relationships as "constant travelling," hence constant change, as with Ship of Love in *Look! We Have Come Through!*, Ship of

Marriage, and Ship of Death. What Lawrence is trying to
register here is that merely to "get on" is *not* the object
of marriage. Marriage is for the two persons to develop
their souls and to have before them, here and now, a
paradisal state, a state of untold revelations enriching one,
coming from the unknown, which is the source and the
moving spirit behind all life; and where the mind is
merely concerned with the mechanical movement of life
from day to day, concerned with somehow getting on,
with merely making things *work*, how could the otherworldly beauty, the otherworldly charm, the otherworldly
wonder be there? The wonder of life can be there only
when the reality of life is accepted. And the reality of
life is—the law of life—that the male should be the lord
and master, the captain of the Ship, and the woman should
be his helpmate.

With ruthless honesty Lawrence describes the reactions
many women may have to this infliction of lordship on
them, but then he at once states that it is not an "infliction"; when he talks of a lord and master, he does not have
a tyrant in mind. It is a kind and a considerate lord that
he is talking about: "I will be lord and master, but ah,
such a wonderful lord and master that it will be your
bliss to belong to me."[57] He compares the man to a phoenix
and refers to the beloved as his nest; the one would be, as
is clear, incomplete without the other. In his view this
does not reduce the woman to a subordinate position; it
asks, rather, large-heartedness from her, and gives her
virtually a more important place. For how would the
bird survive without his nest, asks Lawrence? But the
dominant note, or rather the elementary note from which
the harmony of the rest of the music of marriage arises,
is that the ascendency of the male must be accepted first
by the female, implicitly and without any reservations:

Yet he stuck to his guns. She was to submit to the mystic

man and male in him, with reverence, and even a little awe, like a woman before the altar of the great Hermes. She might remember that he *was* only human, that he had to change his socks if he got his feet wet, and that he would make a fool of himself nine times out of ten. But—and the but was emphatic as a thunderbolt—there was in him also the mystery and the lordship of—of Hermes, if you like— but the mystery and the lordship of the forward-seeking male. That she must emphatically realise and bow down to. Yes, bow down to. You can't have two masters of one ship: neither can you have a ship without a master.[58]

Most modern women would perhaps object to this. At least one of them, Katherine Anne Porter, has publicly voiced her protest about Lawrence's ignorance of sexual psychology. In a review of *Lady Chatterley's Lover* published in *Encounter*, February 1960, Miss Porter writes: "I think from start to finish he was about as wrong as can be on the whole subject of sex." Another woman, Simone de Beauvoir, though not so outspoken, also condemns him for the implicit supremacy of the male that all his stories presume. But an interesting point comes out, if we compare the remarks of Katherine Anne Porter with those of Mlle de Beauvoir.

Simone de Beauvoir's brief section on Lawrence is not very well known. It occurs in her monumental book on the female sex, called *Le Deuxieme Sexe, The Second Sex*. She quotes Lawrence, along with Montherlant, Claudel, Breton and Stendhal, as the authors who typify the general approach of men to women in our society. The burden of her whole thesis is that men prefer to regard women as what she terms "the Other," as subordinate to man, *inferior* to him. We cannot take up here de Beauvoir's treatment of the other writers listed, but one fails to understand her conviction of D. H. Lawrence along with the rest. For though Lawrence regarded woman as "the Other"—she *is* "the Other" even by de Beauvoir's own long account of her special temperament and special bodily needs as differentiated from that of man (see Book II, Part V, Chapters I to VI of *The Second Sex*) —he never said that she was *inferior* to man; he only said she was *different*. There is absolutely no suggestion of bondage in the union that he conceives between a man and a woman. Simone de Beauvoir herself notices this, when she records that in the ecstasy that results among Laurentian men and women there is no question of "sacrifice" or "abandon" or the "surrender" of the one partner to the other, and "the sexual act is . . . a marvellous fulfillment of each one by the other."

> When Ursula and Birkin finally found each other, they gave each other reciprocally that stellar equilibrium which alone can be called liberty.[59]

In the two pages that follow, de Beauvoir examines *Women in Love* and her assessment clearly shows that Lawrence as a matter of fact recognizes all the things in a man-woman relationship that she would herself like to see recognized. But she then takes up her whip and starts lashing at Lawrence:

> Reciprocal gift, reciprocal fidelity: have we here in truth the reign of mutuality? Far from it. Lawrence believes passionately in the supremacy of the male. The very expression "phallic marriage," the equivalence he sets up between "sexual" and "phallic," constitute sufficient proof. Of the two blood streams that are mysteriously married, the phallic current is favoured.[60]

Here plainly de Beauvoir misreads Lawrence. But it is essential to notice that, unlike Katherine Anne Porter, she does *not* regard Lawrence as ignorant of "the whole subject of sex." On the contrary, she regards him as a far better informed author in the matter than many others could be. Her dispute with him is on social grounds, on

the social status that he awards to his women, and not
on the sexual level. This is a very gratifying conclusion,
coming as it does from a woman; it to a large extent
vindicates Lawrence from attacks on him by other women,
such as Katherine Anne Porter, on similar grounds. With
regard to the supremacy of the male that de Beauvoir
objects to, one can only say that she takes the word phallic
rather too literally. For whenever she refers to the expression, she takes it for granted that Lawrence implies by it
the virility in man, that it refers to the penis; and thus,
by her line of reasoning, it presupposes the submission of
the woman to the man. She writes at the end of her essay
on him: "In so far as man is a phallus and not a brain,
the individual who has his share of virility keeps his
advantages; woman is not evil, she is even good—but sub-
ordinated."[61]

But it does not. Even the man with "brains" or with
"sex in the head" has a phallus attached to his body, and
even he can be as virile and potent and even he can mate
with a woman and give her sexual satisfaction; and the
very fact that Lawrence endlessly labors to make a distinction between "phallic consciousness" and what he
calls "cerebral sex-consciousness" shows that by "phallic"
he decidedly means something else, or something more,
than either the male organ or the virility in man. What
exactly he does mean by it is better described by alluding
to a text of his dealing with a different subject, a text
from a collection of travel essays, *Etruscan Places*. Commenting on the architecture of the Etruscan tombs, he
writes there:

> On the whole, here all is plain, simple, usually with no
> decoration, and with those easy, natural proportions whose
> beauty one hardly notices, they come so naturally, physi-
> cally. It is the natural beauty of proportion of the phallic
> consciousness, contrasted with the more studied or ecstatic
> proportion of the mental and spiritual Consciousness we

are accustomed to. . . .[62] The Greeks sought to make an impression, and Gothic still more seeks to impress the mind. The Etruscans, no. The things they did, in their easy centuries, are as natural and as easy as breathing. They leave the breast breathing freely and pleasantly, with a certain fullness of life. Even the tombs. And that is the true Etruscan quality: ease, naturalness, and an abundance of life, no need to force the mind or the soul in any direction.[63]

We gather from this that "phallic consciousness" has a sort of symbolic meaning with Lawrence which, as we can see, need not necessarily refer to the sexual moments alone of our life and which covers the whole span of our existence, organic and inorganic. Applied to sex, it would mean an implicit acceptance of the power and the glory of the body and a sense of love for this power and glory. Virility is one of its aspects, but that it passes beyond virility and is with Lawrence more a projection of the beauty of the union is obvious from the tenderness, from the softness of his theme of marriage.

Instead of living in "subjection," the woman in Lawrence is lifted to an extremely high place. Lawrence certainly thought of the woman as "the Other," but in her "otherness" he saw her greatest charm. It was this otherness, according to him, that earned her an independent recognition, on her own strength and her own beauty, *apart* from man. Take, for instance, the following passage from *Kangaroo*:

> "To any true lover, it would be the greatest disaster if the beloved broke down from her own nature and self and began to identify herself with him, with his nature and self. I say, to any genuine lover this is the greatest disaster, and he tries by every means in his power to prevent this. The earth and sun, on their plane, have discovered a perfect equilibrium. But man has not yet begun. His lesson is so much harder. His consciousness is at once so complicated and so cruelly limited. This is the lesson before us. Man has loved the beloved for the sake of love, so far, but

rarely, rarely has he *consciously* known that he could only love her for her own separate, strange self: forever strange and a joyful mystery to him. Lovers henceforth have got to *know* one another. A terrible mistake, and a self delusion. True lovers only learn that as they know less, and less, and less of each other, the mystery of each grows more startling to the other. The tangible unknown: that is the magic, the mystery, and the grandeur of love, that it puts the tangible unknown in our arms, and against our breast: the beloved. We have made a fatal mistake. We have got to know so much *about* things, that we think we know the actuality, and contain it. The sun is as much outside us, and as eternally unknown, as ever it was. And the same with each man's beloved: like the sun. What do the facts we know *about* a man amount to? Only two things we can know of him, and this by pure soul-intuition: we can know if he is true to the flame of life and love which is inside his heart, or if he is false to it. If he is true, he is friend. If he is false, and inimical to the fire of life and love in his own heart, then he is my enemy as well as his own."[64]

Lawrence was totally against the annihilation of the one partner by the other in marriage, and there should be no doubt on that issue. We have here to go back to what we quoted from the Ship of Marriage chapter in *Kangaroo*: "I will be lord and master, but ah, such a wonderful lord and master that it will be your bliss to belong to me." There is not a trace of any coercion or force implied in this type of statement. Biologically, physically, psychically, it is the bliss of a woman to *belong* to a man. Her fulfillment lies in this, in her surrender. It is a surrender not so much to the "maleness" in the man, as to the divinity, the life-furthering power in him. In the Ship of Marriage chapter itself this is conclusively brought out—the element to which the woman has to surrender or submit:

But he kicked against the pricks. He did not yet submit to the fact which he *half* knew; that before mankind would accept any man for a king, and before Harriet would ever accept him, Richard Lovatt, as a lord and master, he, this self-same Richard who was so strong on kingship, must open the doors of his soul and let in a dark Lord and Master for himself, the dark god he had sensed outside the door.[65]

The demand for a woman to submit to him is, therefore, dependent in Lawrence on the man's first having in him the ability, the power, the creative power to think and act as if he were in direct communication with the unknown. As Lawrence elucidates in *Fantasia of the unconscious*: "And you'll have to fight very hard to make a woman yield her goal to yours, to make her, in her own soul, *believe* in your goal beyond, in her goal as the way by which you go. She'll never believe until you have your soul filled with a profound and absolutely inalterable purpose, that will yield to nothing, least of all to her. She'll never believe until, in your soul, you are cut off and gone ahead, into the dark."[66] In Hindu society, for instance, when a woman is asked to look upon her *pati*, her husband, as an equal of *parmishwar*, a living God, the expectation is that he, in his day-to-day life, will show himself to be worthy of that trust. In the *Ramayana* and the *Mahabharata*, when Sita gives limitless love and devotion to Rama and Daraupadi to Yudhishthira respectively, it is unmistakably brought out that Rama and Yudhisthira are human beings great enough to be incarnations of God, human beings with a purpose in life. Radha's love for Krishna, again, shows devotion on the same ground. These are all illustrations not of servile submission but of joyful surrender—surrender to the glory in the man.

The symbol of the phallus, as we know, has been used for centuries by almost all races in the world to signify the source of energy. In *Priapic Divinities and Phallic Rites*, by J. A. Dulaure, we have an interesting history of the origin and the extent of those ancient legends. As the author says: "When the ancients wished to represent the life-giving power of the Sun and the action of this power on all living creatures, they adopted the emblem of masculinity, called by the Greeks *phallus*."[67] It is this source of energy, stored more conspicuously in the male than in the female throughout nature, that induced Lawrence to insist that in marriage, in centralized sexuality, the husband should have a leading role and the woman must obey him. But it does not involve tyranny at any level, domestic or social. Lawrence's women are socially equals of men. Only on natural grounds did he feel the husband's word should be final in the house—the word of the husband who had the living God in him, who had realized his Self.

But both the man and the wife are independent of each other, as unique. Their souls are constantly in a state of development, influenced not only by the factors within the power of their faculties, but by many unknown cosmic factors as well—their common rhythm has their own separate seasons. And out of this mutual willingness to accept each other's "otherness," to accept the constant change in each other, the husband, the Phoenix, and the woman, his nest, make the conjunction that is a temple of beauty and joy; beauty and joy not in some remote, future state but within the grasp of their hands and their feet and their loins now—their physical bodies replenished and fed by the sun, and the stars, and the planets; drawing life from the universe, passing on life to each other; creating new life.

Marriage is the clue to human life, but there is no marriage apart from the wheeling sun and the nodding earth, from the straying of the planets and the magnificence of the fixed stars. Is not a man different, utterly different, at dawn from what he is at sunset? and a woman too? And does not the changing harmony and discord of their variation make the secret music of life?

And is it not so throughout life? A man is different at

thirty, at forty, at fifty, at sixty, at seventy: and the woman
at his side is different. But is there not some strange conjunction in their differences? Is there not some peculiar
harmony, through youth, the period of child-birth, the
period of florescence and young children, the period of the
woman's change of life, painful yet also a renewal, the
period of waning passion but mellowing delight of affection, the dim, unequal period of the approach to death,
when the man and woman look at one another with the
dim apprehension of separation that is not really a separation: is there not, throughout it all, some unseen, unknown
interplay of balance, harmony, completion, like some
soundless symphony which moves with a rhythm from
phase to phase, so different, so very different in the various
movements, and yet one symphony, made out of the soundless singing of two strange and incompatible lives, a man's
and a woman's?

This is marriage, the mystery of marriage, marriage
which fulfils itself here, in this life. We may well believe
that in heaven there is no marrying or giving in marriage.
All this has to be fulfilled here, and if it is not fulfilled
here, it will never be fulfilled.[68]

In no other literature are love and marriage treated
on so high a level as in that of the ancient Hindus. And
in no other literature is woman given so high a place.
Men and women had freedom to marry whom they
wanted, and the right of final consent rested with the
woman. A *swayamvara* (gathering) was held where all the
suitors for the hand of a particular woman were invited,
and she was asked to make her choice, the belief being
that her intuition would guide her in her selection. In
reality, she was already in love with one of them, and
she was thus free to choose her lover. As Mulk Raj Anand,
one of the leading Indian novelists and thinkers, remarks,
in the works of ancient and mediaeval Hindu writers,
"woman does not appear as she does in European literature of that time, in the role of a mere landscape which
is adorned and loved, but as the essential partner of the

ritual of life. Her generative faculties are accepted as
primary human facts and not open to the insinuations,
ridicule and obscene jokes of those who despise sex."[69]
Just as Helen is the symbol of glorious womanhood in
Western literature, in Indian literature the symbol of
womanhood is Sita. Sita is not only as beautiful as Helen
is; she is something more; she is considered the equal of
Rama, her husband, in status. Both Indian epics, the
Ramayana and the *Mahabharata*, revolve around battles
fought to defend the honor of womanhood. Sita in the
Ramayana is abducted by Ravana, the King of Lanka (the
present Ceylon), against her wishes and desires; Draupadi
in the *Mahabharata* is insulted by Duryodhana, the head-
strong Kaurava prince. The books describe in detail the
forces marshalled and the vengeance sought for those acts
of injustice. In *Manusmriti*, Manu, the famous lawgiver
of India, discusses at length the rights and privileges a
woman should have. To summarize his approach:

> In *Manusmriti* woman attains her apotheosis, as wife,
> mother and dependent relation, serving and radiating her
> love. The gods rejoice when women are honoured, and
> rites in their honour yield no rewards in homes in which
> women are not cherished and revered. The tears of de-
> pendent women blight a family, their grateful smiles make
> it blossom into fortune; their curse, when treated with con-
> tumely, withers the home. Honour and cherish your
> women, therefore, for your own good, on holidays and in
> festivals, with gifts of dainty fare, raiment and jewels! Joy
> dwells in the home in which there is conjugal love. Let a
> woman cherish her beauty that she may retain her hus-
> band's love and become fruitful. With her radiance the
> house will be alit, and without it, be dark and dismal.[70]

Marriage undoubtedly is given a high place in the Christian religion, but a high and equal status for women is
relatively a very modern phenomenon in Christian civilization.

II

1. *SONS AND LOVERS*

It has to be acknowledged that Lawrence's views on marriage, as consolidated in the first part of this chapter, acquired their present proportion only after his own centralized sexuality with a woman, his own marriage. As he wrote to Mrs. Hopkin in 1912, after he had left for Europe along with Frieda, "I never knew what love was before . . . . The world is wonderful and beautiful and good beyond one's wildest imagination. Never, never, never could one conceive what love is, beforehand, never. Life *can* be great—quite god-like. It *can* be so."[71] His early letters to Frieda, included in *Not I, But the Wind. . .*, (pp. 9-28) have the same note of awe, of amazedness, of the marvel of the new feelings, particularly this passage:

> It's a funny thing, to feel one's passion—sex desire—no longer a sort of wandering thing, but steady, and calm. I think, when one loves, one's very sex passion becomes calm, a steady sort of force, instead of a storm. Passion, that nearly drives one mad, is far away from real love. I am realizing things that I never thought to realize. Look at that poem I sent you—I would never write that to you. I shall love you all my life. That also is a new idea to me. But I believe it.[72]

In this connection, we will not concentrate on Lawrence's novels written prior to his own marriage. As a matter of fact, Lawrence seems to believe, and rightly so, that only a married man (married happily or otherwise) has the insight to write and talk about marriage. Writing to Dr. Trigant Burrow, commenting on a book that the latter had sent to him, he says, "But you're wrong, I *think*, about marriage. Are you married?"[73] Dr. Burrow was not only married but had two grown-up children as well, a son aged 22 and a daughter, 18. (See his reply to Lawrence's letter in Nehls' Vol. III—"What I said of marriage, I said of marriage as ownership. And marriage *is* ownership—let's face it."[74] Lawrence, as this chapter makes clear, radically differed from this.)

Our main concern in this chapter accordingly, will be with *The Rainbow* and *Women in Love*—more particularly with the love and marriage of Tom Brangwen and Lydia Lensky, and of Rupert Birkin and Ursula Brangwen, as developed in these two novels. For these novels typify to a large extent Lawrence's whole concept of the man-woman relationship. They are the fruit of the direct experiencing of such relationship.

This is not to deprecate Lawrence's work written before the eventful years of his union with Frieda; far from it. As was shown in the last chapter, *The White Peacock*, the very first novel that Lawrence wrote, has a remarkable gift of vitality and power in it. As a story in praise of the essential beauty of life, regardless of the hostility and adversity involving one or more characters, it remains unrivaled. Similarly, *Sons and Lovers* is a great novel and the study of Paul's mind is a superb creative achievement. His anguish of mother-love, his horror of girl-love, and his passion of woman-love are captured and conveyed with an immediately transferable (transferable to the reader) power. Even the basic idea of a marriage as a conjunction at a level deeper than that of ordinary sex, even this basic idea itself, is seen there and stated. Paul and Miriam are talking, discussing the failure of Clara's marriage with Baxter Dawes:

"What has happened, exactly?" asked Miriam.
"It's so hard to say, but the something big and intense that changes you when you really come together with somebody else. It almost seems to fertilize your soul and make it that you can go on and mature."

"And you think your mother had it with your father?"
"Yes; and at the bottom she feels grateful to him for giv-
ing it her, even now, though they are miles apart."
"And you think Clara never had it?"
"I'm sure."[75]

But these works deal with love and sex in the customary,
restricted sense and the wider horizon of *The Rainbow—
Women in Love* canvas is definitely lacking in them. They
are built on the premise that sex by itself, with any one,
is beautiful; we have a sufficient glimpse of it in the Lettie
and Leslie union in *The White Peacock* and in the affair
of Paul and Clara in *Sons and Lovers*. Lettie in her marriage also signifies the truth of what Lawrence was later
to say in *Apropos*, that in many a marriage, "in among
the counterfeit there flickers a little flame of the true
thing, on both sides," and that one could fan the little
flame and always make a success of it. There never was
the type of love between her and Leslie that we are to
see in *The Rainbow* between Tom and Lydia. If anything,
she had a sort of intuitive affection for George, but it
does not materialize in marriage; in spite of that she
responds to the new life around her and creates a meaningful existence.

But "centralized sexuality" in the form that Lawrence
later conceives of it is not present in these novels, nor is it
present in *The Trespasser*, where the suicide of Siegmund
in the end indicates a denial of the whole action of the
story; Siegmund refuses to accept responsibility for what
he has done. Paul's love for Miriam in *Sons and Lovers*
is a characteristic illustration of the conventional type of
love-in-the-head, which Lawrence was to despise in times
to come. It is a love that grows on what has been described
earlier as the habit of intimacy. Paul and Miriam had
one thing common between them—their love of wild
countryside and the beauty of nature, and it was this—a
material factor, a factor other than their basic desire for

each other—on which their love rested. "So it was in this atmosphere of subtle intimacy, this meeting in their common feeling for something in nature, that their love started,"[76] we are told. An interval of two years has passed meanwhile, when they have been meeting each other off and on, and we are not shown that there was any joy in those meetings, any feeling of communion between them in their sheer togetherness; on the other hand, at most of those meetings, we read, "The boy took no notice of her, and "he scarcely observed her." It is true that Paul was not yet a man at that age, not sure of his feelings, but even when he is grown up, even when Miriam has declared her fondness for him and he is old enough to see and sense that fondness, it is a bullying, a torture, indeed a meaningless sadism that he most often shows her, rather than tenderness, sensitivity, or responsiveness. On her side, Miriam is over-sentimental ("the girl was romantic in her soul"), and willing to subordinate and reduce herself in her love to a subjection amounting to extinction of her own self. And such reactions are incompatible with the idea of love that we have been discussing in this chapter. The dominant mood of their whole relationship is that of tension; and though they become fond of each other—the fonder the more often they meet—the relationship itself is not rooted in spontaneity.

By Laurentian standards, both Paul and Miriam should have recognized the unpleasant truth of it and broken away from each other; at least Paul should have, whose growth is depicted as that of a man living by his intuitive urges. On the contrary, they continue to see each other, and out of sheer nearness, physical nearness, Paul begins to desire her physically. Lawrence takes great pains in the chapters that follow—"Lad-and-Girl Love," "Strife in Love," "Defeat of Miriam," and finally that banal chapter "Test on Miriam"—to explain why the relationship of Paul and Miriam failed. While one can obviously sense

something solid and genuine in the conflict with the
mother that he depicts, the strain of the mother's pull on
the son in keeping him to herself and her responsibility
to a large extent for destroying his relationship with
Miriam, Lawrence's attempt to shift the blame for the
death of the Paul-Miriam friendship to Miriam and her
frigidity, is to me, by Lawrence's own later standards,
unconvincing. Jessie Chambers, we know, has accused
Lawrence of dishonesty in the treatment of Miriam: "His
mother had to be supreme, and for the sake of that
supremacy every disloyalty was permissible."[77] But even
in the tale as it grows in *Sons and Lovers*, there seems to
me to be no justification, on the artistic level, for the final
damnation of Miriam that the story portrays.

> Miriam plunged home over the meadows. She was not
> afraid of people, what they might say; but she dreaded the
> issue with him. Yes, she would let him have her if he in-
> sisted; and then, when she thought of it afterwards, her
> heart went down. He would be disappointed, he would find
> no satisfaction, and then he would go away. Yet he was so
> insistent; and over this, which did not seem so all-important
> to her, was their love to break down. After all, he was only
> like other men, seeking his satisfaction. Oh, but there was
> something more in him, something deeper! She could trust
> to it, in spite of all desires. He said that possession was a
> great moment in life. All strong emotions concentrated
> there. Perhaps it was so. There was something divine in it;
> then she would submit, religiously, to the sacrifice. He
> should have her. And at the thought her whole body
> clenched itself involuntarily, hard, as if against something;
> but Life forced her through this gate of suffering, too, and
> she would submit. At any rate, it would give him what he
> wanted, which was her deepest wish. She brooded and
> brooded and brooded herself towards accepting him.[78]

The passage is perhaps typical of how Miriam feels on the
issue of physical intimacy between Paul and herself, but
it is cited here not to condemn her but to defend her. In

that defense alone lies the defense of Lawrence's art itself, the defense of its cogency. For if we accept this passage at its face value—if we accept this collapse of the Paul-Miriam relationship in general as a valid example of Lawrence's view on life on the whole—we can only agree with those of his critics who say that with him sexual union *is* the end of his art.

Paul, we cannot help admitting, is a sexual rat (at least at this stage of his life), (1) who makes sexual union with Miriam as a *condition* of his love, and (2) who *compels* her, forces her against her wishes, to have that union with him. Both of these conditions amount to compulsion, which is contrary to the impulses of the soul; love, according to Lawrence, can flourish only in freedom. The attempt by Paul throughout is not to win Miriam, or to respect her sentiments, but to subject her to his forceful will:

"We belong to each other," he said.

"Yes."

"Then why shouldn't we belong to each other altogether?"

"But — — —" she faltered.

"I know it's a lot to ask," he said; "but there's not much risk for you really—not in the Gretchen way. You can trust me there?"

"Oh, I can trust you." The answer came quickly and strong. "It's not that—it's not that at all—but — —."

"What?"

She hid her face in his neck with a little cry of misery. "I don't know!" she cried.

She seemed slightly hysterical, but with a sort of horror. His heart died in him.

"You don't think it ugly?" he asked.

"No, not now. You have *taught* me it isn't."

"You are afraid?"

She calmed herself hastily.

"Yes, I am only afraid," she said.

He kissed her tenderly.

"Never mind," he said. "You shall please yourself."

Suddenly she gripped his arms round her, and clenched her body stiff.

"You *shall* have me," she said, through her shut teeth.

His heart beat up again like fire. He folded her close, and his mouth was on her throat. She could not bear it. She drew away. He disengaged her.

"Won't you be late?" she asked gently.

He sighed, scarcely hearing what she said. She waited, wishing he would go. At last he kissed her quickly and climbed the fence. Looking round he saw the pale blotch of her face down in the darkness under the hanging tree. There was no more of her but this pale blotch.

"Good-bye!" she called softly. She had no body, only a voice and a dim face. He turned away and ran down the road, his fists clenched; and when he came to the wall over the lake he leaned there, almost stunned, looking up the black water.[79]

It is obvious: the force behind these arguments is not the force of love but the compelling urgency of passion, of sex-in-the-head. This passage immediately precedes the one quoted earlier and one can now see the cause of Miriam's reluctance when she is repelled by Paul's endless coercion. "Yet he was so insistent; and over this, which did not seem so all-important to her, was their love to break down." It is the type of meditation Ursula Brangwen in *The Rainbow* would have indulged herself in in her affair with Anton Skrebensky, except that she yielded herself to him physically first and realized afterwards that Skrebensky had no genuine love for her, only the force of his will; and it was the consciousness of the fact that the bodily desire had only been induced in her by the will of the man, induced by an outsider—the realization that sex "did not seem so all- important to her"—that made her throw him away in the end. Miriam is going through a similar feeling. Paul is wrong when he tells her "we belong to each other"; he knows that at least he does not; there is no love between them as such; he is only forcing himself on her. The relationship fails in the end on account of that, from lack of true love, and not from Miriam's failure in the "test" inflicted on her. Miriam stands vindicated on that charge; it is Paul whom we convict.

The whole episode of Paul and Miriam is fortunately colored by personal prejudice, by Lawrence's friendship with Jessie Chambers. "Fortunately," because the prejudice forces this particular phase in *Sons and Lovers* so outside the range of artistic noninvolvement with the story as to save Lawrence's concept of love from the charge of contradiction. Perhaps in actual life Jessie Chambers was a bit prudish; Lawrence's mother certainly was overbearing in actual life; most definitely there was a conflict of emotional allegiance in him. So we observe that involuntary responses of Laurentian love never exist between Paul and Miriam. But the cause for the breakdown is discovered afterwards; it is an act of calculated self-justification. In "centralized sexuality," the success of sexual intercourse becomes of a secondary nature; nay, as described earlier, there may be periods where there is no sex at all between the man and the woman; it is the conjunction, the union-in-spite-of-differences, the harmony-in-spite-of-dissimilarities that matters there.

But that sex was not the end of this conjunction for Lawrence is seen even in *Sons and Lovers*, from the passage quoted above. It is further seen in the affair of Paul with Clara. With all the success of their relationship at the sexual level, there is no accord between them; there is no intuitive love in their case either. "So there went on a battle between them. She knew she never fully had him. Some part, big and vital in him, she had no hold over; nor did she ever try to get it, or even to realise what it was. And he knew in some way that she held herself still as Mrs. Dawes." Hence even their love-making becomes mechanical and joyless, in course of time:

Gradually they began to introduce novelties, to get back some of the feeling of satisfaction. They would be very near, almost dangerously near to the river, so that the black water ran not far from his face, and it gave a little thrill; or they loved sometimes in a little hollow below the fence on the path where people were passing occasionally, on the edge of the town, and they heard footsteps coming, almost felt the vibration of the tread, and they heard what the passers-by said—strange little things that were never intended to be heard. And afterwards each of them was rather ashamed, and these things caused a distance between the two of them. He began to despise her a little, as if she had merited it![80]

Clearly the passage brings out the paucity, the emptiness of a relationship that is just physical and nothing else! The joy is in the soul; and in their souls these two are apart. As indeed were Paul and Miriam.

2. *THE RAINBOW, WOMEN IN LOVE*

But it is different with *The Rainbow* and *Women in Love*. By the time these books were written, Lawrence was married; not just married, but married to a woman of Frieda's qualities. Unfortunately, the contribution Frieda might have made to Lawrence's general understanding of woman is hardly ever stressed, at least hardly stressed to the extent that it should be. In fact, it will not be an exaggeration to say that but for Frieda, Lawrence's comprehension of sex might not have been at all as it is known to us. For she was a woman with a dynamic personality, and had an understanding of the physical side of life that Lawrence perhaps lacked. One of the causes of their—Frieda's and Lawrence's—disputes in later life was that whereas Lawrence was admired and feted by his personal friends, Frieda's existence was almost ignored by most of them; and Frieda resented this—resented that Lawrence should win laurels, whereas a substantial source

of the inspiration of his work, she herself, should go unnoticed. (S. S. Koteliansky was one of such defaulters and
writing to him in February 1915, Frieda said: "But you
see I am also his wife on this earth, the wife of the *man*
as distinguished from the *artist*; to that latter I would
always submit. But you see some things I just *know* and
he doesn't.") [81] In any case, her influence on him during
the early days of their life together was considerable, and
even Lawrence at that stage recognized this. It is striking
that, whereas in all his novels and short stories the "wise
man," the person who solves most of the problems, offers
advice, and undoes knots, is a *man*, in one of Lawrence's
plays, *The Married Man*, and in *The Rainbow*, the task
is performed by a *woman*: it is she who provides the main
clue to the problem. The play was written in 1914, was
never performed, and was published by Frieda Lawrence
in *The Virginia Quarterly Review* in 1940 (now published in *The Complete Plays of D. H. Lawrence*, in 1965).
The character we refer to, Elsa Smith, undoubtedly resembles Frieda.

It is the conventional-enough story of a married man
involved in a relationship with another woman. The wife
finds him out at last and dumps herself on him, all angry
and indignant. The man has a friend staying with him
at that time, William Brentnall, and Elsa Smith is Brentnall's fiancée. She arrives at the final scene, when the
Married Man's wife is having a row with her husband,
and pacifies the lot of them. (Elsa Smith is, incidentally,
German.) She has a pleasant word for her future husband,
William, to whom she says, "Promise me you won't have
one philosophy when you are with men, in your smoke
room, and another when you are with me, in the drawing
room. Promise me you will be faithful to your philosophy
that you have with other men, even before me, always."[82]
To Annie Calladine, the girl with whom the Married
Man has been flirting, she says, "Well, I who am a woman,

when I see other women who are sweet or handsome or charming, I look at them and think, well, how can a man help loving them, to some extent? Even if he loves *me*, if I am not there, how can he help loving them?" The following dialogue then ensues:

Annie: But not a married man.
Elsa: I think a man ought to be fair. He ought to offer his love for just what it is—the love of a man married to another woman—and so on. And, if there is any strain, he ought to tell his wife—"I love this other woman."
Sally: It's worse than Mormons.
Brentnall: But better than subterfuge, bestiality, or starvation and sterility.
Elsa: Yes, yes. If only men were decent enough.
Brentnall: And women.
Elsa: Yes. Don't fret, Mrs. Grainger. By loving these two women, Dr. Grainger has not lost any of his love for you. I would stay with him.[83]

Lawrence never agreed fully with Frieda on many of these things, but the desire for complete frankness on the part of the man and the woman, complete honesty in emotional matters was as much Frieda's aim of living as Lawrence's. Frieda was not sexually faithful to him and Lawrence knew it. As a matter of fact, only a little while after their union, she had one of her lapses (when she was away from him). Lawrence wrote to her: "If you want H . . . . , or anybody, have him. But I don't want anybody, till I see you. But all natures aren't alike. But I don't believe even *you* are your best, when you are using H . . . . as a dose of morphia—he's not much else to you. But sometimes one needs a dose of morphia, I've had many a one. So you know best."[84] These lines to a large extent explain even further what we have termed centralized sexuality. Lawrence had no set clauses wherein the centralization must take place. So far as he was concerned— and as his later life was to show—it meant for him fidelity, sexual fidelity as well. As he makes Rupert Birkin tell Ursula in *Women in Love,* "Love is a direction which excludes all other directions";[85] and he was devoted to the fulfillment of the idea. But—and herein lies the strength and the wide span of centralized sexuality—since "sex" for Lawrence was decidedly something more than the mere sexual act, if a lapse did occur at that particular level in one partner, it was not supposed to imply the end of the centralization; the strength, the creative strength of the two—that is, if they had been genuinely in love initially when they came together—lay in accepting the reality of that factor and still continuing together. It is regrettable that these lapses on the part of Frieda were quite frequent. But we are not arguing about the merit of Lawrence's concept on the basis of his personal life; the beauty and the scope of his vision are independent of that. The personal factor is brought in to explain the fresh air, the vigor, the physical pleasure Frieda, in spite of her limitations, must have brought into his existence. Indeed, in spite of her limitations at one particular level of the relationship, she must certainly have given him every-thing of herself, must certainly have centralized so much of herself with him as to have elicited the following re-mark from him on a day when he was very ill: "But if I die, nothing has mattered but you, nothing at all."[86] So Frieda's part in Lawrence's life should be taken as an important constituent in the appreciation of Lawrence the man, and Lawrence the thinker.

It is debatable whether *The Rainbow* or *Women in Love* is the greater work of art. F. R. Leavis thinks *Women in Love*; I would suggest *The Rainbow.* Leavis's main arguments are: (1) *Women in Love* is a "finished" work, so far as the contents are concerned, whereas *The Rainbow* is not complete in itself, but needs a sequel; (2) *Women in Love* is more analytical, *The Rainbow* less.[87] My com-ments are: (1) Lawrence was an artist who believed in the constant change of life. For such an artist there never could be, thematically, a completely self-contained work. As Lawrence's poetry was of the immediate present, his fiction too dealt primarily with the immediate present. What he writes in defense of his poetry thus could equally be applied to his fiction:

> In the immediate present there is no perfection, no consummation, nothing finished. The strands are all flying, quivering, intermingling into the web, the waters are shaking the moon. There is no round, consummate moon on the face of running water, nor on the face of the unfinished tide. There are no gems of the living plasm. The living plasm vibrates unspeakably, it inhales the future, it exhales the past, it is the quick of both, and yet it is neither. There is no plasmic finality, nothing crystal, permanent.[88]

If *The Rainbow* leaves unsolved, as Leavis alleges, the problem of Ursula, *Women in Love* leaves unsolved the man-to-man relationship bothering Rupert Birkin. In their artistic effect, they do not leave an "unfinished" impression on the reader; both strike us as equally complete. (2) Just because *The Rainbow* is less analytical, it captures more sharply, more artistically, the intensity of the experience it describes, whereas in *Women in Love*, the diagnostic element (to use Leavis's expression) at times extinguishes the very life of the novel.

I have elsewhere described *The Rainbow* as the finest novel of marriage in the whole history of English literature. At the same time, it is the greatest prose hymn coming from a man in praise of the mystery of woman (again in the whole history of English literature). Not only love and marriage in three successive generations are described and explored here, but also generation after generation of the wonder of womanhood, the magic of the secrets lying hidden behind fold after fold of female flesh, the unintelligibility of it and yet the spell of it, the flowering of it, the musky grandeur of muliebrity that is magnificently registered, too. The span of the rainbow covers both man and woman, but it is the woman who lends the arc its glittering colors. The man is a restless wanderer, groping blindly for comfort and re-assurances, always demanding too much from life. It is the woman who sits serene and quiet, poised on the center of her being. With a touch of her hand she lifts the man's face and reveals to him the splendor of the firmaments; with another touch she absorbs him into the heat and the moisture in her body and returns him reborn. But the sign invariably comes from her. It is she who comes forward, she who withdraws, she who sets the pace of their common pulsation; the man must just wait. *The Rainbow*, of course, is the story of a number of men who come and go in it—Tom Brangwen, Will Brangwen, and Anton Skrebensky. But more sharply it is the story of Lydia Lensky, Anna Brangwen, and Ursula Brangwen—in short, of "woman"; woman with her hundred faces and hundred limbs and a hundred thousand moods; woman as a child, woman as an adolescent, woman as a wife, woman in love, woman in labor, woman as a mother, woman as a widow, woman in joy, woman in sorrow. So captivated by the theme at the moment was Lawrence that in each of the generations it is the female child on whom he concentrates, going over the same ground again and again to see if there were things in the wonder of a wonder called woman that he could have missed, and every time returning with a new discovery, a new physical joy, a new marvel, a new depth. The novel begins and ends with meditations on womanhood. In the middle as well, it is womanhood it deals with.

The Rainbow thereby is an acceptance *par excellence* of the otherness of woman, of her independence. It is this recognition of her separate independent existence that perpetuates the love between Tom Brangwen and Lydia

Lensky in the first generation of marriage in the story, and the approach is upheld throughout the novel. The moral behind this is obvious. Acceptance of the woman's independence, her separateness, enables Lawrence to develop his point that love is something which should be there between two persons, not because of this, that, and that, in a list of similarities, but in spite of the differences, in spite of the dissimilarities, in spite of the material disparities. It should just happen, in spite of oneself; and once it does happen, it should enrich the self, make the self deeper, make one's whole outlook on life pregnant with understanding. It is safe to presume that Frieda brought this sort of understanding into Lawrence's own life. *The Rainbow* thus also marks the final assimilation of Frieda into Lawrence's consciousness. As Dorothy M. Hoare comments on the novel, "Nothing Lawrence ever wrote afterwards has this tone of sensuous ease, of *gratification*, in Blake's sense."[89] In fact, the theme of the novel came to Lawrence's mind only after he had known Frieda physically, as he admits in a touching letter to her during the days when they were away from each other for a while: "And I've been a rippling walk— up a great steep hill nearly like a cliff, beyond the river. . . . And I smoked a pensive cigarette, and philosophized about love and life and battle, and you and me. And I thought of a theme for my next novel."[90] And when the novel was finished, he imagined it was a new glimpse of reality that he had had himself and was passing on to others—"It is really very good. It really puts a new thing in the world, almost a new vision of life."[91]

Of the loves described in *The Rainbow,* it is in the case of Tom Brangwen and Lydia Lensky that we find the union most successful. In a way, the relationship of Rupert and Ursula runs parallel to that of Tom and Lydia, except for a few new developments, important developments, that I shall mention later. Both Tom and

Rupert have one aim in life: to find a woman and to remain with her all their lives; and this is the main purpose of their search. Rupert Birkin, we read in *Women in Love,* believes in the "finality of love," in having "one woman" only, and in the fact that however confused hitherto his life may have been, he will at last come all right "through marriage." Tom Brangwen too begins his male career with similar objectives. With meticulous care Lawrence builds his character and shows us how the young man has "warmth" in him, how his nature is "generous," how there is "innate delicacy in him," how there is a lot of mad "desire" in him as well, passion, but how he has at the same time the most sensitive of all characteristics a man could possess, an "instinctive regard for women." Through his experience with a prostitute, we are made to realize that sheer physical satisfaction is not what Tom is looking for in life. "He despised the net result in him of the experience—he despised it deeply and bitterly." Instead, as we have just been told, what his soul wants is "to find in a woman the embodiment of all his inarticulate, powerful religious impulses." He is not a man on the loose; though young and impetuous, he has a hold on himself. For "the business of love was, at the bottom of his soul, the most serious and terrifying of all to him."

We need not enlarge further upon the early life of this young man—upon how he meets the woman of his choice, Lydia Lensky; how he courts her; and how he marries her. F. R. Leavis has analyzed their coming together and their courtship with thoroughness, and the reader is referred to Chapter 3 of his *D. H. Lawrence: Novelist.* But we have to see the resoluteness of the faith portrayed by the artist, when the motive force of a man's actions is the "soul." This actually is the anchor of the whole story, the weight upon which the integrity of the story depends. Tom Brangwen and Lydia Lensky have no rules or regulations to go by; they have no means of "knowing" each other; their relationship is built practically on nothing, except this: the urge of the soul. Either the urge is to be proved right, or it is to be proved wrong. Lawrence's answer has been given earlier. If the urge is spontaneous, if it is unpremeditated and unplanned, it is then the urge from the unknown, and is, therefore, creative and healthy—is a genuine urge. If, on the other hand, it is the result of a desired end, if it is prompted by a fixed design in the mind, it is sham and undependable. The decisive factor is "desireless" spontaneity—or what Lawrence calls "mindless" spontaneity.

An interesting way to appreciate this might be a comparison of the first meetings of some of Lawrence's men and women. To confine ourselves to the two novels we are discussing, we shall briefly go over the first encounters between Tom and Lydia, Will and Anna, Anton and Ursula (*The Rainbow*), and between Rupert and Ursula, and Gerald and Gudrun (*Women in Love*). To be sure, in all those encounters the element of attraction is there, but it is the validity of the attraction in the light of what we have said above that is to be tested. What we have to see is whether the action perpetuated is spontaneous, that is, whether it is creative action, or whether it is a mere reaction, reaction as the result of a desired end in the mind.

When Tom sees Lydia on the road for the first time, his involuntary response is: "That's her." Leavis points out the value of this exclamation. He writes that when Tom "meets and passes in the road the strange foreign woman, and says involuntarily, 'That's her,' we have a very specific sense, even so early in the book, of the forces registered in the exclamation—the complexity speaking."[92] The complexity, admittedly, concerns the forces which go to make love and marriage in Lawrence's books, but the intensity, the dramatic intensity of their meeting that Leavis stresses, is almost as marked when Ursula meets Anton, or when Gudrun sees Gerald for the first time.

> But she wanted to turn to the stranger. He was standing back a little, waiting. He was a young man with very clear greyish eyes that waited until they were called upon, before they took expression.

> Something in his self-possessed waiting moved her, and she broke into a confused, rather beautiful laugh as she gave him her hand, catching her breath like an excited child. His hand closed over hers very close, very near, he bowed, and his eyes were watching her with some attention. She felt proud—her spirit leapt to life.[93]

And—

> Her son was of a fair, sun-tanned type, rather above middle height, well-made, and almost exaggeratedly well-dressed. But about him also was the strange, guarded look, the unconscious glisten, as if he did not belong to the same creation as the people about him. Gudrun lighted on him at once. There was something northern about him that magnetised her. In his clear northern flesh and his fair hair was a glisten like sunshine refracted through crystals of ice. And he looked so new, unbroached, pure as an arctic thing. Perhaps he was thirty years old, perhaps more. His gleaming beauty, maleness, like a young, good-humoured, smiling wolf, did not blind her to the significant, sinister stillness in his bearing, the lurking danger of his unsubdued temper. "His totem is the wolf," she repeated to herself. "His mother is an old, unbroken wolf." And then she experienced a keen paroxysm, a transport, as if she had made some incredible discovery, known to nobody else on earth. A strange transport took possession of her, all her veins were in a paroxysm of violent sensation. "Good God!" she exclaimed to herself, "what is this?" And then, a moment later, she was saying assuredly, "I shall know more of that man." She was tortured with desire to see him again, a

nostalgia, a necessity to see him again, to make sure it was not all a mistake, that she was not deluding herself, that she really felt this strange and overwhelming sensation on his account, this knowledge of him in her essence, this powerful apprehension of him. "Am I *really* singled out for him in some way, is there really some pale gold, arctic light that envelopes only us two?" she asked herself. And she could not believe it, she remained in a muse, scarcely conscious of what was going on around.[94]

These two extracts undoubtedly convey one thing: that the feeling in the characters described even in these cases is one of intensity. We read that Ursula's spirit leaps "to life" when she meets Anton, and Gudrun experiences "a keen paroxysm, a transport" on meeting Gerald. We therefore are not going to look for the dramatic intensity of Leavis in the first encounters we wish to discuss. What we have to see is the validity of this intensity: not the intensity itself but the state of the person who experiences the intensity, the motive behind it. We need not examine them in detail, but a study of these two characters, Ursula in *The Rainbow* and Gudrun in *Women in Love*, shows that at the time they met these men, they had formed a certain preconceived notion of the type of man they would like to be wooed by, and of his characteristics. And Skrebensky and Gerald, in the particular circumstances that they come into the story, fill that self-projected image of the lover these two women have in mind. Their intensity thus is the result of their ego, and hence is deceptive and unreliable. And as the succeeding events show, their relationships come to a sad end.

But that is not the case when Tom meets Lydia. He has no other self-projected image than "to find in a woman the embodiment of all his inarticulate, powerful religious impulses." He is not looking for a particular type of woman. Unlike Ursula, he has not been dreaming of a special "Daughter of God" to come and mate with him. When Ursula met Anton in *The Rainbow*: "She laid hold of him at once for her dreams. Here was one such as those Sons of God who saw the daughters of men, that they were fair" (p. 272). Nor, unlike Gudrun, is Tom a "social success," or has a taste for "the arts" (*Women in Love*, p. 16) to look for and be dazzled by similar accomplishments in his counterpart. He is just in a state of readiness, without knowing the particularities of his wants. He has no other "desire" fixed in his mind, except the creative desire to be united to a woman who may stir his soul. Hence the significance of the finality he feels when involuntarily, on meeting Lydia, he cries out "That's her." It decidedly is an expression of the complexity of his feelings, as Leavis asserts, but even more, the exclamation is a symbol of the unprepared for, unforeseen urge of the soul. We are told that after the encounter, "he went on, quiet, suspended, rarefied." So skillful was Lawrence's artistic grasp of the impact of external experiences on the human heart that, within a few sentences, within the space of a single sentence, he conveys the sudden depth, the sudden profundity, that is at times created by such impacts. Every single adjective here—"quiet," "suspended," "rarefied"—gives us a broader picture of the emotional range of Tom Brangwen. The effort of the artist, as may be obvious by now, is not so much to mark the force of the experience as to establish the tone of that force, the tone of that intensity, the inherent authenticiy of it. We read on:

> He could not bear to think or to speak, nor make any sound or sign, nor change his fixed motion. He could scarcely bear to think of her face. He moved within the knowledge of her, in the world that was beyond reality.
> The feeling that they had exchanged recognition possessed him like a madness, like a torment. How could he be sure, what confirmation had he? The doubt was like a

sense of infinite space, a nothingness, annihilating. He kept within his breast the will to surety. They had exchanged recognition.[95]

When much later in the book, Anna, the child of Lydia, meets Will Brangwen, the scene is a long one, and it takes one some time to appreciate the enormity of the impact between the two of them. Both of them are very young, and, so far as we understand from the story, have had no emotional involvement earlier. They are thus nervous and unsure of themselves; for them even to think in terms of "love" and "marriage" produces bashfulness of high order. It is however through other, circumstantial touches that Lawrence makes the reader aware of what is passing between them, or, to be more precise, what has come to pass. Technically speaking it is not a "first" meeting between them; they have known each other as children. But it is the first time they see each other as grown-ups, as a young man and a young woman conscious of the new needs of their bodies. Very subtly, we are informed of the maturity in Anna, of the silence of the ego in her, when we are told: "She knew plenty of young men, but they had never become real to her. She had seen in this young gallant a nose she liked, in that a pleasant moustache, in the other a nice way of wearing clothes, in one a ridiculous fringe of hair, in another a comical way of talking. They were objects of amusement and faint wonder to her, rather than real beings, the young men."[96]

If we recall, Lawrence's major invective against "love" in the modern Western world was that men and women did not fall in love with each other, they fell in love with the personalities of each other (see Part I); they were attracted by the physical and mental accomplishments of each other, the type of physical and mental accomplishments they had already built in their mind. To quote him, "Our consciousness is pot-bound. Our

ideas, our emotions, our experiences are all pot-bound.
For us there is nothing new under the sun. What there
is to know, we know it already, and experience adds
little. The girl who is going to fall in love knows all
about it beforehand from books and the movies. She
knows what she wants and she wants what she knows."[97]
In this case the Indian approach to life shows a meaningful advantage over that of the West. For though
most marriages are arranged in India in these days, the
concept of love, as it does exist and as it is reviewed
and presented in the great classics of the country, is one
that would have been applauded by Lawrence: instinctive and uncalculated urge of two persons for each other.
Rama's and Sita's love for each other in the *Ramayana*
begins in this fashion: "Sri Rama felt utter peace at the
radiance of Sita. He praised her in his heart, but failed
to find an expression for what he praised. She stood before
him, as if the Gods had enclosed the very secret of the
universe in her beautiful body" (*Ramacharitmanas,* I,
ccxxix,3). "Her eyes became heavy at the sight of Rama.
She couldn't move; her whole body went taut; she was
bewitched like a peahen watching the moon. She closed
her eyes and saw Rama inside her shut lids. Her friends
looked at her and knew it was love. They were all a
little frightened at this" (*Ramacharitmanas,* I, ccxxxi,
3, 4). The *Mahabharata* is full of love stories of the same
nature, one of them being the love of Shakuntala for
Dushyant, which was later dramatized by Kalidasa in his
renowned play *Shakuntala,* and the regional literature of
most states in India has its separate classics with similar
themes. The young man and the young woman come
together, often in hostile circumstances; they know
nothing of each other, have never met before, have
never spoken a word; and they look at each other, suddenly conceive of a great longing for each other, and a
deep attachment ensues.

When Anna meets Will in *The Rainbow,* she is not
looking for anything particular either. She had seen
the particularities in other men, but as we are told, she
had not found them "real beings." But "somehow, this
young man gave her away to other people," she feels.
The experience is very different with Will Brangwen.
Through the long scene that follows, the quality of the
experience is explored, and just as in the case of Tom
Brangwen, we are made to realize that here is something
happening which is vitally changing the individual concerned: something so precious that the words fail to
grasp it, something that can only be communicated in
reflex action.

They go to Church together, and sit next to each other.

> The colour came streaming from the painted window
> above her. It lit on the dark wood of the pew, on the
> stone, worn aisle, on the pillar behind her cousin, and on
> her cousin's hands, as they lay on his knees. She sat amid
> illumination, illumination and luminous shadow all
> around her, her soul very bright. She sat, without knowing
> it, conscious of the hands and motionless knees of her
> cousin. Something strange had entered into her world,
> something entirely strange and unlike what she knew.
> She was curiously elated. She sat in a glowing world of
> unreality, very delightful. A brooding light, like laughter,
> was in her eyes. She was aware of a strange influence en-
> tering in to her, which she enjoyed. It was a dark enriching
> influence she had not known before. She did not think of
> her cousin. But she was startled when his hands moved.[98]

She remains absorbed in the nimbus of his nearness,
acutely aware of him, and yet not knowing what she
is actually aware of. When the singing starts, she bursts
out into an uncontrolled hysterical laugh, and Lawrence
then goes on to give us a lengthy picture of this reaction
of the body, a picture that in itself is some indication of
Anna's present feelings and that the artist in Lawrence
puts to an effective use. For though it is at the strong

and loud sound of Will's singing that the laughter begins,
the spirit behind the scene is the spirit of release—the
body, Anna's body, giving an utterance to the flood of
new and ungraspable emotions that the young man's
presence near her has generated, and that her mind
somehow finds impossible to assess in rational terms;
emotions for which the normal vehicles of expression fail
and some uninhibited action of the body alone can give
an outlet: the uncontrolled laughter.

> Then suddenly, at the very first word, his voice came
> strong and over-riding, filling the church. He was singing
> the tenor. Her soul opened in amazement. His voice filled
> the church! It rang out like a trumpet, and rang out
> again. She started to giggle over her hymn-book. But he
> went on, perfectly steady. Up and down rang his voice,
> going its own way. She was helplessly shocked into laugh-
> ter. Between moments of dead silence in herself she shook
> with laughter. On came the laughter, seized her and shook
> her till the tears were in her eyes. She was amazed, and
> rather enjoyed it. And still the hymn rolled on, and still
> she laughed. She bent over her hymn-book crimson with
> confusion, but still her sides shook with laughter. She pre-
> tended to cough, she pretended to have a crumb in her
> throat. Fred was gazing up at her with clear blue eyes. She
> was recovering herself. And then a slur in the strong, blind
> voice at her side brought it all on again, in a gust of mad
> laughter.
> She bent down to prayer in cold reproof of herself. And
> yet, as she knelt, little eddies of giggling went over her. The
> very sight of his knees on the praying cushion sent the little
> shock of laughter over her.
> She gathered herself together and sat with prim, pure
> face, white and pink and cold as a christmas rose, her hands
> in her silk gloves folded on her lap, her dark eyes all vague,
> abstracted in a sort of dream, oblivious of everything.
> The sermon rolled on vaguely, in a tide of pregnant
> peace.
> Her cousin took out his pocket-handkerchief. He seemed
> to be drifted absorbed into the sermon. He put his handker-
> chief to his face. Then something dropped on to his knee.

There lay the bit of flowering current! He was looking down at it in real astonishment. A wild snirt of laughter came from Anna. Everybody heard: it was torture. He had shut the crumpled flower in his hand and was looking up again with the same absorbed attention to the sermon. Another snirt of laughter from Anna. Fred nudged her remindingly. Her cousin sat motionless. Somehow she was aware that his face was red. She could feel him. His hand, closed over the flower, remained quite still, pretending to be normal. Another wild struggle in Anna's breast, and the snirt of laughter. She bent forward shaking with laughter. It was now no joke. Fred was nudge-nudging at her. She nudged him back fiercely. Then another vicious spasm of laughter seized her. She tried to ward it off in a little cough. The cough ended in a suppressed whoop. She wanted to die. And the closed hand crept away to the pocket. Whilst she sat in taut suspense, the laughter rushed back at her, knowing he was fumbling in his pocket to shove the flower away.

In the end, she felt weak, exhausted and thoroughly depressed. A blankness of wincing depression came over her. She hated the presence of the other people. Her face became quite haughty. She was unaware of her cousin any more.

When the collection arrived with the last hymn, her cousin was again singing resoundingly. And still it amused her. In spite of the shameful exhibition she had made of herself, it amused her still. She listened to it in a spell of amusement. And the bag was thrust in front of her, and her sixpence was mingled in the folds of her glove. In her haste to get it out, it slipped away and went twinkling in the next pew. She stood and giggled. She could not help it: she laughed outright, a figure of shame.

"What were you laughing about, our Anna?" asked Fred, the moment they were out of the church.

"Oh, I couldn't help it," she said, in her careless, half-mocking fashion. "I don't know *why* Cousin Will's singing set me off."

"What was there in my singing to make you laugh?" he asked.

"It was so loud," she said.

They did not look at each other, but they both laughed again, both reddening.[99]

They return home and the routine of life—having tea, making small talk with other members of the family, and the like—goes on. But we read about Will: "He was very much excited and filled with himself that afternoon. A flame kindled round him, making his experience passionate and glowing, burningly real." And we read that, after he left,

> the glow remained in him, the fire burned, his heart was fierce like a sun. He enjoyed his unknown life and his own self. And he was ready to go back to the Marsh.
>
> Without knowing it, Anna was wanting him to come. In him she had escaped. In him the bounds of her experience were transgressed: he was the hole in the wall, beyond which the sunshine blazed on an outside world.[100]

Before we return to the story of Tom Brangwen and Lydia Lensky, let us lightly touch on the meeting of Ursula and Rupert in *Women in Love*. In spite of the repetition of the theme of love and marriage in these two novels, it goes to Lawrence's credit as an artist that no two relationships are handled by him in a similar manner; in each, there is a clearly discernible variation. Ursula is a very different girl from her grandmother, Lydia; she is the product of the Grammar School education. By the time she meets Rupert, she is a teacher in one of the schools, he an inspector. The long time they take before they can reconcile themselves to a union stands, in a way, for the corruptive influence of modern education, which slowly builds an ego, builds an ideal in each of them and hence makes it difficult for the mind to relax. This is further borne out in Lawrence's criticism of the modern educational system in *Fantasia of the Unconscious,* where he says: "We talk about education—leading forth the natural intelligence of a child. But ours is just the opposite of leading forth. It is a ramming in of brain facts through the head, and

a consequent distortion, suffocation, and starvation of
the primary centres of consciousness. A nice day of
reckoning we've got in front of us."[101] Tom in *The Rainbow* has no uncertainty about his choice; Lydia accepts
him the same evening that he proposes to her, for she
has no uncertainty, either. But two thirds of *Women in
Love* is over before Ursula and Rupert are relaxed
enough mentally to arrive at a similar conjunction:

> She had her desire of him, she touched, she received the
> maximum of unspeakable communication in touch, dark,
> subtle, positively silent, a magnificent gift and give again,
> a perfect acceptance and yielding, a mystery, the reality of
> that which can never be known, vital, sensual reality that
> can never be transmuted into mind content, but remains
> outside, living body of darkness and silence and subtlety,
> the mystic body of reality. She had her desire fulfilled. He
> had his desire fulfilled. For she was to him what he was to
> her, the immemorial magnificence of mystic, palpable, real
> otherness.[102]

It happens on page 337 of a novel that runs to the total
length of 508 pages. Obviously, as the story shows, the
"distortion, suffocation, and starvation of the primary
centres of consciousness" by education has quite a major
hand in this delay. In any case, in spite of these adverse
influences, when Ursula meets Rupert in the beginning,
somewhere in her consciousness she feels that he is the
man for her—"She wanted to know him more. She had
spoken with him once or twice, but only in his official
capacity as inspector. She thought he seemed to acknowledge some kinship between her and him, a natural, tacit
understanding, a using of the same language. But there
had been no time for the understanding to develop."[103]
The understanding comes slowly but the urge of the
soul is present even here. Shortly afterwards, in a scene
in Ursula's classroom, the two give a convincing proof
of it when in a curious, dramatic situation Lawrence

brings together Ursula, Rupert, and Rupert's present friend, Hermione. It is a valuable encounter, in the sense that through the veiled hostility of Rupert toward Hermione in the presence of a third person, Ursula, the artist in Lawrence makes the reader (and makes Ursula) aware of the repulsion that Rupert has for Hermione and the kinship that he feels for Ursula. It is left unexplained by Lawrence—a serious defect in the story—how a man of Rupert's character and views originally came to be attached to Hermione. But the scene in the classroom clearly establishes the bond, the beginning of the bond, between Rupert and Ursula.

> They were gone. Ursula stood looking at the door for some moments. Then she put out the lights. And having done so, she sat down again in her chair, absorbed and lost. And then she began to cry, bitterly, bitterly weeping: but whether for misery or joy, she never knew.[104]

That it was for joy, we are left in no doubt as the story develops.

In the silence of their souls, in the "pureness" of their intensity, and in the creative awareness of it, Tom and Lydia accept each other and their marriage comes into being. Lawrence here—as indeed in every other case—makes a fine distinction between "impulse" and "instinct." The two are not to be confused; impulse is not very reliable, and often is even hostile to instinct; it is the instinct one must follow and not impulse. We recall here Eliot's description of Lawrence as "impatient and impulsive."

Talking about Lydia, Lawrence writes:

> She got to know him better, and her instinct fixed on him—just on him. Her impulse was strong against him, because he was not of her own sort. But one blind instinct led her, to take him, to have him, and then to relinquish

herself to him. It would be safety. She felt the rooted safety
of him, and the life in him. . . .[105]

So they are married and their life together starts. Lydia
would have given herself to him even before the actual
ceremony of marriage. Not that Lawrence approved of
free love. But the precise argument is that once the
recognition is exchanged between two persons, it is final;
it doesn't necessarily need the ceremony to sanctify it.

> She did not know this, she did not understand. They had
> looked at each other, and had accepted each other. It was
> so, then there was nothing to balk at, it was complete
> between them.[106]

But Tom holds back nevertheless, until the ceremony
is over. And then the duel, the long fight, the slow and
painful recognition (painful for Tom) of separateness
in togetherness begins. Their Ship of Marriage is on its
way.

It is perhaps necessary to go over the details of a part
of their married life together. They are not Tom and
Lydia now, they are "husband" and "wife" (Lawrence
makes a point of using those expressions for them at the
present juncture) :

> It made a great difference to him, marriage. Things
> became so remote and of so little significance, as he knew
> the powerful source of his life, his eyes opened on a new
> universe, and he wondered in thinking of his triviality
> before. A new, calm relationship showed to him in the
> things he saw, in the cattle he used, the young wheat as it
> eddied in a wind.
> And each time he returned home, he went steadily, ex-
> pectantly, like a man who goes to a profound, unknown
> satisfaction. At dinner-time, he appeared in the doorway,
> hanging back a moment from entering, to see if she was
> there. He saw her setting the plates on the white-scrubbed
> table. Her arms were slim, she had a slim body, and full

skirts, she had a dark, shapely head with closed-banded hair. Somehow it was her head, so shapely and poignant, that revealed her his woman to him. As she moved about clothed closely, full-skirted and wearing her little silk apron, her dark hair smoothly parted, her head revealed itself to him in all its subtle, intrinsic beauty, and he knew she was his woman, he knew her essence, that it was his to possess. And he seemed to live thus in contact with her, in contact with the unknown, the unaccountable and incalculable.[107]

"The unknown, the unaccountable and incalculable" —here is a description of the mystery of any relationship; the unknown as it keeps becoming manifested from moment to moment. It is for this reason, for the newness, for the "unknownness" of the living moment that we have compared some of the first meetings among Lawrence's men and women, and their responses to the first meetings. To put it in a rather naïve manner, Lawrence would have it that even in marriage, when the man and the woman have started living together, every meeting between them must be treated by both of them, every day, every time every day, as a "first" meeting; every time, the two of them must come afresh to each other. What normally happens is that once a relationship is formed between a man and a woman, the memory—bitter or happy—of that relationship grows, and then the spontaneity of the relationship vanishes; the further action comes to be the result of that memory rather than immediate responsiveness to the moment. It may sound enigmatic, for certainly memory in any relationship plays an important part. But in Laurentian ethics, the fact has to be accepted that memory is an unhealthy influence, as it conditions the mind to prejudices in favor of or against a thing. Once this happens, there can be no freshness in the approach to things. It is against this conditioning of the mind that we must compare the first encounters described earlier: the successful relationships,

such as those of Tom and Lydia and Will and Anna, are
successful because of the absence of that conditioning; "the
unknown, the unaccountable, the incalculable" is experienced by them because, as far as possible, the mind has
made no attempt rigidly to "know" things or to "account"
for them or to "calculate" them in advance.

After the marriage, however, Tom cannot keep up that
flexibility of the mind; it is not the Lydia as she is every
day and every moment that he loves now; it is a special
Lydia that he demands, the Lydia in whose nearness he
finds security ("He was safe with her now, till morning") ,
the Lydia who has in her own way opened new doors of
reality to him and who, he wills, *must* always continue to
do so, to satisfy his need. But herein lies the root of his
misery; despite his demanding ownership of her in marriage, Lydia will be what she will be, from moment to
moment, in her own mysterious way. She has to be appreciated and admired for that, something Tom fails to
see in his early possessiveness. Years afterwards, when
Lydia's granddaughter Ursula asks her, "Will somebody
love me, grandmother?" Lydia's reply is: "Yes, some
man will love you, child, because it's your nature. And I
hope it will be somebody who will love you for what you
are, and not for what he wants of you."[108] Tom does not
appreciate this, does not appreciate the value of the very
quality that had originally attracted him to Lydia—her
"otherness." "It was her curious, absorbed, flitting motion,
as if she were passing unseen by everybody, that first
arrested him"—that was when he first saw her on the
road; later, when again "one day he met her walking
along the road with her little girl," she glanced at him
"almost vacantly," and "the very vacancy of her look in-
flamed him"; when he saw her in the church, "there was
a fineness about her, a poignancy about the way she sat
and held her head lifted. She was strange, from far off,
yet so intimate. She was from far away, a presence, so

close to his soul"; outside the church, immediately after-wards, "the wide grey eyes, almost vacant yet so moving, held him beyond himself"; when she came to fetch butter from his farm she stood before him "like a silence" and "her self-possession pleased him and inspired him, set him curiously free." It was this "otherness" in her, one must see, her complete lack of self-consciousness, her inexplicable independence of him and of everything else that had originally fascinated him and prompted the urge: "He submitted to that which was happening to him, letting go his will, suffering the loss of himself, dormant always on the brink of ecstasy, like a creature evolving to a new birth."

To be sure, he himself is a man of similar bearing, as the novel clearly indicates—a man always open to the new. We read of him earlier in the book, "It was coming, he knew, his fate. The world was submitting to its trans-formation. He made no move: it would come, what would come." And this spirit of expectancy and wonder is re-tained by him—or better still, the spirit of expectancy and wonder stays with him, for "retaining" it would imply a conscious effort—throughout the period of his courtship. But unfortunately, after the marriage, the first reaction is that of shutting off this spirit. He now plans, he now demands, he now expects; and his very insistence that she should always give him the same type of joy, be always the same, is a sign of decay. For a while he ceases to be "on the brink of ecstasy, like a creature evolving to a new birth." For new birth means a state of non-pre-knowingness. It may bring joy, it may bring pain; the force of the argument does not conceive the experience as such, but of the acceptance of the experience, whatever it might be. Tom, however, wants only what *he* wants; he makes conditions for the new to be (the life that Lydia should always give him) ; he wants to measure the new by the old.

What is implied is the height of insensitivity when the lovers aim at a "oneness" after marriage. Tom aims at something like this, to begin with, and feels miserably unhappy when he realizes that Lydia still keeps a part of the secret of her unknowable self to herself. "And he remained wrathful and distinct from her, unchanged outwardly to her, but underneath a solid power of antagonism to her. . . . He walked about for days stiffened with resistance to her, stiff with a will to destroy her as she was." He fails to realize that her beauty lies in this endless unknowability, so that he could go in to her again and again, yet again and again, and come back refreshed, yet come back refreshed. Slowly the truth comes to him. He must be patient; he must wait, he must wait for the "sign" from her (we must notice how Lawrence picks up symbols of everyday Christianity and uses them in his own way to extend and deepen his meaning: sign, confession, new birth, and so on). He must not rush her or drive her. He must leave her alone, let her slumber on in the knowledge of her own consciousness, until she could receive him.

> She was sure to come at last, and touch him. Then he burst into flame for her, and lost himself. They looked at each other, a deep laugh at the bottom of their eyes, and he went to take of her again, wholesale, mad to revel in the inexhaustible wealth of her, to bury himself in the depths of her in an exhaustible exploration, she all the while revelling in that he revelled in her, tossed all her secrets aside and plunged to that which was secret to her as well, whilst she quivered with fear and the last anguish of delight.
>
> What did it matter who they were, whether they knew each other or not?[109]

And so the cycle goes on. A child is born to them, and for a while, Lydia becomes so preoccupied with the new arrival that she cannot pay any attention to Tom. Here is the constantly growing, constantly changing relationship, a new phase emerging all the while, and obviously the success of a marriage depends on a recognition of these phases. Tom again fails to see this; for him the new arrival simply means his relegation to a relatively minor position in his claim to his wife's affection. And this again upsets him. We read:

> When Brangwen saw her nursing his child, happy, absorbed in it, a pain went over him like a thin flame. For he perceived how he must subdue himself in his approach to her. And he wanted again the robust, mortal exchange of love and passion such as he had had at first with her, at one time and another, when they were matched at their highest intensity. This was the one experience for him now. And he wanted it, always, with remorseless craving.[110]

How penetratingly Lawrence conveys Tom's longing for something that is past and his inability to accept the new—the new that is not pleasant to him! "This was the one experience for him now. And he wanted it, always, with remorseless craving." In the "remorseless craving" is the bond of an earlier memory, and how can "new" be always the same as what had once come to pass? That an experience can never be the same again is remarkably well expressed by Lawrence in the next paragraph, where he describes Lydia as trying to oblige Tom in his physical desire, and comments: "And it was almost as before." The introduction of the word "almost" colors the tone of the paragraph, for it shows that the experience is different this time. We go on to read "Perhaps it was quite as before"—the element of doubt still persisting. Tom, however, is satisfied with even this and thinks it complete, so far as he is concerned. But he does not see that Lydia is not there as a vessel for his sexual outlets, a machine to constantly satisfy him. She is a Woman, with a Self of her own, with her own mysterious needs and demands, and he must learn to receive only what she can give. For she is tired of his constant demands and can no longer give him the physical satisfaction he so persistently wants.

It is now that Tom's comprehension really begins to widen; now that he realizes that the end of marriage is not the sheer satisfaction of the sexual urge:

> So he had to begin the bitter lesson, to abate himself, to take less than he wanted. For she was Woman to him, all other women were her shadows. For she had satisfied him. And he wanted it to go on. And it could not. However he raged, and, filled with suppression that became hot and bitter, hated her in his soul that she did not want him, however he had mad outbursts, and drank and made ugly scenes, still he knew, he was only kicking against the pricks. It was not, he had to learn, that she *would* not want him enough, as much as he demanded that she should want him. It was that she could not. She could only want him in her own way, and to her own measure. And she had spent much life before he found her as she was, the woman who could take him and give him fulfilment. She had taken him and given him fulfilment. She still would do so, in her own times and ways. But he must control himself, measure himself to her.
>
> He wanted to give her all his love, all his passion, all his essential energy. But it could not be. He must find other things than her, other centres of living. . . .[111]

And even now he takes a long time before he can finally reconcile himself to this. The move, once again, is made by Lydia. She notices that unless she too accepts him as he is, he may go away to other women. And she calls him one day to herself, and the physical life which had been interrupted for a while between them is renewed. And, after all, Tom recognizes the hard fact that if she is really the "other" ("She was the awful unknown"; "She was beyond him, the unattainable"), he must learn to accept her with her otherness; he should not try to remold her, or expect her to be what she is not. And this completes his marital bliss.

Their coming together now, after two years of married
life, was much more wonderful to them than it had been
before. It was the entry into another circle of existence, it
was the baptism to another life, it was the complete confirmation. Their feet trod strange ground of knowledge,
their footsteps were lit-up with discovery. Wherever they
walked, it was well, the world re-echoed round them in
discovery. They went gladly and forgetful. Everything was
lost, and everything was found. The new world was discovered, it remained only to be explored.

They had passed through the doorway into the further
space, where movement was so big, that it contained bonds
and constraints and labours, and still was complete liberty.
She was the doorway to him, he to her. At last they had
thrown open the doors, each to the other, and had stood in
the doorways facing each other, whilst the light flooded
out from behind on to each of their faces, it was the transfiguration, the glorification, the admission.

And always the light of the transfiguration burned on in
their hearts. He went his way, as before, she went her way,
to the rest of the world there seemed no change. But to the
two of them, there was the perpetual wonder of the transfiguration.[112]

For indeed Tom has now realized the truth that Lydia
had perhaps always known—the significance of the living
moment. The impact of the living moment alone constitutes the breath of life, and this impact if felt without
inhibitions, if received with openness, immediately wipes
out the past moments and the memory of those moments.
For Lydia precisely this—the metamorphosis to the new,
the wiping out of the old—had happened when she had
met Tom and agreed to marry him ("When she opened
and turned to him, then all that had been and all that
was, was gone from her, she was as new as a flower that
unsheathes itself and stands always ready, waiting, receptive") .[113] But Tom had been wallowing in and worried
about her past and the other things that might be in her
mind in addition to her love for him, and he had been
too exacting in the demands that he placed on her, the

affection that he expected from her. Now, after this new coming together, he sees the devastating effect of these thoughts on the health of his soul. He feels that even if Lydia had had other attachments earlier, he, Tom Brangwen, was the actuality to her and hence the reality. Memory, he suddenly comes to grasp, was there in the mind mostly because of an unfulfilled wish: "What was memory after all, but the recording of a number of possibilities which had never been fulfilled? What was Paul Lensky to her, but an unfulfilled possibility to which he, Brangwen, was the reality and the fulfilment?"[114] Hence, he sees the value of his present with her and forgets everything else. He joins Lydia in her reverence for the passing moment and is humble before it.

Having realized this, they almost realize God, whatever that recognition may mean, right here and now:

> Now He was declared to Brangwen and to Lydia Brangwen, as they stood together. When at last they had joined hands, the house was finished, and the Lord took up his abode. And they were glad.
> The days went on as before, Brangwen went out to his work, his wife nursed her child and attended in some measure to the farm. They did not think of each other—why should they? Only when she touched him, he knew her instantly, that she was with him, near him, that she was the gateway and the way out, that she was beyond, and that he was travelling in her through the beyond. Whither?—What does it matter? He responded always. When she called, he answered, when he asked, her response came at once, or at length.[115]

How successful their union remained thereafter is woven long into the story, along with the other developments in the plot concerning other characters; the effect is achieved by Lawrence in a most accomplished manner right till the end of their marriage on Tom's death. We are given a glimpse of it when, many years afterwards,

Anna is wanting to marry Will, and Tom is a little sorry
to lose the girl he has so affectionately brought up and is
thus in a dejected mood. Then in a thoughtful mood he
reminds himself of the ultimate joy he still gets only from
the "marital embrace with his wife": "He would say so
to anybody, and be proud of it. He lay with his wife in
his arms, and she was still his fulfilment, just the same
as ever. And that was the be-all and the end-all. Yes, and
he was proud of it."116 Again we see a glimpse of it in the
speech Tom makes—a speech delivered rather clumsily,
but which has in a nutshell considerable Laurentian
thought on the subject, and the substance of which Lawrence himself was to repeat almost word for word in
Apropos of Lady Chatterley's Lover fourteen years later—
the speech he makes at the wedding of Will and Anna
(he is in a "mood of inspiration," we are told) :

> Marriage is what we're made for. . . . A man enjoys
> being a man: for what purpose was he made a man, if not
> to enjoy it? . . . And likewise a woman enjoys being a
> woman: at least we surmise she does. . . . Now, for a man
> to be a man it takes a woman, and for a woman to be a
> woman, it takes a *man*. . . . Therefore we have marriage. . . .
> There's no marriage in heaven, but on earth there is mar-
> riage. . . .   There's very little else on earth, but marriage.
> You can talk about making money, or saving souls. You
> can save your own soul seven times over, and you may have
> a mint of money, but your soul goes gnawin', gnawin',
> gnawin', and it says there's something it must have. In
> heaven there is no marriage. But on earth there *is* marriage,
> else heaven drops out, and there's no bottom to it.117

And lastly we have a glimpse of it, a confirmation of it,
from Lydia herself, when after Tom's death she sits
ruminating about the two husbands she had had (in the
order that they come into her life) :

> She, Lydia Brangwen, was sorry for him now [for Paul

Lensky]. He was dead—he had scarcely lived. He had never known her. He had lain with her, but he had never known her. He had never received what she could give him. He had gone away from her empty. So, he had never lived. So, he had died and passed away. Yet there had been strength and power in him.

She could scarcely forgive him that he had never lived. If it were not for Anna, and for this little Ursula, who had his brows, there would be no more left of him than of a broken vessel thrown away, and just remembered.

Tom Brangwen had served her. He had come to her, and taken from her. He had died and gone his way into death. But he had made himself immortal in his knowledge with her. So she had her place here, in life, and in immortality. For he had taken his knowledge of her into death, so that she had her place in death. "In my father's house are many mansions."

She loved both her husbands. To one she had been a naked little girl-bride, running to serve him. The other she loved out of fulfilment, because he was good and had given her being, because he had served her honourably, and become her man, one with her.

She was established in this stretch of life, she had come to herself. During her first marriage, she had not existed, except through him, he was the substance and she the shadow running at his feet. She was very glad she had come to her own self. She was grateful to Brangwen. She reached out to him in gratitude, into death.[118]

The story of Tom Brangwen and Lydia Brangwen comes to an end here, and is sufficient demonstration of the kind of love and marriage Lawrence conceived of in his creative writings. Mark Spilka discounts Tom's character as "still unformed at the time of his death,"[119] which is an unfortunate critical assessment of Tom and of Lawrence. For in the character of Tom, Lawrence reveals his conception of all fulfillments in life: the assertion that the joy of living lies in vulnerability, in being unformed and unfinished, in being open to the new. The quality that Mark Spilka intends to condemn in Tom, is something worthy of praise in him. His unformedness is not the result of restless yearning. It is the result of his receptivity to the unknown. There is no fear of the unknown in him, as Spilka wrongly states ("though he shares his wife's belief in a vague and indefinable God, he is still afraid of the unknown") ,[120] but instead a reverence. He sees the unknown in his wife, he sees the unknown in the child Anna, he sees the unknown around him in all forms, each form a different form of manifestation. And he remains open to it in all its manifestations.

The story of Ursula and Rupert in *Women in Love* follows the same pattern. But in *Women in Love* we hear more—from the lips of Rupert—about the doctrine of Laurentian love. It is somewhat beautifully conceived by him at one place, when he says to himself: "It must happen beyond the sound of words."[121] Ursula and Rupert take a long time before they can arrive at this level of understanding, but the process does not consist of adjustments at the mental level, it consists of negation of mental curiosities and doubts. As Rupert tells Ursula: "While ever either of us insists to the other, we are all wrong. But there we are, the accord doesn't come."[122] Finally, however, the accord does come—when they are capable enough to let things take their own shape; and they are married. That their marriage too was a success, like that of Tom Brangwen and Lydia Lensky, we are made to see right at the end of the novel. Gerald is dead and Rupert is mourning the loss. Both Rupert and Ursula have been watching Gerald's body:

"It's a bitter thing to me," he said.
"What—that he's dead?" she said.
His eyes met hers. He did not answer.
"You've got me," she said.
He smiled and kissed her.
"If I die," he said, "you'll know I haven't left you."
"And me?" she cried.

"And you won't have left me," he said. "We shan't have any need to despair, in death."[123]

It is the ultimate tribute that a man and a woman in love could pay to each other. In *The Rainbow*, Lydia Brangwen pays the same tribute to Tom Brangwen, as already quoted: "For he had taken his knowledge of her into death, so that she had her place in death." Lawrence did not believe that one could visualize beforehand what might follow after death; the expression is a figurative one. And yet it shows his faith in the validity of love. Rupert Birkin, by making this confession to Ursula, is acknowledging the depth of their love and the triumph of their marriage. This is not a place to discuss the man-to-man relationship that Rupert wanted with Gerald and which he is sorry he cannot have now since Gerald is dead. But we must repudiate the charge that it signifies the attraction of a homosexual relationship. Lawrence believed that every man should have a "purpose" in life, which he must try to fulfill in collaboration with other individuals having a similar purpose, hence the man-to-man relationship. He makes it sufficiently explicit in *Fantasia of the Unconscious* that this relationship between men is a "non-sexual" union. The sexual relationship exists only with the woman, but that fulfillment by itself generates excessive creative energy in the man, which later he must use to enhance his what Lawrence calls "purposive activity." The man-to-man relationship comes only *after* a successful man-to-woman relationship. To quote from *Fantasia of the Unconscious*, "Men, being themselves made new after the action of coition, wish to make the world new. A new, passionate polarity springs up between men who are bent on the same activity, the polarity between man and woman sinks to passivity. It is now daytime, and time to forget sex, time to be busy making a new world."[124] As it follows a little later, "This meeting of many in one great passionate purpose is not sex, and should never be confused with sex. It is a great motion in the opposite direction."[125] The following remarks of Birkin to Ursula corroborate this; that for Birkin Ursula comes first and the friendship with Gerald afterwards, as a consequence of the new life that Birkin derives from Ursula: " 'Having you, I can live all my life without anybody else, any other sheer intimacy. But to make it complete, really happy, I wanted eternal union with a man too: another kind of love,' he said."[126] Why it should be the man alone who should seek for this further friendship with a man, and not a woman with another woman as well, is again quite clear from the passages just referred to. The "purposive activity" in Lawrence's world is confined to men alone; a mission together between like-minded men.

It should be asserted however that *Women in Love* is not, as *The Rainbow* is, essentially a novel of marriage. Forcefully Lawrence pushes ahead to new fields of experience in it. Having absorbed the physical knowledge of the female into him, and having glorified it in the earlier novel, in *Women in Love* Lawrence takes the opportunity to assert that that absorption (of the woman into the man) is not the final force of life, is not the be all and the end all. The goal indeed is the realization of Self as we have it page after page in *Women in Love*. The coming together of a man and a woman is the way, the way to the beyond, and in *The Rainbow*, though most certainly this "beyond" is often referred to, it is not so definitely stressed as in *Women in Love*. Or rather, whereas the "beyond" in *The Rainbow* is described in terms of positive statements, in *Women in Love* it is approached in negative phraseology, a higher form of understanding according to Vedantic thought in the East. The phrase "positive statements" of *The Rainbow* is again a somewhat misleading expression. It is not suggested that Lawrence

in *The Rainbow* anywhere defines *what* the "beyond" is
(that would be contrary to the Laurentian myth of life).
Actually, we are clearly reminded there by Lawrence of
what he describes as the "unthinking knowledge" of Lydia
Brangwen: "It was as if she worshiped God as a mystery,
never seeking in the least to define what He was."[127] And

> To this she had reduced her husband. He existed with
> her entirely indifferent to the general values of the world.
> Her very ways, the very mark of her eyebrows were symbols
> and indication to him. There, on the farm with her, he
> lived through a mystery of life and death and creation,
> strange, profound ecstasies and incommunicable satisfactions,
> of which the rest of the world knew nothing. . . .[128]

But in *Women in Love,* the mystery that Lydia and Tom
live without attempting to define it is brought to prominence by explicitly negative affirmations. When finally
Ursula and Rupert arrive at a complete acceptance of
each other as the initiation to the reality beyond, we read,
"This was release at last. She had had lovers, she had
known passion. But this was neither love nor passion."[129]
And again, shortly afterwards:

> There were strange fountains of his body, more mysterious
> and potent than any she had imagined or known, more
> satisfying, ah, finally, mystically-physically satisfying. She
> had thought there was no source deeper than the phallic
> source. And now, behold, from the smitten rock of the man's
> body, from the strange marvellous flanks and thighs, deeper,
> further in mystery than the phallic source, came the floods
> of ineffable darkness and ineffable riches.[130]

Herein lies the reason why Ursula and Rupert take so
long to accept each other in marriage. Partly, as stated
before, it is the conditioning of their minds by education,
by "ideas," that is responsible for it. But also the delay
is because Rupert wants Ursula to see the "negative"

acceptance that a union with him would imply. Having taken in from the "woman" all that he could in *The Rainbow,* the man now has a turn to give something back to her, something that she fails to comprehend. Ursula has to see—what she in the end does see—that the union with Rupert has to be not on the basis of love, or of passion, or on that of phallic power of the man. "He knew she had a passion for him, really. But it was not finally interesting. There were depths of passion when one became impersonal and indifferent, unemotional. Whereas Ursula was still at the emotional personal level —always so abominably personal."[131]

The shortest and the most important saying of the Upanishads in respect of reality is *"Na iti,"* which means *not this.* Negative understanding—as indeed the Existentialists in the West have started putting forward now—has been the heart of Vedantic philosophy for the last five thousand years in India; it is believed there that this is the *highest* form of perception. *"Na iti," "Na iti," "Na iti"*; not this, not this, not this; not love, not passion, not phallic vigor; none of these is the "beyond." The beyond is there only when one is—to repeat Rupert Birkin's words—"impersonal," "indifferent," "unemotional." Lawrence, thus, in *Women in Love* catches the mystery to Self, which he was to restate years afterwards—after having gone through devious experiences of self-adjustments to the "new" in his own life—as the only valid human discernment in *The Man Who Died* (see next chapter) ; and in this field—as also in the field of man-to-man relationship—*Women in Love* goes ahead of *The Rainbow*. But once the conjunction between Ursula and Rupert is formed, we are left to believe that the succeeding details of their marriage are identical with those of Lydia and Tom in *The Rainbow*; they find the gateway to the unknown. How forceful the joy of such a union is imagined to be in Hindu thought can be seen from the following text from one of the Upanishads, where the bliss of a man come into the knowledge of Self is compared retrospectively with the type of bliss a man enjoys when he comes in to his woman: "Now as a man, when embraced by a beloved wife, knows nothing that is without, nothing that is within, thus this person when embraced by the Self, knows nothing that is without, nothing that is within. This indeed is his form in which his wishes are fulfilled, in which the Self is his wish, in which no wish is left."[132] The fulfillment conceived of in *The Rainbow* and *Women in Love* is of a similar nature.

3. AARON'S ROD

From the discussion so far it is clear how vital a part what Aaron in *Aaron's Rod* calls "Providence" or "Fate" ("I see you are like Lilly—you trust to Providence," said Sir William. "Providence or fate," said Aaron)[133] plays in the affairs of Lawrence's characters. The "Providence" of Lawrence should be distinguished from the Calvinist concept of God's will on one hand and the Hindu theory of *Karma* on the other. Both God's will and *Karma* preclude spontaneity; both "fix" the movement of destiny to a predetermined design. God's will presupposes a master of the universe, apart from the universe. But as analyzed by me in Chapters 2 and 4, in Lawrence's scheme of things no such master exists. The Hindus do not believe in a master like that, but their faith in *Karma* as well imposes a somewhat too rigid pattern on day-to-day living, and, at times, gives the individual a feeling of suffocation.

We may briefly see what *Karma* stands for in the Hindu mind. The theory of *Karma* simply says that just as most organic and inorganic life has certain properties attached to it, with certain action-and-reaction characteristics, so too do a man's actions. Thus an act once performed must bring its results or consequences, and no power on earth can wipe out or forgive or stop the reaction that an action puts into motion. There is a noteworthy *shaloka* (verse) in the *Gita*, which says: *Karmany eva 'dhikaraste, ma phalesu kadacana* (II, 47). Translated, it reads: "Man has the right to action alone, and never to the result." This does not suggest that the result will be decided by a God, or a power outside the universe; it suggests that the result is automatic on the basis of that action. Thus, an action performed, the man has of necessity to accept the result. And this goes on beyond more than one life; the same soul is born again and again, and the cycles are repeated almost endlessly—action and reaction, action and reaction. A stage may finally arrive when the individual is free of the cycles, and through enlightenment of the Self launches out into the unknown.

This may sound logical enough, but if we look at it carefully, it binds the individual in a huge grinding machine, where the cogs and the wheels move with a regularity that is not the regularity of freedom but the regularity of restriction. An action performed is not an independent action, an end in itself, but by some hidden force gets adjusted against previous actions—of this birth and of previous births—and the result may not well become obvious for still many births to come. Isn't this miserably smothering? Doesn't this extinguish the joy of the living moment? Doesn't this bind one, enclose one, put one in a cell within a cell within a cell?

It does. But then the theory of *Karma* is a subsequent development of Hindu thought and does not form a conspicuous part of the Vedantic teaching. In the Upanishads, if there are passages that speak of rebirth and *Karma* (see *Brhadaranyaka Upanishad*, IV, iii,37-38; IV,iv,1-5), there are also passages, more forceful passages, that completely reject the concept (see *Mandukya Upanishad*, 1-12), In any case, it is clearly stated there that rebirth and *Karma* is an illusion, which exists only for the man who moves at a lower level of consciousness. The enlightened one, the man with *vidya,* knows that it is all an illusion, *maya,* and rises above it. What matters in life, according to the Upanishads, is the immediate reality, the moment-to-moment comprehension. The theory of *Karma,* though it has now come to be a part and parcel of Hindu thought, is not the heart of Hinduism. The heart of Hinduism is the *Atman,* the Self, which comprehends, absorbs, and throws out the reactions to life as they come and go. It is in this sense that Providence or Fate is accepted by Hindu scriptures, and it is in this sense that Lawrence makes use of the term. Providence or Fate is the unknown revealed to the Self—at a particular time and in a particular circumstance, irrespective of the past or the future. As Lawrence says in the Foreword to the American edition of *Women in Love*: "The creative, spontaneous soul sends forth its promptings of desire and aspiration in us. These promptings are our true fate, which is our business to fulfil. A fate dictated from outside, from theory or from circumstance, is a false fate."[134] Providence or Fate thus is the living Present: it is what actually happens.

This is fairly well illustrated by Lawrence in the novels that have been considered so far, but in *Aaron's Rod* the same response is approved of and presented even when adverse circumstances befall a man. Love and marriage should be prompted by Providence; but even separation in love, or separation in marriage, should be prompted by the same source. The novel is a splendid study of a man in despair; it conveys the hopelessness and the despondency of an individual who, at a certain time in life, comes to so absolute a state of feeling as to realize that no alternative is left open to him but to act exactly in the manner that he actually does. There is no question of God's will here, or of *Karma.* The consistent effort by

Lawrence throughout the book is to bring out that whatever comes to happen in the case of Aaron and his wife Lettie was the only thing that could have happened in that particular juncture in their life. As the story unfolds, we are led to believe that when Aaron leaves his wife and children and goes away, he has realized the meaninglessness of arguments, either with his wife or with himself. It is a new form of inertia, the effortless inertia of not fighting the reality of existence, however unpleasant the reality may be, that overcomes him. And the response suggested, the response of the moment is: "leave," "go away." (It is unfortunate that the children should have to suffer because of this catastrophe; but one should not overlook the fact that they would in any case have suffered, suffered more, in what Aaron later on terms "the tension of barrenness" of their home, if Aaron and Lettie had not parted.)

An expressive passage dealing with the subject comes when Aaron is spending a few days in Italy at the place of Sir William Franks, a friend of Lilly, and where the very first evening of his arrival his host and other guests assembled there question him about his family.

"Indeed! Indeed! Well. May we ask you another question, Mr. Sisson. I hope you don't object to our catechism?"

"No. Nor your judgment afterwards," said Aaron, grinning.

"Then upon what grounds did you abandon your family? I know it is a tender subject. But Lilly spoke of it to us, and as far as I could see . . ."

"There were no grounds," said Aaron. "No, there weren't. I just left them."

"Mere caprice?"

"If it's a caprice to be begotten—and a caprice to be born—and a caprice to die—then that was a caprice, for it was the same."

"Like birth or death?—I don't follow."

"It happened to me: as birth happened to me once—and

death will happen. It was a sort of death too: or a sort of birth. But as undeniable as either. And without any more grounds."

The old, tremulous man, and the young man, were watching one another.

"A natural event," said Sir William.

"A natural event," said Aaron.

"Not that you loved any other woman?"

"God save me from it."

"You just left off loving?"

"Not even that. I went away."

"What from?"

"From it all."

"From the woman in particular?"

"Oh, yes. Yes. Yes, that."

"And you couldn't go back?"

Aaron shook his head.

"Yet you can give no reasons?"

"Not any reasons that would be any good. It wasn't a question of reasons. It was a question of her and me and what must be. What makes a child be born out of its mother, to the pain and trouble of both of them? I don't know."

"But that is a natural process."

"So is this—or nothing."

"No," interposed the Major. "Because birth is universal process—and yours is a specific, almost unique event."

"Well, unique or not, it so came about. I didn't even leave off loving her—not as far as I know. I left her as I shall leave the earth when I die—because it has to be."[135]

It is clear from this and other similar statements by Aaron in the novel—from the "qualms and emotions concerning his abandoned family" that he feels all along, from his brief return to his wife, from his apparent restlessness at his other sexual affairs—it is clear from all these that he did not really wish to leave his family. But what Aaron wishes to communicate to Sir William and the others here is that just as "birth" or "death" happen without any conscious desire on the part of the individual, in like manner he had not consciously planned or plotted to leave his family; innumerable little criss-cross threads of strain had grown between him and Lettie, and on their own these little threads had at last led to this inevitable result. There was nothing else for him to do then but submit to the force of the urge. If he were to give Sir William a reason for leaving his wife, he would only be rationalizing about the event and making out a case for himself. He and Lettie were both to be blamed for the failure of their marriage. But Aaron could not have gone on living a day longer with her, when he actually did leave her; the relationship would take the strain no more.

Concerning *Aaron's Rod,* Eliseo Vivas comments: "The worst defect of the book is its radical incoherence. This defect shows itself in two closely connected senses: in its utter lack of form and in its failure to elucidate an important point in which the reader is legitimately interested, the grounds on which Aaron leaves his wife and children."[136] It is fairly well recognized that as a novel *Aaron's Rod* is not one of Lawrence's best, and Vivas is right in speaking of its "lack of form" (we might omit the word "utter"; the book is about a man in a confused state of mind, and hence part of its incoherence and lack of form is essential to the portrayal of Aaron's character); but Vivas is inaccurate in his statements concerning "the grounds." The ground is made sufficiently clear by Lawrence. Fate or Providence in its own mysterious way communicates an urge from moment to moment to every individual and this urge, if accepted with a silent mind, is always the right one to follow. Reasons and arguments in defense of it may be marshaled after the actual event has taken place, but at the moment of inception it is beyond reason, beyond the domain of arguments.

So far as the motivating power behind Aaron's dramatic action is concerned, the evidence undoubtedly is in favor of what Lawrence says in his other novels: that things should happen with a natural ease and natural inevitability. Achsah Brewster narrates a remark of Lawrence, his once telling her that "the Hindus were right to believe that the hand of Fate deals out three events—birth, marriage and death—and that no man can escape his fate."[137] If we apply the same to the desertion of Aaron, his action acquires the right proportion and falls well within the range of Lawrence's famous "urge of the soul."

Lawrence, rather, deserves praise for his still-persisting trust in marriage, which is outlined even in *Aaron's Rod*. "Trust" is the only word one can think of for his strong convictions. For we see that, though Aaron leaves his family and goes away, that is not the end of the marriage. The view taken by Lawrence is that marriage is eternal, and perhaps after a long separation Aaron and Lettie may evolve toward a better understanding of themselves and hence towards a new relationship between themselves. He records in *The Captain's Doll*: "All our troubles, says somebody wise, come upon us because we cannot be alone. And that is all very well. We must all be *able* to be alone, otherwise we are just victims. But when we *are* able to be alone, then we realize that the only thing to do is to start a new relationship with another—or even the same—human being."[138] A similar hope is conceived by Lawrence for Aaron and Lettie, for some remote date. How much self-searching, how much self-groping the two would have to go through before they could arrive at that stage is observable from the hardness of the wills that has come in them and that is described in the chapters "Wie es Ihnen gefaellt," when Aaron sits thinking about his domestic life, and "More Pillar of Salt," when Aaron returns home for a brief visit. The extremity of their case, however, is in itself sufficient to show Lawrence's unshaken belief that, however badly things may turn between a man and a woman, there is always the hope of new life's coming into being between them.

4. THE JOURNEY TO THE BEYOND

But the "physical," as ever, remained the entrance for Lawrence to the unknown, and it was in his reverence for that passage, that door to the beyond, that he laid the stress he did on the sanctity of marriage. For the intensity of physical love could be there only when it was centralized, with one particular person. The beyond, the unknown, the Self could never be realized without this "centralization." Briefly, it is a sort of Pilgrim's progress and Lawrence's Pilgrim has to progress through physical conjunction to reach his own Self. To continue the analogy, this Pilgrim has many pitfalls and obstructions on his way, from which he should save himself or emerge successfully. There is the Barrier of the Mind, there is the Castle of Cheap Bodily Desire, and there are the Hill of Love and the Cave of Marriage. He must climb the Hill of Love and enter the Cave of Marriage, for that is the only way the road lies to proceed further. However good and pious the Pilgrim, even as good as Jesus, his quest would remain incomplete and fruitless if he did not go through this experience. Inside the Cave of Marriage, the Pilgrim must join himself physically with another kindred Spirit, whose hand he should hold. It is an endless Cave, growing ever wider and lighter, and the two Pilgrims could spend their whole life in it. They would have to pass through Showers and Fires of Experience, which are bound to alter and change them considerably. They must recognize and accept this change. There are Dragons in this Cave who would try to destroy their identity, but they must walk warily and see that this identity is not lost in any circumstances. If victorious, the Pilgrims are sure to be rewarded by a deeper inner consciousness. And so it is that Lawrence describes the journey of the Self through Sex (phallic) to deeper Self.

Though his account differs from that of Bunyan's Pilgrim, it is as austere, moral, and invigorating.

Dorothea Krook remarks that the type of love Lawrence advocates is selfish; it nowhere envisages a position where an individual may be willing to sacrifice everything he has for the sake of his beloved, as one should in love: "For when, as in Lawrence, an extraordinary capacity for love (and need of love) is combined with as extraordinary a capacity to resist and resent the necessary condition of love, that to find one's self one must lose it, it is indeed inevitable that he should suffer perpetually from the fear of a total loss of identity in the act of loving, which seems to have haunted Lawrence all his life and is one of the central experiences repeatedly enacted in his novels and stories."[139] But then, the kind of physical conjunction Lawrence has in mind does not depend on conventional love. That "to find one's self one must lose it," the biblical line that Dorothea Krook quotes, Lawrence agreed with too. He says in *Fantasia of the Unconscious* (as he says in all his novels, even in *Aaron's Rod*: "to be alone, to be oneself, not to be driven or violated into something which is not oneself, surely it is better than anything") :[140] "To be alone with one's own soul. Not to be alone without my own soul, mind you. But to be alone with one's own soul! This, and the joy of it, is the real goal of love. My own soul, and myself. Not my ego, my conceit of myself. But my very soul. To be at one in my own self. Not to be questing any more. Not to be yearning, seeking, hoping, desiring, aspiring. But to pause, and be alone."[141] It is this that "to find one's self one must lose it" suggests; not subjection to another, as Dorothea Krook reads it, but a state of nonworry, nonanxiety, nonegoism—so that one may accept whatever comes without a murmur.

The physical conjunction that Lawrence puts forward in his novels is thus based on this relaxed state of mutuality between the husband and the wife. Although we are not discussing *Lady Chatterley's Lover* in this chapter (see Appendix), the reason why Constance's marriage with Clifford fails is because of the growing tension between them (on grounds of permanent sexual failure there). Similarly in *Aaron's Rod,* or in *The Captain's Doll,* or *The Ladybird,* it is tension, on one ground or another, that leads to trouble. Whereas the aim, in Lawrence's words, is: "two people who can be silent together, and not conscious of one another outwardly. Me in my silence, she in hers, and the balance, the equilibrium, the pure circuit between us."[142]

Thus there is no "holding back" in Lawrence's men and women, no selfishness or self-seeking, and Dorothea Krook is merely restating a comment often made about Lawrence. As Lawrence himself states in *Fantasia* (just before the preceding extract), "Because really, being alone in peace means being two people together."[143]

In *Fantasia* also, Lawrence says: "The best thing I have known is the stillness of accomplished marriage, when one possesses one's soul in silence, side by side with the amiable spouse, and has left off craving and raving and being only half one's self."[144] The peace and the bliss coming out of a successful union is precisely what is highlighted in the Indian culture. In the *Rig Veda* one reads: "Man longs for woman, natural as the parched frogs longing for the rains." In fact, as stated earlier, sexual gratification was considered so important a part in man's emancipation that it is conspicuously and prominently mentioned as one of the "ways" to understand reality in Indian thought; the fourfold scheme of man's liberation as conceived there is: (1) *Dharma* (social behavior), (2) *Artha* (economic prosperity), (3) *Kama* (sexual gratification), and (4) *Moksha* (spiritual realization). Vatsyayana, who was the contemporary of Kalidasa, treats of sex, in his well-known book *Kama Sutra,* as an independent branch of philosophy. As Mulk Raj Anand comments, the hypothesis behind this gradation seems to be that before an individual can reach reality, he has to go through and be aware fully of all his bodily curiosities, so that "no hidden longings should remain in the mind of the seeker after *Moksha*, which might prove to be a hindrance to spiritual progress afterwards."[145] There was an actual period in Indian history when the sexual was so highly exalted that huge temples were erected depicting various poses of sexual union between the man and the woman. Those temples still exist in four of the cities, Khajuraho, Konarak, Puri and Bhuvaneshwar—all historic cities and venerated places of pilgrimage. The ease and grace of the figures in those temples is beyond description. The volume called *Kama Kala*, published at Geneva in 1958, contains reproductions of some of these figures and in them one can catch a glimpse of the relaxed joy these shapes of stone possess. Not only this, but as Mulk Raj Anand observes in his introduction to this volume, "the whole of Indian folk art is replete with sexual motifs and, from the metal and wood images of Bengal to the wood carvings on the ceremonial Rathas, or carriages for gods, attached to each temple, there is the most intricate and tender embellishment of the theme of human love perhaps in all world art."[146] Lawrence knew of the grace of these postures, as he had seen some of the reproductions of the Ajanta frescoes. He wrote to Lady Ottoline Morrell in 1915, to whom he had sent a folio of these reproductions as a Christmas present:

Did you like the Ajanta frescoes? I *loved* them: the pure fulfilment—the pure simplicity—the complete, almost perfect relations between the men and the women—the most perfect things I have *ever* seen. Botticelli is vulgar beside them. They are the zenith of a very lovely civilisation, the crest of a very perfect wave of human development. I love them beyond everything pictorial that I have ever seen—the perfect, perfect intimate relation between the men and the women; so simple and complete, such a very perfection of passion, a fulness, a whole blossom. That which we call passion is a very one-sided thing, based chiefly on hatred and *Wille zur Macht*. There is no Will to Power here—it is so lovely—in these frescoes.[147]

In these words of unlimited praise, Lawrence captures the apt tonality of Indian art. "There is no Will to Power here," he says; and so it is. There is, on the other hand, to take the expression from *Fantasia*, "the stillness of accomplished marriage." The ancient Hindu philosophy gave a place to love and marriage that corresponds, in many details, to what Lawrence was to express on the subject centuries later in a different part of the hemisphere. And Lawrence, to the extent that he knew of Hindu thought, recognized this affinity and applauded it. For the above-quoted passage from him on the Ajanta frescoes is the gist of his own views on love between a man and a woman.

4

Self-Realization

I

1. INTUITION AND REASON

To appreciate fully the Self as conceived by Lawrence, one has to appreciate clearly the problem of spontaneous comprehension. The list of people who have looked upon spontaneity with suspicion is a formidable one and the names there, from Plato downwards, cannot be dismissed lightly. Men like T. S. Eliot and Wyndham Lewis and Bertrand Russell, when they accuse Lawrence of being sentimental and, in the words of one of them, "a positive force for evil"[1] (because he lays more emphasis on intuition than reason), are serious-minded scholars who say what they say because of their convictions. It is clear that people with this type of approach genuinely consider intuition as dangerous and unprofitable to man and society, just as Lawrence, as genuinely, considered reason a menace. An understanding of Lawrence in this respect, therefore, involves some measure of readjustment on the part of many of his readers.

It should be noticed in the first place that Lawrence does not look upon intuition as something *opposite* of reason and knowledge. The opposite of reason is unreason; and Lawrence, like any sensible person, was forcefully repelled by unreason. To regard intuition as implying *absence* of reason is a mistake that many highly intelligent men make (T. S. Eliot on "inner-light": "the most un-trustworthy and deceitful guide that ever offered itself to wandering humanity") .[2] Lawrence, however, makes a clear distinction between intuition and unreason. He says: "Men are not free when they are doing just what they like. The moment you can do just what you like, there is nothing you care about doing. Men are free only when they are doing what the deepest self likes."[3] Thus intuition, or following the "inner-light," is not so easy as following the first impulsive thought that comes to one's mind; it presupposes a state of mind wherein the mind comes to be implicitly aware of the genuine merit of an impulse.

Leon Vivante offers a cogent defence of Lawrence in *A Philosophy of Potentiality*, where he comments:

> Lawrence's conception can be better understood and becomes all the more convincing if we admit that even the simplest sensation contains in germ, as I think is legitimate to presume, this rich unity—quite apart from acquired habits and stored up experiences. Indeed a sensation, in so far as it is instrumental, a means to practical or to extrinsically cognitive ends, is or may be—we all agree—unreliable, deceitful, only provisional, and of little value. Yet the same sensation, considered in and for itself, in its own reality, opens the problem of subjectivity! There is in it—we must presume that there is—a unity, which is not that of the stimuli. There is, we must presume, an overcoming of material multiplicity.[4]

It should be stressed, since it is a point Vivante does not make, that there is a clear warning in Lawrence against giving way to, or submitting to, every impulse that one may have. To quote from him:

> And there is getting down to the deepest self! It takes some diving.
> Because the deepest self is way down, and the conscious

self is an obstinate monkey. But of one thing we may be sure. If one wants to be free, one has to give up the illusion of doing what one likes, and seek what IT wishes done.[5]

We see from this that for Lawrence intuition is a certain force beyond reason and unreason both. He refers to it as IT here. In *Aaron's Rod* he speaks of it as "this obstinate black dog"; in *The Plumed Serpent* as "the Star of the Beyond." At many other places, it is simply called "the dark source of life"; in the unpublished preface to the *Collected Poems*, "the ghost" or "the demon"; in *Etruscan Places*, "the vivid life-electron"; in "The Crown," "the lion"; in the essay "Thinking about Oneself," "the tiger." Most often he refers to it by the Christian symbol, "the Holy Ghost." The terminology keeps changing, but we know that invariably it signifies the Self in each created being, the primal power within us. To summarize its essence, according to Lawrence:

> It is the thing that prompts us to be real, not to push our own cravings too far, not to submit to stunts and high-falutin, above all, not to be too egoistic and wilful in our conscious self, but to change as the spirit inside us bids us change, and leave off when it bids us leave off, and laugh when we must laugh, particularly at ourselves, for in deadly earnestness there is always something a bit ridiculous.[6]

Does this sound hysterical? And yet, a usually wise American critic observes: "In D. H. Lawrence the hysteria of direct sensual experience destroys every structure of sensibility."[7] We have to go into this charge very carefully, step by step. Does really deep sensual experience destroy every structure of sensibility? What is sensibility? Is it not the power to feel, the power to "sense" things, the power to be aware of life? Are not sensibility and sensuality intimately allied, therefore? Can one ever become aware of one's sensibility except through sensual experience? There is, thus, a basic contradiction in the statement of R. P. Blackmur, the critic quoted. His remarks indicate the same error as that noted earlier: the error of considering anything that is not measured by reason, by the factual evidence, to be measured by unreason, or what he terms "hysteria." Unless this is clearly grasped, we cannot see the value of the "readjustment" that we have in mind. Reason and unreason are, to a great extent, similar; they are both based on "factual evidence" —one on the correct type of evidence, the other on the incorrect—but nevertheless, essentially they are both things of the mind. They are the result of what one knows— the sum total of environment, tradition, and mental arithmetic, of the influence of science, religion, and culture. The final split (into reason and unreason) will depend on whether the knowledge acquired is accurate or inaccurate. But their source, the origin of their growth, is the same.

Naturally Lawrence nowhere minimizes the value of healthy mental growth. To do so would be incompatible with that genius with which even his adverse critics associate him. Without a healthy mind one cannot make a single decision, and for Lawrence there was a decision to be made by each individual—in his self-awareness— from *moment* to *moment*, every day. The individual can live in the present (as was discussed in Chapter 1) only by living intelligently, self-introspectively. In the case of a man with an active "faith" in some organized religion, most of the decisions of life are already made for him by the religion, or the society, or the creed to which he may belong. But thinking from day to day, from moment to moment, *without* leaning on and finding security in an outside authority is a more arduous task. We must acknowledge that any dependence on authority—tradition, religion, God—is primarily the outcome of fear. We are not certain of the future; we are afraid of the unknown; most of all we are afraid of losing the known.

In authority we find security and protection, and most of all we find a hope of continuation of the known. Not much common sense is required to see that any such hope is purely illusory. But we would rather cling to a pleasant illusion than face an unpleasant reality. And let it be understood once and for all that in this quest there is not much difference between the man who goes to God and the man who goes to the Devil. They are both, in their own way, trying to run after security, trying to run away from what *is*, away from reality. To live with the present as it is, to face sorrow and happiness as they come, without making an effort to find an escape from present misery in an imaginary and distant heaven, and without trying to perpetuate forever the brief "happy" spell that one may be passing through, that is the aim of a true seer of Self as conceived by Lawrence. And in this aim, obviously, a mind must be healthy and vigorous, must be uniquely receptive and healthy, and to imagine that Lawrence was against mental consciousness is to assert that Lawrence was against himself.

But the point is that for Lawrence mental consciousness has its limits. He enlarges on it in his two volumes of deliberative thought, *Psychoanalysis and the Unconscious* and *Fantasia of the Unconscious*. Any one who has any doubt about Lawrence's approach to reason and intuition has only to go through these volumes to see the truth of the matter. In both these books, Lawrence unhesitatingly accepts the part the mind plays in our lives. But at the same time he asserts there as well the limitations of the mind, limitations that cannot be disputed. He writes in *Psychoanalysis and the Unconscious*:

True, we must all develop into mental consciousness. But mental-consciousness is not a goal; it is a cul-de-sac. It provides us only with endless appliances which we can use for the all-too-difficult business of coming to our spontaneous-creative fullness of being. It provides us with means to adjust ourselves to the external universe. It gives us further means for subduing the external, materio-mechanical universe to our great end of creative life. And it gives us plain indications of how to avoid falling into automatism, hints for the *applying* of the will, the loosening of false, automatic fixations, the brave adherence to a profound soul-impulse. This is the use of the mind—a great indicator and instrument. The mind as author and director of life is anathema.[8] (Lawrence's emphasis)

The debate is carried on by him in *Fantasia of the Unconscious*:

The business of the mind is first and foremost the pure joy of knowing and comprehending, the pure joy of consciousness. The second business is to act as medium, as interpreter, as agent between the individual and his object. The mind should *not* act as a director or controller of the spontaneous centres. These the soul alone must control: the soul being that forever unknowable reality which causes us to rise into being. There is continual conflict between the soul, which is forever sending forth incalculable impulses, and the psyche, which is conservative, and wishes to persist in its old motions, and the mind, which wishes to have "freedom," that is spasmodic, idea-driven control. Mind, and conservative psyche, and the incalculable soul, these three are a trinity of powers in every human being. But there is something even beyond these. It is the individual in his pure singleness, in his totality of consciousness, in his oneness of being: the Holy Ghost which is with us after our Pentecost, and which we may not deny. When I say to myself: "I am wrong," knowing with sudden insight that I *am wrong*, then this is the whole self speaking, the Holy Ghost. It is no piece of mental inference. It is not just the soul sending forth a flash. It is my whole being speaking in one voice, soul and mind and psyche transfigured into oneness. This voice of my being I may never deny. When at last, in all my storms, my whole self speaks, then there is a pause. The soul collects itself into pure silence and isolation—perhaps after much pain. The mind suspends its knowledge, and waits. The psyche becomes strangely still. And then, after the pause, there is fresh beginning, a new

life adjustment. Conscience is the being's consciousness, when
the individual is conscious *in toto,* when he knows in full.
It is something which includes and which far surpasses
mental consciousness. Every man must live as far as he
can by his own soul's conscience. But not according to any
ideal. To submit the conscience to a creed, or an idea, or
a tradition, or even an impulse, is our ruin.[9] (Lawrence's
emphasis)

The implication is that there comes a stage in the life
of each one of us, a time when mind cannot lead us any
farther. The known world the mind can evaluate for us;
but in the search for Self, the journey is so deep and un-
conventional that the known world must come to an end
at a point. And it is here that the sharp distinction
between one set of values and the other comes in. For
according to the devotees of the Knowledge-cum-Reason
cult, mind is the author and director of life. They cannot conceive of an experience—even one's experience of
God—which cannot be completely measured by the mind.
It is the mind which selects and rejects; which sifts
evidence, makes conclusions, decides issues. Hence, according to such people, at no level can one ignore, or
subordinate, the logical deductions of the mind to the
vague and undefinable promptings of the instinct. Things
must be proved before they are accepted, they declare.

At this stage we should take note in some detail of
the Indian philosopher, J. Krishnamurti. It is commonly believed by the Knowledge-cum-Reason intellectuals that anyone speaking of intuition, particularly in
our present century, must be an undisciplined, untutored
man, ignorant of the rich heritage of culture; that he must
not have been highly educated; that he would have had
no great "influences" in his life, and would be a rather
slipshod and clumsy thinker. An impression of this type
is still widely held by many people about Lawrence, and
to some extent the impression is superficially justifiable.

Students of Lawrence know that he was a phenomenally well-read man, but the surface facts do indicate a humble upbringing, a somewhat mediocre formal education, and a somewhat mediocre career as a teacher before he became a professional writer. This therefore could lend support to the conclusion that a man with such a background could hardly appreciate the grandeur and the beauties of the human mind, and would perhaps turn to the easier, all-too-simple yardstick of the heart and intuition.

But let us look at J. Krishnamurti. The facts of his life have become a legend by now and are too well known to be recorded in detail here. Jiddu Krishnamurti was born in 1897 in a small village in South India called Madanapalle, near Madras. He was the son of an employee in the revenue department of the Government. The father, Jiddu Naraniah, was an ardent theosophist, and that was how the family was introduced to Mrs. Annie Besant, the president of the Theosophical Society, when she was visiting the area in 1909. From his early days, the father had noticed exceptional gifts in the son and Annie Besant was similarly impressed by the young boy's intuitive faculties and his remarkable independence of mind. She was not alone in this assessment; she was accompanied by an associate, C. W. Leadbeater, who fully agreed with her. In fact, she became so thoroughly convinced of the boy's latent capabilities that she offered to adopt him and look after his further education. She felt certain that the boy's profound mind could produce, in course of time, a new message for humanity. So they— Mrs. Besant and Mr. Leadbeater—persuaded the father to hand over the future care of the child to them. Mrs. Besant took Krishnamurti with her to Europe in 1911, formed an organization called "The Order of the Star in the East," and announced that she had discovered a new Messiah, who in due course would come to head and lead the organization. For years now Krishmamurti was given the best possible training to prepare him for his task and in the end, in 1925, he was duly installed as, what Annie Besant called him, the "World Teacher."

It is from here that the really interesting history of J. Krishnamurti begins. At twenty-eight he had a following running literally into thousands, in all parts of the world. His personality was magnetic, and those who met and heard him carried the word far. A halo thus came to be attached to his name almost everywhere. He was coming in contact with important people in every country; he was formally welcomed wherever he went; he was listened to with respect and conviction. And yet in 1929 he shocked his followers by disbanding the Order of which he was the head and by formally denying the value of any spiritual authority. It was an unusual development, but Krishnamurti was firm. He said he was convinced that messiahs, instead of leading men, misled them; that reliance on any authority *outside* man was the spiritual death of the individual, as the individual was an entity by himself, inherently capable of feeling the glory of creation. And so he stepped aside and refused to be any more the messiah his Society said he was.

Since 1929 Krishnamurti has traveled widely and has preached extensively. He does not confine himself to any particular philosophical system and has repeatedly declared that he has no "system" if his own. His talks have been collected and published, but he has written no books. Wherever he goes the subjects of his talks are the same: "knowledge," "meditation," "self," "reality." And wherever he goes he says practically the same things. The marvel of the whole thing is that there is an almost word-for-word similarity between the views on life of this deeply religious thinker and those of the volatile and restless man from Eastwood, D. H. Lawrence.

It is surprising that astute critic Aldous Huxley, who has written on both of them (Introduction to *The*

Letters of D. H. Lawrence, and Foreword to *The First and Last Freedom,* a collection of talks by J. Krishnamurti), should have failed to notice this. To quote from Huxley's introduction to the *Letters,* he says that Lawrence "was always intensely aware of the mystery of the world, and the mystery was always for him a *numen, divine.*"[10] A few pages afterwards he records, "Most men live in a little puddle of light thrown by the gig-lamps of habit and their immediate interest; but there is also the pure and powerful illumination of the disinterested scientific intellect. To Lawrence, both lights were suspect, both seemed to falsify what was, for him, the immediately apprehended reality—the darkness of mystery."[11] And on Krishnamurti's teaching, he has the following to say: "It is not . . . a system of beliefs, a catalogue of dogmas . . . It is not ritual, not a church, not a code, not uplift or any form of inspirational twaddle."[12] What is it then? In Huxley's words, it is a sense of awareness of "a transcendent spontaneity of life, a 'creative Reality.' "[13] Huxley's introduction to the *Letters* was written in 1932 and he was perhaps at that time not familiar with the talks of Krishnamurti. But the "Foreword" dates from 1954, and one can only put it down to oversight that he makes no reference to the deep affinity between the thoughts of these two thinkers.

Endlessly, Krishnamurti has spoken for the past several decades against every form of known authority. For authority means rigidity; it implies division, seclusion, the good and the not-good, *my* method and *his* method, *this* and *that.* And wherever there is division, reality cannot be. Therefore, reality, by Krishnamurti's understanding, can be approached only by freeing the mind from the past or the future, and even the present by totally "silencing" it and listening to the clear, still voice of intuition. "To understand the highest, there must be liberation from time, the continuous past, present, and future, from the fears of the unknown, failure, and success."[14]

We will come back to this later. We have not yet finished the details of the "readjustment" necessary to the understanding of Lawrence. The case of Krishnamurti is cited as a reply to those who allege that dependence on intuition is advocated only by impulsive people. Here is the example of a man who is universally accepted as an extremely sober and sensible individual. And systematically, logically, almost like a scientist, he argues and builds a case for the complete repudiation of intellect and a complete faith in intuition.

And what path should an individual then follow in this perilous but so important voyage, the voyage of self-realization? The answer of both J. Krishnamurti and D. H. Lawrence is that there is no path, there is no way, there is no solution. For it is a journey, they say, where the end is not known.

It must be seen, and seen certainly, that this answer is quite different from the inference one may, in a moment of enthusiasm, be led to draw from this. It does *not* suggest the religious or intellectual tolerance which some of the broadminded sects advocate: that all paths lead to the same God, and that one religion is as good as the other. God is the same no doubt everywhere, but no one knows how to get to Him, and, according to Krishnamurti, the man who talks of many paths to God is at heart an intolerant person: "The many paths to one reality are the invention of an intolerant mind; they are the outcome of a mind that cultivates tolerance. . . . Wisdom is the understanding of what *is* from moment to moment."[15] What Krishnamurti means is that such a man is merely suggesting that he should be left alone to follow *his* path; he too is displaying rigidity of mind and lack of openness. Reality is shapeless, timeless, and illimitable, and the moment we set up a fixed path it is gone. The thing to acknowledge is that *all* paths are wrong, and that is what the Upanishads, in fact, assert. As J. Krishnamurti said to me in one of his conversations with me:

> Man's discovery of God ceases to be a discovery if he begins with a foregone conclusion in his mind. Most religions impose a certain image of the type of God they would want their followers to worship. Whereas to my mind, in the search for truth, which to me is the search for God, the choice does not rest with us as to what to reject or accept. Truth, God, call it what you will, is an awareness of the totality of existence, of our hopes and desires, our ambitions, our greed, our loves and thousands of other emotions which constitute what passes for the living individual. I believe organised religions stand in the way of this awareness of the totality of existence.[16]

In the concluding chapter of *Aaron's Rod*, Lilly is talking to Aaron. In spite of the rough time he has had in life, Aaron has not seen much light and he is still thinking in terms of finding out some definite way, some definite clue, which may, once and for all, solve this great riddle of existence for him. He feels that, if there is a goal to be achieved, there must be the key to it; and he must seek it. Lilly reproaches him for this, and says: "I'm rather sick of seekers. I hate seekers."

> "What," said Aaron rather sarcastically—"those who are looking for a new religion?"
> "Religion—and love—and all that. It's a disease now."
> "Oh, I don't know," said Aaron. "Perhaps the lack of love and religion is the disease."
> "Ah—bah! The grinding of the old millstone of love and God is what ails us, when there's no more grist between the stones. We've ground love very small. Time to forget it. Forget the very words religion, and God, and love—then have a shot at a new mode. But the very words rivet us down and don't let us move. Rivets, and we can't get them out."

"And where should we be if we could?" said Aaron.

"We might begin to be ourselves, anyhow."

"And what does that mean?" said Aaron. "Being yourself —what does it mean?"

"To me, everything."

"And to most folks, nothing. They've got to have a goal."

"There is no goal. I loathe goals more than any other impertinence. Gaols, they are. Bah—jails and jailers! gaols and gaolers—."[17]

The passage is very clear but its substance is reasserted, somewhat vehemently, a little later, when Lilly bursts out:

"The responsibility is on your own shoulders all the time, and no God which man has ever struck can take it off. You *are* yourself, and so *be* yourself. Stick to it and abide by it. Passion or no passion, ecstasy or no ecstasy, urge or no urge, there's no goal outside you, where you can consummate like an eagle flying into the sun, or a moth into a candle. There's no goal outside you—and there's no God outside you. No God, whom you can get to and rest in. None."[18]

The last eight pages or so of this novel display an extraordinary subtlety of mind on the part of Lawrence, an extraordinary power of penetration. It is not the purpose here to offer Lawrence as an illustration of a consistent philosopher, nor are we trying to search for any consistent philosophy in him. He was an artist, moved by a philosophy of life, no doubt, but mainly an artist. But the beauty of the openness of his mind, the vast spaces, the yawning gaps of untouched grandeur which his imagination beheld and roamed in, and the spell of his fearless visions have to be realized to accept him as an artist. The implication of the passages just quoted is farreaching. For they intimate that even the hope of a goal at the end, or the hope of a path to that goal, detracts from the joy of immediate living, and hence from the joy of the Self. There is no goal, and there is no path, and only when that is irrevocably accepted does the meaning of existence become clear.

Very well, we say, there is no goal, there is no path, so what is one to do? How could one ever realize this unknowable reality? The answer—the simple and brief answer that both J. Krishnamurti and D. H. Lawrence give is: by direct experiencing. Says Krishnamurti: "How can there be understanding when the mind is agitated? Earnestness must be tempered with the swift play of spontaneity."[19] It is in direct experiencing alone, when the knowledge-hunting part of the mind has gone to sleep, that reality can strike and the self become alert to the Self. Krishnamurti adds: "You will find . . . that truth will come in moments when you are not expecting it."[20]

If we have allowed ourselves to go through this "re-adjustment" dispassionately, we see that we can now come to the following conclusions: (1) Intuition is *not* the opposite of reason; the opposite of reason is unreason. (2) D. H. Lawrence rejects unreason and rash impulses and acknowledges the power of reason and intellect. (3) He, however, feels that reason cannot lead man to a final awareness of Self, and that for that intuition alone can help. (4) Intuition means silencing of all fixed ideas in the mind and being completely open and vulnerable to the new.

In his essay "The Real Thing," when Lawrence questions himself, "What *is* the real thing?" his reply is: "the answer will be difficult. Some trick with glands or secretions, or raw food, or drugs won't do it. Neither will some wonderful revelation or message. It is not a question of knowing something, but of doing something. It is a question of getting into contact again with the *living* centre of the cosmos."[21] The essay ends on a note of interrogation, "And how are we to do it?" Hints of the solution are scattered all over in his creative work, but in his critical writings they are set down even more boldly (since he speaks in his own right as a person there). "When we have become very still, when there is an inner silence as complete as death, then, as in the grave, we hear the rare, superfine whispering of the new direction; the intelligence comes. After the pain of being destroyed in all our old securities that we used to call peace, after the pain and death of our destruction in the old life comes the inward suggestion of fulfilment in the new."[22] This quotation from "The Reality of Peace" is typical. "Both desire and impulse tend to fall into mechanical automatism: to fall from spontaneous reality into dead or material reality. All our education should be a guarding against this fall,"[23] he says in "Democracy." We notice, therefore, how unfair R. P. Blackmur is when he cites Lawrence as an illustration of "the deracinated, unsupported imagination, the mind for which, since it lacked rational structure sufficient to its burdens, experience was too much."[24] Lawrence's mind did not lack a rational structure; witness the enormity and the variety of his creative output, and the main discussion above pertaining to this subject. The point is simply that the type of experience in which Lawrence was most deeply interested just could not be comprehended by any rational structure alone. Writing to Lady Ottoline Morrell in 1915, he exemplifies this when he advises her of the utter futility of hanging on to the rigid notions in her mind and tells her how this hardness can never lead her to peace: "Do not keep your will in your conscious self. Forget, utterly forget, and let go. Let your will lapse back into your unconscious self, so you move in a sleep, and in darkness, without sight or understanding. Only then you will act straight from the dark source of life, outwards, which is creative life."[25] It is this that must be understood.

This section on the subject of intuition will conclude with the following from Sri Aurobindo, where he makes the observation that even a man's senses—the sense of touch, of sight, of hearing—can function in two different ways. Governed by reason, the rational structure, alone, the senses reflect the material aspects of the phenomenal world. Governed by intuition, they reflect the basic truth of the phenomenal world:

> Intuition has a four-fold power. A power of revelatory truth-seeing, a power of inspiration or truth-hearing, a power of truth-touch or immediate seizing of significance, which is akin to the ordinary nature of its intervention in our mental intelligence, a power of true and automatic discrimination of the orderly and exact relation of truth to truth,—these are the fourfold potencies of Intuition. Intuition can therefore perform all the action of reason—including the function of logical intelligence, which is to work out the right relation of things and the right relation of idea with idea,—but by its own superior process and with steps that do not fail or falter.[26]

The problem becomes clearer when illustrated with the famous distinction J. Krishnamurti makes between Meditation and Concentration. According to him what most people consider to be meditation is nothing but concentration, a class-room exercise, a focusing of the attention on one thing in exclusion to the others. They try hard to still their minds, but they soon get out of control once again. The real meditation is where one looks into oneself and is willing to uncover one's deepest urges. That exposure may lead to many unpleasant discoveries about the self, but they must be faced. On the other hand if one merely trains one's mind to be still, one is only imposing a discipline on it, an obstruction that will prevent self-knowledge. Says Krishnamurti: "Disciplines are mere impositions and so can never be the means of denudation."[27]

We see from this that genuine intuition and meditation would mean absorption of the mind in nothing except the present. The stress is thus on leaving the mind absolutely open. To quote Krishnamurti again:

> There is freedom when the entire being, the superficial as well as the hidden, is purged of the past. Will is desire; and if there is any action of the will, any effort to be free, to denude oneself, then there can never be freedom, the total purgation of the whole being. When all the many layers of consciousness are quiet, utterly still, only then is there the immeasurable, the bliss that is not of time, the renewal of creation.[28]

Anyone familiar with the writings of Lawrence can see the value of this distinction: intuition reveals itself not in the silence of the Flesh, but in the silence of the Mind, as Lawrence tells Lady Ottoline Morrell. The Flesh is a part of our whole, and hence essential for the health of the psyche. If everything is from God, everything is of God. In one of the texts of the recently discovered Dead Sea Scrolls, there appears a delicate reference to what is described as the "primeval divine predestination": "From the God of knowledge comes everything that is and shall be. And *before* their [men's] existence he has determined all their reflections and thoughts. And *during* their existence . . . all their deeds are irrevocably fulfilled."[29] Even on that line of reasoning —that of predestination—there should be no question of sin and fall and the triumph of the "sons of light" over "the sons of darkness" (as the Scrolls, on the other hand, go on to argue).[30] Everything that is is from God and therefore the mind is to be free and not to offer any resistance to any one set of values. These values are not to be striven for in themselves (egoism), but only to be lived, and then with the passing moment be discarded and the new values as they emerge be accepted. That is the intuition of D. H. Lawrence—the complete silence of the mind, the freedom from preferences, and, at the same time, the openness to the new (the "choiceless awareness" and "alert passivity" of J. Krishnamurti). That is what Rupert Birkin means when he says to himself that one should "abandon oneself utterly to the *moments*" alone;[31] not a heedless, thoughtless abandon, but an egoless abandon, mindless abandon, preference-less abandon. That is the kind of look that Aaron sees on Lilly's face: "It was something quite different from happiness: an alert enjoyment of rest, an intense and satisfying sense of centrality."[32] In the introduction to the American edition of *New Poems*, Lawrence puts the whole thing rather sharply: "Eternity is only an abstraction from the actual present. Infinity is only a great reservoir of recollection, or a reservoir of aspirations: man-made. The quivering nimble hour of the present, this is the quick of Time. This is the immanence. The quick of the universe is the *pulsating, carnal self,* mysterious and palpable. . . ."[33] In short, genuine intuition means the silence of the mind in "the immediate present, the Now"; intuition guided by the past or the future is only a pseudo variety of it. And even this silence of the mind is not to be deliberately cultivated; anything that is deliberately made can at any time be unmade, at any time be lost. The natural silence of the mind is an automatic consequence of the mind absorbed in the Now; and, as can be seen, even the remotest attachment to a mental image of God, or a godhead like Christ or Krishna, will interfere with the natural silence, hence with natural intuition. The first is what one may call Meditation; the second is only Concentration. And it is the first type that leads one to an awareness of Self.

2. GOD AS "IS"

Before we examine a few illustrations from Lawrence's creative work to show how his characters aim at the Self-realization described above, it is necessary to consider briefly the question of the nomenclature of God in Lawrence. It is a question we cannot escape. According to E. W. Sinnott, this is a natural, or—to borrow from the title of his *The Biology of the Spirit*—a biological impulse, an impulse of every species toward a "goal-seeking."[34] Lawrence believed neither in a personal God nor in a "goal" as such ("All goals become graves," he says in one of his essays).[35] The best of his characters live without defining either for themselves. But as an artist, Lawrence knew that an imaginative reconstruction of life could not be complete without some concept of this enigmatic maker of the universe called God. Consequently, though he wrote to S. S. Koteliansky in 1916, "I am most sick of this divinity of man business,"[36] he was at heart absorbed with nothing else so much as to come to terms with it.

In Lawrence the answer to this question is very simple: God is what *is*. His recognition of "the immediate present, the Now" as the only conceivable reality, and his constant effort to enforce that point in every single piece of fiction or poetry that he wrote, reinforce this. God is what *is*. Language and expression, he says, cannot go beyond that.

There are three men in our century who have employed this particular expression in their final nomenclature of reality. They are J. Krishnamurti, Martin Heidegger, and D. H. Lawrence. God is whatever *is*; that is the limit, according to these three, of the frontiers of human understanding. Every talk of J. Krishnamurti revolves around this. Denial of whatever *is* is a denial of God; acceptance of whatever *is* is an acceptance of God. According to the German existentialist, Heidegger, "The 'being' uttered in 'is' means: really present, permanently there, takes place, comes from, belongs to, is made of, stays, succumbs to, stands for, has entered upon, has appeared."[37] "It remains difficult," he goes on, "perhaps impossible, because contrary to the essence of being, to pick out a common meaning as a universal generic concept under which all these modes of 'is' might be classified as species. Yet a single determinate trait runs through them all. It directs our contemplation of 'being' to a definite horizon, in which understanding is effected. The limitation of the meaning of 'being' remains within the sphere of actuality and presence, of permanence and duration, of abiding and concurrence."[38] This makes sufficiently clear the *is* we are speaking of.

We should appreciate, however, that Heidegger's absorption with what *is* is that of a professional philosopher, hence is mainly intellectual (see the verbosity and unduly created complications of the essays collected in his volume *Existence and Being*). Krishnamurti talks of *is* as a religious thinker, intuitively. D. H. Lawrence accepts *is* in the spirit of Krishnamurti, as a religious thinker, but takes it up and makes use of it as an artist. But one can say that the differences are only marginal; the approach is the same. As such, whereas one thus finds Lawrence close to Indian thought, he is, if one were to give a parallel illustration from the West, closer to the Existential thinkers in his manner of reasoning. (John Middleton Murry, in his new introduction to *Son of Woman*, has similarly noticed this: "he was the living embodiment of yet another theory which is part of the intellectual climate of today: the philosophy of existentialism.") [39]

The whole issue, in the final analysis, boils down to an understanding of two words: "being" and "becoming." Most religions of the world emphasize the importance of

becoming, spiritual becoming. Vedantic thought in the
East, and Existentialism in the West, are the only two
bodies of opinion where "being" is the sole center of
interest. To quote from Martin Heidegger: "What becomes is not yet. What is need no longer become. What
'is,' the essent, has left all becoming behind it if indeed it
ever became or could become."[40] It does not depreciate
the value of action, or of becoming. There can never be
a state of total inaction. But when the being, the me, is
totally absorbed and morbidly submerged in the desire
to become, the being never knows the beauty of what it
means to be. There has been a past, and there will be a
future. But there is also a present; and the existence, the
actuality at the moment is not of what has been or what
is to come, but what *is* now. The God, if at all it has any
actuality, can therefore be, as can be seen, in what *is*; in
the being, being a being. To quote from Krishnamurti:
it is "not through the 'me' becoming, but through the
'me' completely coming to an end—that there is the new."[41]
And to quote from one of the characters of D. H. Lawrence: "There is no Before and After, there is only Now."[42]
And since this "being" is always in a state of flux, a dynamic change, its concreteness, its completeness, exists
only in its independent existence in that briefest spell of
time before it has changed itself to another being of
another briefest spell, which in turn changes itself to
another being, and so on. The interest lies, one may
observe, not in the process of change, but in the new and
changed being that emerges every second: the universe
reborn and refashioned and reshaped from moment to
moment, by a process inherent in it—the physical, visible,
graspable image of life. That is, the interest lies in the *is*.

   The *is*, the God, in the manifested form is visualized
by Lawrence as an urge, a desire, manifested in created
matter in its spontaneous outbursts. It is there in each
one of us, only man because of his own foolishness has

lost touch with it, for man has lost the art of following his intuition. But there it sits inside us, coiled up and sending messages to us, and its glory is so great that often it dazzles us, blinds us with its revelations. Instead of following it, we often run away from it; we are afraid of the hidden recesses of our own depths that it may suddenly open to us. But with patience, an infinite amount of patience, we see beauty and radiance seldom beheld otherwise. Let the *is* show us anything, lead us anywhere, send any urge; it is like a tiger, unpredictable. Only, as Lawrence says in his essay "Thinking about Oneself," we must be prepared to look straight into the eyes of this tiger boldly.[43] And we must be prepared to accept that anything that comes from it is holy, is God itself—that urge, that command, that desire.

The *is*, the God, in the unmanifested form, is, as said before, unknowable. The nearest that man can visualize it, it would be a state of complete mindlessness, when the known is totally forgotten. Lawrence gives the metaphor of Dreamless Sleep to illustrate that state of existence (this explains his continuous stress on "Darkness" in his work). But enough that man can never know it.

And since the artist's world—the world of a novelist, a poet, or a painter—is the world of the manifested, it is in its image as *urge* that we see God in Lawrence's art; the push, the thrust, the shove—the shove that creates and destroys; and the joy of it, the endless delight of it, the romance of it. The delight of the created world, the delight of love and physical union, and the final delight of the self feeling the Self, all knit together in composite stories of men and women, with their needs and their hungers, and all seen in the wider setting of social and economic background, yet essentially localized in the individuals concerned in their attempt to live with their surroundings come what may: this is the field of D. H. Lawrence. In one of his letters to Koteliansky, he once said: "It is sad, but the world seems wider and freer when one is alone."[44] In a society where man is practically lost in the weltering confusion of the times, Lawrence is thus the great artist of the Self. For it is the storm within the individual rather than the one outside that is his concern. Once, he seems to imply, the storm within is accepted properly, the outside world on its own acquires a different shape. It is not so much a question of fighting the storm as of facing it, accepting it; for until the deep desires of the self are understood, there will always be confusion in the outward action, hence confusion in society. "You see it is impious for us to assert so flatly what *should be*, in face of what *is*. It is our responsibility to know how to accept and live through that which *is*,"[45] he wrote to Eunice Tietjens in 1917 (Lawrence's emphasis). And these seem to be very nearly his last words on the subject. As he says in the preface to his play *Touch and Go*: "The essence of tragedy, which is creative crisis, is that a man should go through with his fate, and not dodge it and go bumping into an accident. And the whole business of life, at the great critical periods of mankind, is that men should accept and be one with their tragedy."[46] Once that is grasped, once one has gone through and squarely faced what *is*, once one has accepted the reality of one's own being, understanding comes, joy comes, widening of the horizon comes. It is as such that the best of Lawrence's characters live. It is as such that they grow up, fall in love, procreate, get angry, get sick, roar with fun, or dry up in grief. It is as such that they make their exit. But the reverence for the new always remains with them so long as they are alive. The freedom of the Self is not a goal with them, to be achieved at the end of the voyage; freedom of the Self is *now*.

Richard Rees in *Brave Men* has drawn our attention to the affinities between D. H. Lawrence and Simone Weil, and the comparison stands so far as Simone Weil believed as well in the universality of religion and did not attach much importance to the figure of the historical Christ. But the otherworldliness, in complete contrast to the beauty and the joy of this world, on which she insisted was foreign to Lawrence's temperament. Rees maintains: "However that may be, there have been few writers in any age who possessed to such a high degree the power to convey the truth that 'everything that lives is holy'; his failure—in so far as he can be said to have failed —was in not doing justice to the complementary truth, which is the keynote of Simone Weil's religious thought: that holiness is not of this world."[47] Where Richard Rees sees Lawrence's failure, there lies Lawrence's strength. Everything that *is* is holy; because everything that is is of God. Does Lawrence ever say, anywhere, that the other world is not holy? There is, on the other hand, hardly an artist to compare with him in his veneration for the unknown. Only he asserts that whereas the unmanifested is holy, the manifested is holy too. And the manifested is nearer at hand.

It would be complacency on my part to imply that everything I say here is being practiced in the East, or in India, to be more precise. It is not. But "detached action," nevertheless, continues to be the main dictum of Indian philosophy. As the Vedas say, it is the unattached mind, the free mind, only that can feel the joy of the Self. The *Ramayana*, for instance, is the story of an *uttum purusha*, a great man, who all his life bowed to what *is*, the truth as it appeared from moment to moment. So many nations having invaded it one after the other, India at present is a hotch-potch of several amalgamations. Gandhi tried to reintroduce, when he was alive, some of the innocence of earlier times there; his experiments in community living were a bold attempt to establish the old harmony between the individual and the universe in which he lived. Lawrence knew of Gandhi's efforts and wanted to do the same in the West. Earl Brewster records, "We spoke of Gandhi's *ashram* and his enthusiasm for hand spinning and weaving, of which Lawrence said: 'He is right. We might start such a place with a few people: only I ought to do it in my own country: southern England perhaps.' "[48] Brewster goes on to say that Lawrence once wrote to him: "All we possess is life—weaving, carving, building—this is the flow of life, life flows into the object—and life *flows out again* to the beholder. So that whoever makes anything with real interest, puts life into it, and makes a little fountain of life for the next comer. Therefore a Gandhi weaver is transmitting life to others—and that is the great charity."[49]

These are all issues, however, that need not be discussed here. Discussions about society must be left to sociologists. Lawrence was primarily an artist and he knew it was not his field to go into intricate details of social problems. To quote him: "The great social change interests me and troubles me, but it is not my field. I know a change is coming—and I know we must have a more generous, more human system based on the life values and not on the money values. That I know. But what steps to take I don't know. Other men know better."[50] As an artist, he merely establishes the value of the raw material, of the individual and the universe; and he leaves it at that.

II

1. SELF IN EARLY NOVELS

By the time Lawrence neared his death, his sensibility was heightened and his work of those last years displays an unusually keen awareness of the mystery and the strangeness of the whole process of life. This awareness is a common and natural development and is seen in most people approaching their end. My attempt will be to show how in the case of Lawrence the result of this special psychic alertness, the creative endeavor of this phase, was consistent with the vision of his earlier days and that the coming death—with all its accepted implications of fear, of restlessness—neither blurred, nor made him alter in the least, his stand on the related issues of the known and the unknown.

There is, however, a clearly marked shift of emphasis. Whereas previously the artist in him was preoccupied with the beauty and the joy of the observable world in isolation—paying homage to this beauty, recognizing its rich glory and its zest; whereas previously the artist approached it on terms of equality, with a desire of mutual sharing and mutual recognition of each other's entity; now we see that the artist approaches it with humility, almost in submission. The interest of the artist is, as it were, transferred from the mystery of life to the mystery of death. It must be kept in sight, however, that for Lawrence death was not an event in time, which came only once in life. There was death every day, in the life of each one of us, and I have discussed this bent of his thought earlier. There is death every day, and hence death as Death is not a permanent event; death and life alternate; death is not the end. So Lawrence does not treat of death and God (the two themes he handles during this phase of life) as something *approaching* him, coming toward him in the future when he may be initiated into their mysteries. No, they are already there—both death and God—in everyday life. So even within the heightened interest that Lawrence displays toward these two subjects, there is no shift in the angle of the proposition. But the proposition now is handled with technical skill and feelings bordering on virtuosity. The microcosm acquires a deepening color. The music of the artist, if it becomes

more sad, becomes also more lyrical. The individual as
a character, as an outsider, is completely lost and in the
ensuing picture only the perennial realities remain.

It will be pertinent here to quote in full a letter Lawrence wrote to his sister Ada, as far back as the year 1911.
We do not know the full references, but we conclude from
the first line of the letter that the sister was disturbed
about several problems in her life, more particularly the
problem of religion, and that she had written to the
brother (who was then a teacher at Croydon) asking his
advice. The text of the reply follows:

> I am sorry more than I can tell to find you going through
> the torment of religious unbelief: it is hard to bear, espe-
> cially now. However, it seems to me like this: Jehovah is
> the Jew's idea of God, not ours. Christ was infinitely good,
> but mortal as we. There still remains a God, but not a
> personal God: a vast, shimmering impulse which waves
> onwards towards some end, I don't know what—taking no
> regard of the little individual, but taking regard for hu-
> manity. When we die, like rain-drops falling back again into
> the sea, we fall back into the big, shimmering sea of un-
> organised life which we call God. We are lost as individuals,
> yet we count in the whole. It requires a lot of pain and
> courage to come to discover one's own creed, and quite as
> much to continue in lonely faith. Would you like a book
> or two of philosophy? or will you merely battle out your
> own ideas? I would still go to chapel if it did me any good.
> I shall go myself, when I am married. Whatever name one
> gives Him in worship we all strive towards the same God,
> so we be generous hearted: Christians, Buddhists, Mrs. Dax,
> me, we all stretch our hands in the same direction. What
> does it matter the name we cry? It is a fine thing to establish
> one's own religion in one's heart, not to be dependent on
> tradition and secondhand ideals. Life will seem to you,
> later, not a lesser, but a greater thing. This which is a
> great torment now, will be a noble thing to you later on.
> Let us talk, if you feel like it, when I come home.[51]

When this letter was written D. H. Lawrence was only

twenty-six. Like Keats he seems to have matured early, emotionally. The letter displays not only a ripe understanding, but a sympathetic one. In his zeal to convince others of the validity of his conceptions in his later years, he loses something of the catholicity of his earlier comprehension and becomes a little confined; the vision of the artist comes to be tempered by the earnestness of the preacher, and, for a while, he seriously becomes Lawrence the missionary. But we see that in the last two years of his life he returns to the same spirit of openness as that expressed in this particular letter.

In the last two chapters we discussed some of Lawrence's early works and the reader can appreciate the substance of the theory as applied to them. In *The White Peacock* Lettie and Cyril and Emily and Annable live by intuition; George does not, Meg does not. In *Sons and Lovers* Paul is supposed to follow intuition, so is Clara, Miriam is not. In *The Rainbow* Tom Brangwen and Lydia Lensky both follow intuition and are a striking illustration of the health of the soul and the body, of the "freedom *together*" of *Women in Love*. And so it goes on, novel after novel. The question is not at all of whether a character is violent, or is promiscuous, or is kind, with a discussion of that. The stories are not built on that premise; no character, according to Lawrence, can be uniformly bad or uniformly good. To be sure, one sees Lawrence disposing of certain individuals with a stroke of his pen (good and not-good) , but the implication is not that they are inherently so. The implication is that they are such insofar as they do not abide by their intuition. In other words, the right and wrong in Lawrence is not based on moral or ethical values, but on the voice of the Self; not on what *should* be but on what *is*.

This may sound alarming, for one may very well ask: how can society survive if every individual is to go about following his intuition? But herein lies its strength. For being aware of one's intuition, being aware of the Self, tackles the problem of society at its very root. Being aware of the Self means being completely impersonal, and hence errorless, pure; and thus the birth of any relationship in society, based on such an approach, would mean, at least in principle, a permanent and binding relationship. "As a matter of fact," says Rupert Birkin in *Women in Love*, "if you enter into a pure unison, it is irrevocable, and it is never pure till it is irrevocable."[52] For otherwise the relationship will be arrested before it is formed; it will not come into being; intuition will lead the parties away from each other. We have an example of it in the affair between Gerald and Gudrun in *Women in Love*, where Gudrun accepts Gerald as a lover *against* her instincts (note her reactions when Gerald creeps up to her bedroom and she allows him to sleep with her, pp. 361- 69) , and how the relationship comes to a miserable end later on: "When you first came to me, I *had* to take pity on you. But it was never love" (Gudrun to Gerald, p. 467) . So society, which is a combination of relationships, stands to gain rather than lose from intuition; it is all sentimental piffle that intuition will breed chaos. For hundreds of years by now, civilization in the West has been based on the moral and ethical right and wrong, and has it succeeded in attaining a flawless society?

So the history of such free men is continued in Lawrence's fiction, each time with a new problem to face, a new background, but with the same covering. The ripening process of the artist in Lawrence becomes fairly obvious, if one goes through the novels in the order that they were written. And before the zeal of the prophet overtook him, the flowering of his genius displayed itself in two masterpieces of English fiction, *The Rainbow* and *Women in Love*, which mark a culminating phase of one cycle in his development, one that began with *The White Peacock*. Thereafter Lawrence was carried away by his desire to evolve a "doctrine" out of his vision, to be a prophet. Years were to elapse before he was a pure artist again.

As an intellectual exercise one is tempted to fix the years from 1915 to 1916 (for earlier reference to the importance of the year 1915 in the life of Lawrence see Chapter 3) as the moment of departure between the artist and the prophet in him. Events leading up to and subsequent to this time point to that direction—a visionary fusion of the life-and-art realities in his mind. In 1917 we find him writing: "The pure abstract thought interests me now at this juncture more than art";[53] "philosophy interests me most now—not novels or stories";[54] "for the last nine months nothing has interested me but thinking about 'deep subjects,' as you call them" (on December 29).[55] To give an idea of the mellowness which this realization generated in him, before he turned from art to "deep subjects," quotations are given below from the correspondence of the year in which *Women in Love* was completed (1916). The conviction and the ease with which he speaks there of the being and the self, the relationship of the self to what *is* from moment to moment, the truth that this relationship inherently has in it, are indicative of nothing else but ease, beauty, and dignity— in short, holiness. And this holiness rises day after day, is communicated to person after person, endlessly—the same holiness, the same dignity, the same beauty, the same ease, the same conviction. To Ottoline Morrell he writes: "Everything lies in *being*, although the whole world is one colossal madness, falsity, a stupendous assertion of not-being";[56] to Cynthia Asquith: "The world crackles and busts, but that is another matter, external, in chaos. One has a certain order inviolable in one's soul. There one sits, as in a crow's nest, out of it all";[57] to Catherine Carswell: "We must have the courage to cast off the old symbols, the old traditions: at least, put them aside, like a plant in growing surpasses its crowning leaves with higher leaves and buds. There is something beyond the past. The past is no justification. Unless from us the future takes place, we are death only";[58] to Katherine Mansfield: "there is a death to die, for us all . . . . But being dead, and in some measure risen again, one is invulnerable";[59] to Mark Gertler: "Nothing matters, in the end, but the little hard flame of truth one had inside oneself and which does not blow about in the draught of blasphemous living";[60] to John Middleton Murry: "Terribly and cruelly the old self dies in one, the old world cracks up and falls away piece by piece. But it is all beyond one's will and one's control, one can only writhe and wait for the process to hurry up in one. But then there do come the days when the new self bubbles up and makes one happy," and a little later, "we can't dictate the terms, nor the times. It has to come to pass in us."[61]

Then, of course, there is *Women in Love* itself—a penetrating study of the understanding of Self in the character of Rupert Birkin. One cannot add very much to the general analysis of the book by Leavis, except perhaps that unfortunately the distinguished critic moves the emphasis from the individual to the social side of the story: "after reading *Women in Love* we do feel that we have 'touched the whole pulse of social England' ";[62] and again: "The drama as it centres in Gerald, involving as it does the diagnostic presentment of the large movement of civilization, has the effect—one difficult, in the nature of the case, to test in a count of pages—of bulking a good deal more largely in the whole than the Birkin-Ursula theme."[63] Without going into Leavis's dispute with J. Middleton Murry about whether the Birkin-Ursula relationship was a sublimation in art of Lawrence's own failure in life, it may be stated that the diseased, fading pulse of social England has been captured by many other twentieth-century writers as well, and if *that* were the end of *Women in Love*, or, for that matter, the end of Lawrence's art, Lawrence would be no better an author than—than James Joyce, for instance. His accomplishment lies in that, while registering the social pulse, he also suggests how one may be able to live with that pulse. Gerald Crich, the character on whom Leavis hinges his discussion, is the diseased part of society; but the health, of which Leavis admits Lawrence to have been a vigorous representative, the far-reaching realization of living with oneself, is achieved in Rupert Birkin alone. And in the "whole" of the novel, it is the personality of Birkin that "bulks" in itself more of the creative spirit of the novelist than that of Gerald. (So much so that when Birkin moves into the background, since he is now married and has a life of his own to lead with Ursula and can therefore no more act as the mirror to Gerald, Lawrence had to create another character, Loerke, another Birkin, to provide a foil to Gerald.)

But we propose to pass over all this period of Lawrence's life and come to *The Man Who Died*, the last of his novels.

2. *THE MAN WHO DIED*

The Man Who Died is an exquisite piece of workmanship. In Leavis's book on Lawrence, there is, curiously enough, not a single reference to it, and Graham Hough views it as only a polemical piece in his chapter entitled "The Doctrine" in *The Dark Sun*. And yet it is a significant work of art, perfectly conceived and perfectly finished.

The story is supposed to be the story of Jesus, but it is my contention that Lawrence did not intend it to be a criticism either of Jesus or of Christianity. Hough, in his analysis of it as a doctrinal piece of writing, fails to bring out its beauty as a work of art; he is too preoccupied with proving how Lawrence misunderstands the message of

Christianity. He writes that Lawrence here is still concerned with the failure of "Christian" love but now he finds an alternative to it in Christian tenderness. As such, Hough believes *The Man Who Died* "comes nearer to being a reconciliation with Christianity than anything else Lawrence wrote."[64] Hough cannot perhaps imagine how such repeated stress on the "Christian" values as the only point of comparison limits the scope of Lawrence's vision. For, as one may see, in this method of approach it is assumed from the start that no one can ever go beyond the Christian view of life, or rise above it. In his article "The Living Dead—I: D. H. Lawrence," J. Middleton Murry, for instance, refers to Lawrence's attempt to find a basis of consciousness outside Christianity as "retrogression" or "regression."[65] It was precisely this kind of approach that Lawrence actually rebelled against: the claim of Christianity to "exclusiveness" or "uniqueness" of revelation. There are two simple rules by which one may judge how universal a religion is: (1) Any religion that believes in proselytizing—converting people from other sects to its own fold—is a narrow faith, and (2) any religion that resorts to a religious war is, again, a narrow creed. However emancipated a particular faith may be, the moment it says that it is a "better" faith than others, it becomes circumscribed; it has sown the seed of strife, the seed of conflict; it has denied the omnipresent glory of God. It cannot be doubted that the history of Christianity, in its attitude toward other religions, has been mostly a history of intolerance. As Lawrence says in *Apocalypse*: "The instinctive policy of Christianity towards all pagan evidence has been and is still—suppress it, destroy it, deny it."[66] The claim of Christianity to universal love that Graham Hough speaks of is thus not a very sound one; it is a love only for those who embrace the faith, that is, those who are Christians. In this, Christianity is not the only religion that stands condemned; other missionary religions suffer from a similar drawback. Commenting on this in *Eastern Religions and Western Thought,* S. Radhakrishnan says: "These two attitudes are common to all missionary religions. Each claims with absolute sincerity that it alone is the true light while others are will-o'-the-wisps that blind us to the truth and lure us away from it. When it attempts to be a little more understanding, it affirms that the light of its religion is to that of others as the sun is to the stars, and the minor lights may be tolerated so long as they accept their position of subordination."[67]

Lawrence's rejection of Christianity's claim to "exclusiveness," therefore, has quite a force in it, and if we were to treat *The Man Who Died* as a work containing Lawrence's "doctrine" as contrasted with Christianity, we could only arrive at conclusions quite opposed to the Christian faith, for in *The Man Who Died* Lawrence altogether dismisses the idea of "exclusiveness." In *The Plumed Serpent,* in the celebrated interview between the Bishop and Don Ramon, we have a reasonably full summing-up of what Lawrence believes to be the shortcomings of Christianity on this count, and wherein he sees the catholicity of a religion:

"Your Church is the Catholic Church, Father?"
"Surely!" said the Bishop.
"And Catholic Church means the Church of All, the Universal Church?"
"Surely, son of mine."
"Then why not let it be really catholic? Why call it catholic, when it is not only just one among many churches, but is even hostile to all the rest of the churches? Father, why not let the Catholic Church become really the universal Church?"
"It is the Universal Church of Christ, my son."
"Why not let it be the Universal Church of Mohammet as well; since ultimately, God is One God, but the peoples speak varying languages, and each needs its own prophet to speak with its own tongue. The Universal Church of

Christ, and Mohammet, and Buddha, and Quetzalcoatl, and all the others—*that* would be a Catholic Church, Father."[68]

The Bishop sits twiddling with his ring and over and again Ramon asks him, "Should there not be peace between the men who strive down their different ways to the God-Mystery?," "Can you not understand me?," "Is there not sense in what I say? Cannot you understand?" The Bishop, of course, does not understand; he is not open-minded enough. Almost the same line of reasoning is offered by Lawrence in essays like "On Being Religious" in *Phoenix,* where we read:

> From time to time, the Great God sends a new saviour. Christians will no longer have the pettiness to assert that Jesus is the only Saviour ever sent by the everlasting God. There have been other saviours, in other lands, at other times, with other messages. And all of them Sons of God. All of them sharing the Godhead with the Father. All of them showing the Way of Salvation and of Right. Different Saviours. Different Ways of Salvation. Different polestars, in the great wandering Cosmos of time. And the Infinite God, always changing, and always the same infinite God, at the end of the different Ways.[69]

But by the time Lawrence came to write *The Man Who Died,* he had risen above all arguments and come to the conclusion that the very concept of a "path" or a "faith" was wrong, and though earlier he would have accepted that all paths led to the same God, he now believed that even that was a restricted view and that in reality to get to God one needed no path, no faith at all. As such, we should look upon *The Man Who Died* as a work of art rather than a philosophical treatise—a work of art where, instead of going the "closest" to Christianity, as Hough asserts, Lawrence goes completely away from the confines of *all* religions, speaking in a language truly universal, enacting a theme truly humane, and building a drama briefer in length, more pointed in characterization than his earlier work, and yet equally consistent with its insights.

The story is very skillfully written and skillfully told, and its presentation is a tribute to the inventiveness of Lawrence's genius. By one masterly stroke, that of taking over the historical Christ as his central figure, he surmounts the major difficulty all novelists have to face in a story: of "developing" the character. The character is already known to his readers, known for about two thousand years to their cultural consciousness. At the same time, by another stroke, equally masterly, of not naming the character, he cleverly establishes the fact that it is *not* the historical Christ that he is talking about. Thus the appearance of the person is the same; he has the same personality; his past and the events leading up to his present situation are the same. Yet it is a different man.

Unless this is accepted, the value of the story is not seen. But for the fact that Lawrence now wishes to steer clear of all known religions, *The Man Who Died* would not be any different from *The Plumed Serpent*. We have to recognize that *both* of them—*The Man Who Died* and *The Plumed Serpent*—are stories of Resurrection. The theme of *The Plumed Serpent* is about nothing but, as we read there, "The coming and going of things";[70] wandering minstrels go round singing: "Someone will enter between the gates, / Now, at this moment, Ay! / See the light on the man that waits. / Shall you? Shall I?;"[71] and Ramon basically declares only one thing: "What is God, we shall never know! . . . But the Sons of God come and go. / They come from beyond the Morning Star; / And thither they return, from the land of men."[72] Of course, as stated earlier, when Lawrence talked of Resurrection or the Risen Lord, not for a moment had he in mind the coming back of the historical Christ. The idea of repeated manifestations of God is rational and quite compatible with the spirit of the idea of Self that we have been discussing. For if Self is in each one of us, it is only reasonable to presume that those who have realized the Self are deeper and more powerful human beings than the others, and as such, are, in a way, figuratively speaking, manifestations of God. This, as is obvious, paves the way for the people following these Manifestations (Sons of God, Saviors) and taking guidance from them, and for the hypothesis of "many" paths to God. It was with this end in view that *The Plumed Serpent* was written, or that we come across statements like "Obey the man in whom you recognise the Holy Ghost" in Lawrence's essays. But though this approach is more liberal and tolerant than that of "one" path, even this is, as has been seen, a confined and an insular one. For, in the last resort, Self can be discovered only by the individual himself; and the "paths" and the "Saviours" detract from that discovery. It may be stated that even in Hinduism—where reincarnations and recurring manifestations of God are widely accepted—this positive concept of the "many" paths appears much later, in the Epic period, and the often-quoted *shaloka* in favor of it—*Yada-yada hi dharmasya glanir bhavati bharata, abhyutthanam adharmasya tada 'tmanam srjamy aham* ("For whensoever the law fails and lawlessness uprises, O thou of Bharata's race, then do I bring myself to bodied birth") [73]—is only from the *Gita*. (Contrary to the commonly held belief, the *Gita* is not a part of the Hindu scriptures but a section in one of the epics, the *Mahabharata*.) The *Gita* mirrors the Vedic philosophy faithfully, but because of this well-intentioned twist (well-intentioned, as the idea was to be as catholic as possible), the far-reaching significance of what the Vedas say is lost even in India. There are many gods and there are many paths, all a part of *Brahman*, the Great God, but according to the Vedas, the great Seer is one who sees that in reality there are *no* gods and that there are *no* paths, the individual himself being a part of the same *Brahman*; the great Seer is one, the center of whose gravity is his Self. There is a telling conversation pertaining to this between Yajnavalkya and his student Vidagdha Sakalya in *Brhadaranyaka Upanishad*, where when the student asks the teacher, "How many gods are there really, O Yajnavalkya?" the teacher starts with the figure "three thousand and three," comically brings the number down to "one and a half," then "one," and then finally tells him that there are actually "no" gods as conceived by man.[74] It is this kind of supreme awareness that Lawrence reaches in *The Man Who Died,* where he pushes aside all concepts and theories, forgets even his lifelong quarrel with Christianity, not even referring to Christianity by name, and emerges resplendent and glorious in the singleness of the Self, in the "nameless" singleness, of which he had always been a devotee.

The structure of the whole of Lawrence's creative work rests on the kernel of this "God within."

Paul and his mother now had long discussions about life. Religion was fading into the background. He had shovelled away all the beliefs that would hamper him, had cleared the ground, and come more or less to the bedrock of belief that one should feel inside oneself for right and wrong, and should have the patience to gradually realize one's God.[75]

Only what was "more or less" in *Sons and Lovers* now becomes absolutely positive. Not only that; to signify the measure of reliance on the power within, all ideas of leadership, or of the supremacy of one man over the other, are at this stage rejected. "For the whole life-effort of man was to get his life into direct contact with the elemental life of the cosmos, mountain-life, cloud-life, thunder-life, air-life, earth-life, sun-life. To come into immediate *felt* contact, and so derive energy, power, and a dark sort of joy. This effort into sheer naked contact, *without an inter-*

mediary or mediator, is the root meaning of religion. . . ."[76]
(Lawrence's emphasis). Lawrence said this in praise of
the Mexicans, and though he contradicted himself to some
extent in the reestablishment of the rituals of "interme-
diaries" like Quetzalcoatl and Huitzilopochtli in *The
Plumed Serpent* (mostly in order to refute the myth of
Christ as the only Savior), he implements this doctrine
completely now. There was a man who was a great seer,
a man in tune with his Self. Unfortunately this man came
to believe that all other men too should think and live
exactly like him. His object was noble; he only wanted
them to be as at peace with themselves as he was with
himself. But he forgot that the method of one man was
not necessarily the method of the other. And therefore,
while he went about exhorting the masses to follow him,
he was actually imposing a "pattern" on them. His teachings were moving, a relief from the social and political
oppression of his times. But in his enthusiasm he came to
be guilty of the same error as were the oppressors: he
went to excesses. He taught people the doctrine of love,
the doctrine of turning the other cheek, of suffering—
sentiments remarkable in themselves, but liable to mislead the individual when deliberately cultivated. So
though he taught them to follow their Self, he associated
his own voice with that Self when he started defining what
was right and what was wrong, right and wrong according
to *his* Self. His religion was thus a religion of reaction,
reaction against a certain other religion of the time, and
he forgot that anything that began as the result of reaction
was always incomplete. Anyway, he was caught by his
adversaries and was crucified. But they took him down
from the cross a bit too soon, before he was dead, and
after lying for a few days in the cave where they threw
his body, he recovered his consciousness and came back
to life.

It is at this point that the story of *The Man Who Died*

starts. He wakes up "at the same time," "the same hour," on "the same morning," while a cock in a nearby peasant's house gives a fierce and uncontrolled cry of joy as it breaks the cord by which it is tied and flies to freedom. The cock is undoubtedly a symbol—symbol of the endless wave, the strength, the urge of life. The first thing that the man notices on coming back to himself is that the phenomenal world is still as beautiful as ever. In our account of *The White Peacock,* we saw how there is never a mourning in nature; nature in that respect may even be described as "heartless." However great a particular man may be, once he is dead and gone, the cosmos has finished with him. A chapter has been closed, a life has come to an end; but there are other lives, other chapters, in progress right now, new buds opening and growing and flowering; and the flame of life, relentless in its intensity, insists on burning, on glowing, regardless of what may have just preceded. This is the preliminary shock that the man who had died receives on stepping forth once again into the open. Only three days had passed since they had killed him, and yet the universe had already dismissed him and he finds the cogs of its wheel running as forcefully, as beautifully as ever. "The world, the same as ever, the natural world, thronging with greenness, a nightingale winsomely, wistfully, coaxingly calling from the bushes beside a runnel of water, in the world, the natural world of morning and evening, forever undying, from which he had died." The man, bewildered, walks on, and "leaping out of greenness, came the black and orange cock with the red comb, his tail-feathers streaming lustrous." Then he sees the "squawk" and the "flutter" and the "whirring of feathers" of the cock—the spirit of its defiance while it is captured, feels the "cool silkiness of the young wheat under his feet," and sees the "first green leaves spurting like flames" on a fig tree; and he is captivated by this dance of the universe—the pale blue sky, the cool air, the warm sun, the rebellious cock, the rebellious, ringing life all around him, "glowing with desire and with assertion."

> The man who had died looked nakedly on life, and saw a vast resoluteness everywhere flinging itself up in stormy or subtle wave-crests, foam-tips emerging out of the blue invisible, a black and orange cock or the green flame-tongues out of the extremes of the fig-tree. They came forth, these things and creatures of spring, glowing with desire and with assertion. They came like crests of foam, out of the blue flood of the invisible desire, out of the vast invisible sea of strength, and they came coloured and tangible, evanescent, yet deathless in their coming. The man who had died looked on the great swing into existence of things that had not died, but he saw no longer their tremulous desire to exist and to be. He heard instead their ringing, ringing, defiant challenge to all other things existing.[77]

If prose can ever catch the dauntless and daring lilt of life, the beauty and the wonder of its cadence, here is a powerful illustration of it. One is at once reminded of the burial scene in *The White Peacock*, where years before Lawrence had depicted the same effervescence, the hiss and the foam of it, and if perchance Annable were to have risen out of his coffin, he would have been equally dazzled by such a sight. The river of life flows on, the sea of life, in waves bobbing up and down, the waves of which every single living creature is the crest, the tip, hence the pinnacle of glory. Who bothers, who cares, whether Krishna or Buddha or Christ are there or not? The wave is still there, and so is the tip: "the everlasting resoluteness of life," "the tide of life," "the destiny of life," "the surge of life," in Lawrence's words.

It must be observed that it is not merely the beauty of the passing moment that Lawrence is interested in. It is the joy a living being derives by sharing in that moment that is his concern. And there can be no sharing in the "now" when the mind is even remotely preoccupied with what has been and what will be, the past and the future; the two are a contradiction in terms. Sharing in the living moment is, in Lawrence's own words, "an act of pure attention"[78] (in one of his pansies he calls it, "a man in his wholeness wholly attending").[79] And it has, as he goes on, "its own answer":[80] a reward, a harvest to be reaped not later, but instantly, at the same time.

A unique feature of *The Man Who Died* as a story is its compactness, its pithy succinctness. Even in its first draft, the form in which it appeared in *The Forum* in 1928 (under the title *The Escaped Cock*), it is complete in itself and as forceful; and that cuts it down to half its present length. The three facets that I have been delineating here, the three major attributes of Lawrence, (1) Delight of creation, (2) love and marriage and (3) Self-realization, are all faithfully captured and presented within that brief length. With the addition of the second part a year later, the image is expanded and all three qualities are seen once again, reenacted. In his earlier works, the artist was mostly concerned with them one at a time. To be sure, they are there in life *together,* but Lawrence's art had not yet acquired the skill of extracting a homogeneous whole without upsetting the stability of these three forces. In this story, however, they move side by side; they are ideally woven into each other. There is much truth in what Catherine Carswell said in one of her letters about the story, that no one "but a dying man could have written it." (Catherine Carswell, it should be said, was one of his earliest and most observant critics. In the same letter she describes *The Man Who Died* as "the loveliest and most original story of our generation. Its sheer fragrance and freshness made me hold my breath.") [81] The awareness of death certainly made the artist in him see deeply and at the same time intensely—wiping out all desire in him to prove a thing, or to justify it, or to build a case around it. The period of his isolated catharses was over (and he had had a number of them, in the longer novels) ; the time now was for a composite creative restoration.

In his "act of pure attention," in the alertness and intuition brought about by the nullity of death (nullity of his own past), the man who had died sees not only that life is beautiful but that every noticeable object has, as the young wheat under his feet has, "the roughishness of its separate life." Ah, the roughishness of its separate life; its distinct crispness, its own angularity, own charm, own beauty, own sharpness! Thus it strikes him that each individual is unique in his own way, and how he had tried to force a uniform, fixed design on all of them. There is plainly no bitterness in him; he does not criticize himself for what he had at one time done; he is dead to his past. Phrases like "since life must be," "so he let them be," "it is well," "it had to be," "yet even this was as men are made," "Patience! Let destiny move," indicate the man's arrival at that most noteworthy of all stages when he neither condemns an action nor justifies it. We have a skeleton in the cupboard, all of us, but how many of us are brave enough to open the cupboard completely and look at it? We open it only partly, and look, invariably, to approve or to disapprove, eaten as we are with care and worry (care and worry to prove ourselves right). And a mind caught in the snare of condemnation and justification only sees what it wants to see; it does not, it cannot, see the whole. But the man who had died is now beyond "attachments"—"for in the tomb he had slipped that noose which we call care. For in the tomb he had left his striving self, which cares and asserts itself."[82]

And the moment he recognizes this, the moment he sees the independent existence of life-in-itself as it moves on and on, he is free, he is healed, he is a new man: he has risen. Earlier, when the peasant approached him, he had waved him aside by saying: "Don't touch me, brother. I am not yet risen to the Father." To the woman named Madeleine, too, he had said: "I must go to my Father!" When asked to meet his mother, his reply had been: "But now I must ascend to my Father." Graham Hough's assertion that Father in Lawrence's mythology is the Flesh is not true. Father is the realization of the Self. The Self indeed implies an acceptance of everything that exists, and so an acceptance of the flesh; but the flesh is not the end. It is not even the beginning, for that matter. It is one of the features of the phenomenal world, and the emphasis is not so much on immediate participation in it as on its justificationless, condemnationless admission, along with a similar admission of the rest of life in general. It is, therefore, the Self that the man who had died implies when he talks of rising to the Father. For even now he is not yet certain in his mind; the intuition leads, but the past still clings to him. The peasant, Madeleine, his mother —he can see that if he goes back to them, to the world of his early days, they will never leave him at peace and, whereas he had imposed a pattern on them earlier, now they would impose a pattern on him, would expect him to live according to a design that is, so far as he is concerned, dead in him. The tragedy of it is not that he is a changed and a new man; the tragedy is that the others refuse to accept the reality of this change; they have no "rebirth" in them: "Now my own followers will want to do me to death again, from having risen up different from their expectation." And this bites, this worries him, he thinks about it still. But the voice within him is sharp like a razor and he is convinced that "whatever came of touch between himself and the race of men, henceforth, should come without trespass or compulsion." He knows now that compulsion implies a denial of the life-force, is a sign of excess; excess of one type of feeling in disregard of other feelings: "Don't run to excess now in living, Madeleine. It only means another death." He has various extravagances in mind—excessive physical love (Madeleine's earlier lovers) ; excessive spiritual love (Madeleine's love for him, and his own love for others) ; excessive virginity ("He was virgin, in recoil from the little, greedy life of the body. But now he knew that virginity is a form of greed . . .") ; excessive hope ("But the hope was cunning in him"—in the peasant, who looked stupidly hopeful of a reward later for having given him shelter) —but he has done with all of them and is no longer bound. And so he basks in the sun, and so he looks at the carefree radiance of the cock: "Surely thou art risen to the Father, among birds," and lets life tumble by. And he becomes so much absorbed in the "now" that he does not even care to formulate his thoughts in words; he just feels his thoughts and lets them slide away. For he understands that words again bind one to the past: "The Word is but the midge that bites at evening. Man is tormented with words like midges, and they follow him right into the tomb." And it is at this moment, the instant he is taken up with the "wordless-nameless-now," that he rises to the Father, to the Self. At that very moment he becomes whole and healed and restored, and the divinity of life unfolds itself to him in all the richness of its colors.

> So he healed of his wounds, and enjoyed his immortality of being alive without fret . . . . Now his uncaring self healed and became whole within his skin, and he smiled to himself with pure aloneness, which is one sort of immortality.[83] (Note that he is healed and has not yet partaken of the life of the Flesh. Flesh is *not* the Father.)

As the story moves, we become increasingly conscious of the varying shades of the man's feelings; feelings that are registered to convey a sense of acute watchfulness on his part. His intuition and his Self would, in point of fact, be valueless unless he has this sharpness of assimilation— of simultaneous assimilation—of the movement of life at its different levels. We read: "And he said to himself: 'Strange is the phenomenal world, dirty and clean together! And I am the same. Yet I am apart! And life bubbles variously. Why should I have wanted to bubble it all alike?'" Once again the story is *not* a justification of the greater life over the lesser, as Graham Hough seems to read it (*The Dark Sun*, p. 250). The greater life and the lesser life are *both* there, and both taken together are life. It is only the preponderance of one of them over the other that is considered harmful to the individual. The character of the man who had died loses all its force if we do not accept that. The whole story loses its force.

And armed with this realization—no longer to "know," but to "be"—the man who had died issues forth into the world of men and women once again, to be a part of it. (See Lawrence's poem "Conceit" of the same period, where he writes: "Now we have to admit we *can't* know ourselves, we can only know about ourselves. / And I am not interested to know about myself any more / I only entangle myself in the knowing. / —Now let me be myself, / now let me be myself, and flicker forth / now let me be myself, in the being, one of the gods.") [84]

We now deal with the final scene, where at last the man who had died meets his equal in the body and becomes one with her. The peasant woman had tried to give herself to him, crouching before him and letting him see her soft breasts sway, but he had held back. Not that he had anything against her; she was what she was. He simply felt that he could not be one with her in her thoughts and her consciousness. (This is where intuition rises above the desire of the mind.) But with the priestess of Isis he finds it otherwise. She is a woman in search of the "reborn" man, waiting. There is an alluring charm in her expectancy, a subtle calm. The legend of Isis is well known from earlier times, and her remarriage to Osiris every year stands for fertility and the cosmic resurrection (some other names for Isis and Osiris: Dumuzi, Ishtar; and Tammuz, Adonis). And by making the man who had died sleep with the priestess of Isis, Lawrence reenacts the cosmic marriage without which life could not go on.

It should be observed that before their union actually takes place, the calm and the poise, the emotional tranquility, of both of them is repeatedly stressed. It is this only that is to distinguish between intuition and impulse; the urge to meet each other, if it is to be real, has to come from the stillness of the mind. The priestess watches the man in his sleep and although she sees that the man's face is "worn, hollow, and rather ugly," she also notices "the other kind of beauty in it, the sheer stillness of the deeper life." And this is what happens to her

> For the first time she was touched on the quick at the sight of a man, as if the tip of a fine flame of living had touched her. It was the first time. Men had roused all kinds of feeling in her, but never had touched her with the flame-tip of life.[85]

She goes away, disturbed. She is not a woman who could easily be disturbed by men: "Rome and Egypt alike had left her alone, unroused." For "she was a woman to herself, she would not give herself for a surface glow, nor marry for reasons. She would wait for the lotus to stir." Passing fancy had no attraction for her: it is in the quick of her life that she wants to be touched. The lotus, however, has now stirred; she cannot give reasons as to how and why it has happened, but she knows it.

The next morning she summons the man to her presence. But the man comes leisurely, without hurry. He knows he wants a life of the body, but it must come in its own time. The truth of it he had already seen, when the peasant woman had desired him to take her and he was not touched. He wanted a woman who had the "gentle reverence of the return gift," who would take and give and still leave him free, and the peasant woman was not capable of it. The silence of his mind had therefore told him that he must wait: "having died, he was patient, knowing there was time, an eternity of time." And so when the priestess sends for him, he is in no haste. The beauty of the day—the sea and the rocks and the trees—is "like a flower in unruffled bloom," and instead of going in to the priestess, he sits down on the steps of the temple, watching the landscape. It is the priestess who finally comes out and finds him there, sitting, "in the infinite patience of waiting"—patience that had "something almost menacing" in it. She knows, she knows: he is the man destined to woo her and love her. She takes him in and asks him: "Has Isis brought thee home to herself?" But it is obvious to her that the question is superfluous. For if the voice of intuition is to depend on the attitude or the answer of the other, it is no voice but a deception; intuition works independently of all external suggestions. (That is why the chapter "Test on Miriam" in *Sons and Lovers* is a blot on the genius of Lawrence. Paul did not have to go to the extent of knowing Miriam physically to realize whether he loved her or not. Obviously Lawrence was not so clear about the value of spontaneous comprehension at that stage, and those passages in *Sons and Lovers* are a put-up piece of writing to justify his own desertion of Jessie Chambers. He as a man probably clearly saw that he did not love her, but as an artist he was at that time too timid to acknowledge it and foolishly went around building a case to blame her for the breakdown.) And so though the man answers, "I know not," the priestess is sure: "She felt it in the quick of her soul." Her intuition has guided her.

On the other side, there is an equal, spontaneous stirring in the man: the same flame-tip that the girl had felt in him, he feels in her. In wonder he says to himself:

I am a physician, yet I have no healing like the flame of

this tender girl. The flame of this tender girl! Like the first pale crocus of the spring.[86]

Well, his intuition has guided him too. What follows afterwards is but a repetition of the spell of physical union, which need not occupy us here. That spell has been as beautifully outlined by Lawrence in earlier novels and the reader is referred to the last two chapters of this volume. "There are destinies of splendour, and there is a greater power," says the man who had died to himself at the quivering that the woman produces in him, and he knows that his hour is come. My object is to show how he arrives at this realization guided by his own Self and not by passion or desire.

> Now all his consciousness was there in the crouching, hidden woman. He stooped beside her and caressed her softly, blindly, murmuring inarticulate things. And his death and his passion of sacrifice were all as nothing to him now, he knew only the crouching fulness of the woman there, the soft white rock of life . . . . "On this rock I built my life". The deep-folded, penetrable rock of the living woman! The woman, hiding her face. Himself bending over, powerful and new like dawn.[87]

She is the woman of his life and there is no holding him back. It is notable that the main theme of the story, the theme of newness in life and more particularly in the man who had died, is preserved by Lawrence in every minute detail. The man who had died refuses to learn anything more about her; where is the need for any mental calculations, he feels, once the contact, the contact led by the Self, is established? "I will ask her nothing, not even her name, for a name would set her apart." As he had said to himself: "It doesn't need understanding. It needs newness. She brings me newness." And he rests contented in that deeper knowledge.

The woman conceives by him and he is ready to leave,

go away from her. It is not an act of desertion, but something forced on him by necessity. The Romans are trying to recapture him and, having known the life of the body, the man is in no hurry to lose it. But he tells the woman:

> . . . I shall come again: all is good between us, near or apart. The suns come back in their seasons: and I shall come again.[88]

It is infinitely touching: the note of tenderness and hope on which most of Lawrence's novels end. (See the grace and benevolence of the end of *Lady Chatterley's Lover*.) The man knows that having once known a woman through his intuition, he is bound to her for ever (fidelity in love). As Birkin tells Ursula in *Women in Love*: "It is the law of creation. One is committed. One must commit oneself to a conjunction with the other—for ever."[89] The remaining part of this very paragraph is further help in appreciating the conduct of the man who had died, for Birkin goes on to add, "But it is not selfless—it is a maintaining of the self in mystic balance and integrity—like a star balanced with another star."[90] The man who had died is thus bound to the woman of Isis so long as he is alive and yet his Self is free. His temporary separation from her stands as a symbol of this freedom, as do the words with which the story ends: "To-morrow is another day."[91] And so he goes away, linked to the woman of his choice by an invisible cord, and yet free—as indeed she is linked to him and is free too.

The background music to *The Man Who Died* is the melody of *Last Poems*, which were written at about the same time. Over and again the reverence to God as seen in every living life is paid there, almost like the homage of a devotee in a shrine. One must be careful not to misinterpret some of the poems, like "Bodiless God" or "The Hands of God," as implying a return to a personal God in Lawrence. The bloom of his vision rests on the *denial* of a personal God, and even these poems, when read together with other compositions in this volume, reinforce rather than contradict that view.

Let us, for instance, take "Bodiless God":

Everything that has beauty has a body, and is a body;
everything that has being has being in the flesh:
and dreams are only drawn from the bodies that are.

And God?
Unless God has a body, how can he have a voice
and emotions, and desires, and strength, glory or honour?
For God, ever the rarest God, is supposed to love us
and wish us to be this that and the other.
And he is supposed to be mighty and glorious.[92]

One might conclude from this that here is an assertion of God's having a body. And so indeed it is; but of that of a very different sort of living God from the God that conventional Christianity preached. It is *not* an assertion of a God in the flesh, having a body *apart* from the visible universe (whose voice one must listen to in one's heart); it is an avowal of God in the flesh of the living cosmos as it is. Everything that exists, everything that *is*, is God. As we read in the very next poem, "The Body of God": "There is no god / apart from poppies and the flying fish, / men singing songs, and women brushing their hair in the sun";[93] and Lawrence never compromised on that.

That is what he means when he declares: "All that matters is to be at one with the living God / to be a creature in the house of the God of life."[94] It is a recognition of the reality of things as they are, and the man who had died sees this reality without any wish now to alter it. (It is herein that the Man who had Died may be said to be an "improvement" on Birkin: the preacher element is missing in him.) In *Last Poems,* Lawrence takes us through a magnificent array of the productiveness of life, its manifold multiplicity. We are told that any lovely and generous woman is God, any clear and fearless man is God; so is a red geranium, or a mignonette, or a cherry-pie heliotrope, or the lizards and mastodons in the moss and the mud (for that is their nature), or the poppies, the flying fish, or the ribbon-spangled rainbow, or the leaping dolphins, or the mighty whales, and the twinkling butter-fly, the big and dark Bavarian gentians, the cobra, the hyena, the scorpion, the ant, or the nightingale at twi-light, the fox in the dark, the goose in the mist; and so are the elements, the sun like a lion, the moon like a queen, the rolling, breaking sea, or the very heat, the very cold, the earth, and the sky. It is apparent that a God in flesh *apart* from the Universe and a God in flesh *in* the Universe are not reconcilable unless we are willing to give up *one* of these principles. We may play with words, we may offer and put forward cleverly devised doctrines; the fact remains that the living God of Lawrence is not con-ceivable in its full effulgence unless the personal God is disregarded. We have listed in this paragraph, in almost Lawrence's own words, the rhythm of life he venerates, and omits all other power. Until we appreciate this, con-fusion about, and misunderstanding of, his work will continue.

No wonder that Richard Aldington chaffs at him for saying that even a crow, flying beautifully in its might, is God. He quotes his remark, "God doesn't *know* things, He *is* things," and comments: "But, after all, what is the use of being a thing if you don't know it?"[95] Looked upon in the Vedic concept of *Brahaman,* however, such state-ments of Lawrence come to have a definite meaning. Even a crow is God; so is everything else; and things come and go, and they are all God; they do not have to specifically *know* that, or be mentally aware of themselves—they *are* that. In the third hymn of Quetzalcoatl, Lawrence speaks of the "Stone of Change" with which Quetzalcoatl returns to the Mexicans, and in *Last Poems* we read: "The breath of life is in the sharp winds of change." The symbolical clue of such remarks is clear. Everything is for joy, so long as it exists. In course of time, it is replaced by other things. The constant factor is the urge behind—the urge to change, the urge to destroy the old and to bring in the new. And so long as anything lasts, the smallest of small atoms, it is the very God Himself.

> And life is for delight, and for bliss
> and dread, and the dark, rolling ominousness of doom
> then the bright dawning of delight again
> from off the sheer white snow, or the poised moon.[96]

3. DEATH AND DEEP SLEEP

It is but a very brief section of Lawrence's writing that deals with the life beyond, the life after death. Nevertheless, Death remains for Lawrence a highly conspicuous symbol of newness. For the new can only be there when the old is not, when the known is not; and at no time is the known, the old, so completely brought to extinction as at the time of death. It is not within the scope of any artist to convey the newness of the beyond, the newness of the hereafter, as the hereafter is unknowable. But sure enough—and this is important—it is within his power to convey the newness of an individual who can somehow manage to learn to die every day, die every minute, die to his past, die to the known, while he is still alive.

Lawrence has a long section on the subject in "The Reality of Peace," where he says:

> That is how we know death, having suffered it and lived. It is now no mystery, finally. Death is understood in us, and thus we transcend it. Henceforward actual death is a fulfilling of our own knowledge.

Nevertheless, we transcend death by understanding down to the last ebb the great process of death in us. We can never destroy death. We can only transcend it in pure understanding. We can envelop it and contain it. And then we are free.

By standing in the light we see in terms of shadow. We cannot see the light we stand in. So our understanding of death in life is an act of living.

If we live in the mind, we must die in the mind, and in the mind we must understand death. Understanding is not necessarily mental. It is of the senses and the spirit.

But we live also in the mind. And the first great act of living is to encompass death in the understanding.

Therefore the first great activity of the living mind is to understand death in the mind. Without this there is no freedom of the mind, there is no life of the mind, since creative life is the attaining a perfect consummation with death. When in my mind there rises the idea of life, then this idea must encompass the idea of death, and this encompassing is the germination of a new epoch of the mind.[97]

In his treatment of Death, it is the day-to-day death in the life of an individual not yet physically dead that is the chief concern of Lawrence as an artist, and not his physical demise. That is why we observed while analyzing *The Man Who Died* that it was not the story of Christ but of a different man, having the same past. Christ was dead and Lawrence had no use for him; but Lawrence's character never died ("They took me down too soon. So I have risen up"). The resemblance of the man who had died to Christ is unmistakable, but the story acquires its artistic value only if he is recognized to be a different person. The dead Christ is physically extinct and by any standards of intelligence and common sense he can never rise again in the body. A body once deceased is defunct, and the unknown is not within our reach. It is the body alive that can, however, rise to a new life once it is dead to what has been.

Thus, in *The White Peacock* there is no rebirth for

George because he does not know how to die to his past; hence his misery. And in *Sons and Lovers*, it is the very dilemma that Paul is faced with, after the death of his mother. It is not her death that really matters; it is his mind holding on to her memory. In *Women in Love*, when Diana is drowned, Rupert tells Ursula: "I don't mind about the dead once they are dead. The worst of it is, they cling on to the living, and won't let go."[98] It is such a situation that confronts Paul in the last few chapters of *Sons and Lovers*:

> And his soul could not leave her, wherever she was. Now she was gone abroad into the night, and he was with her still. They were together. But yet there was his body, his chest, that leaned against the stile, his hands on the wooden bar. They seemed something. Where was he?—one tiny upright speck of flesh, less than an ear of wheat lost in the field. He could not bear it. On every side the immense dark silence seemed pressing him, so tiny a spark, into extinction, and yet, almost nothing, he could not be extinct. Night, in which everything was lost, went reaching out, beyond stars and sun. Stars and sun, a few bright grains, went spinning round for terror, and holding each other in embrace, there is a darkness that outpassed them all, and left them tiny and daunted. So much, and himself infinitesimal, at the core a nothingness, and yet not nothing.
>
> "Mother!" he whispered—"mother!"[99]

It is the death of his memories that he is avoiding that is the chief concern of Lawrence the artist. For the young man cannot have a rebirth until he goes through that death. Fortunately, before the novel ends, Paul sees the light and we are left with the hope that he will continue to see it.

> But no, he would not give in. Turning sharply, he walked towards the city's gold phosphorescence. His fists were shut, his mouth set fast. He would not take that direction, to the darkness, to follow her. He walked towards the faintly humming, glowing town, quickly.[100]

The rebirth now is certain.

It must not be assumed, however, that Lawrence was incapable of describing a death scene in a moving manner. If he wished, his art could as easily narrate the sense of tragedy a death generates. We have a good illustration of it in the drowning of Tom Brangwen in *The Rainbow,* where the return of the farmer to his house at night in heavy rain, his floundering while he is unharnessing the horse, his fall in the flooding water and his death, and the bellowing, heart-rending cries of his wife, are very stirringly and touchingly done. The death of Gerald Crich in *Women in Love* is another striking illustration of the same type. It is the after-effect of death that we are speaking of; the immediate and the long-range impact of it on others. A situation like, for instance, Heathcliff's pining for Emily in *Wuthering Heights,* is simply unthinkable—and as we notice, entirely absent—in Lawrence. According to Lawrence such a renunciation would be a meaningless waste of the life-force, and in this scene of the drowning of Tom Brangwen he describes how by the very next morning the spell of death was already waning. " 'I shared life with you, I belong in my own way to eternity,' said Lydia Brangwen, her heart cold, knowing her own singleness": these are the comments of his wife to herself when she sees his body. One is fascinated by the limitless adjustability to life that Lawrence tries to communicate, here and elsewhere, in his writings; for otherwise, he would say, the health of the being could not be maintained. Life must bubble, whatever the havoc or the tragedy, and it is only with this understanding that one can absorb the truth of the other passages that follow after the death of Tom Brangwen:

At the funeral, and after the funeral, Will Brangwen was madly in love with his wife. The death had shaken him. But death and all seemed to gather in him into a mad, overwhelming passion for his wife. She seemed so strange and winsome. He was almost beside himself with desire for her.

And she took him, she seemed ready for him, she wanted him.[101]

In his essay "On Human Destiny," Lawrence says: "And that's the human destiny. The light shall never go out till the last day. The light of the human adventure into consciousness, which is, essentially, the light of human God-knowledge."[102] In the same essay, a little later, he remarks: "I live and I die. I ask no other. Whatever proceeds from me lives and dies. I am glad, too. God is eternal, but my idea of Him is my own, and perishable. Everything human, human knowledge, human faith, human emotions, all perishes. And that is very good; if it were not so, everything would turn to cast-iron."[103] Change, the "Stone of Change," is the very basis of Lawrence's creative force. And this leaves no room for any long beating of the breast, or pulling of the hair, or endless sorrow, or endless grief.

And so, all along in his creative work, it is the death in the living individual, death in the mind, that he insists on. It is herein that Rupert has his wisdom and Gerald his folly in *Women in Love*; it is this exactly that Don Ramon is supposed to typify in *The Plumed Serpent*; it is this—the recognition of the death of her marriage to Clifford—that Constance's surrender to Mellors is supposed to show in *Lady Chatterley's Lover*. Rupert tells Gerald in *Women in Love*: "You've got very badly to want to get rid of the old, before anything new will appear—even in the self,"[104] for Gerald *won't* let go the past. Much later in the story, Rupert rebukes him again, for what he calls "a mill-stone of beastly memories round your neck."[105] Rupert is himself put to the test when Gerald in the end dies and he is torn with grief at the loss of such a friend. But, overcome though he is at the sight of the frozen corpse of his friend, his sanity does not desert him: "He turned away. Either the heart would break, or cease to care. Best cease to care. Whatever the mystery which has brought forth man and the universe, it is a non-human mystery, it has its own great ends, man is not the criterion. Best leave it all to the vast, creative, non-human mystery. Best strive with oneself only, not with the universe."[106] As he tells himself: "To rant, to rave, to be tragic, to make situations—it was all too late. Best be quiet, and bear one's soul in patience and in fullness."[107] For as he has just grasped, though one life, or more than one, may come to an end, the fountainhead goes on forever and the fulfillment of the individual is in his continuation with the flow of the spring:

> The game was never up. The mystery of creation was fathomless, infallible, inexhaustible, forever. Races came and went, species passed away, but ever new species arose, more lovely, or equally lovely, always surpassing wonder. The fountain-head was incorruptible and unsearchable. It had no limits. It could bring forth miracles, create utter new races and new species, in its own hour, new forms of consciousness, new forms of body, new units of being. To be man was as nothing compared to the possibilities of the creative mystery. To have one's pulse beating direct from the mystery, this was perfection, unutterable satisfaction. Human or inhuman mattered nothing. The perfect pulse throbbed with indescribable being, miraculous unborn species.[108]

Jack in *The Boy in the Bush* reflects similar thoughts when he ruminates: "The two are never separate, life and death. And in the vast dark kingdom of afterwards, the Lord of Death is Lord of Life, and the God of Life and creation is Lord of Death."[109] It is in this light that Death has to be seen in Lawrence.

But in the brief sequence of poems coming in the final section of *Last Poems,* Lawrence decidedly devotes him-

self unreservedly to the subject of physical Death, death
of the body, and it is to that section that we propose to
direct our study of Lawrence's appreciation of the "hereafter."

The metaphor that Lawrence uses for Death in all those
poems is "dark oblivion." In two of the poems, "Sleep"
and "Sleep and Waking," he compares this dark oblivion
with the "dreamless sleep" of the individual while he is
still alive. While asleep—in a sleep without any dreams—
the mind comes to a state of stillness that otherwise can
never be achieved. "In sleep I am not, I am gone / I am
given up," he says;[110] not an ordinary sleep, the sleep of a
worried man, filled with the hallucinations of his worry,
but "dark, dreamless sleep, in deep oblivion!" That is the
only state where the mind is completely dead to the
known; in short, when the individual is in total contact
with the unknown. Even here Lawrence is aware of the
inadequacy of words to capture or to describe that state—
aware of the fact that even "deep sleep" and "dark oblivion" are but expressions—and he warns us of the danger
of hurrying to attach familiar attributes or familiar qualities to these words. In the poem "Tabernacle," where he
talks of the "temple" of oblivion and the oblivion "dwelling" there, and the soul's "passing" into that temple, he
therefore makes it clear that these words are not supposed
to raise a picture of the type of temples we know of or of
the type of ordinary meaning that we associate with dwelling and living, and so on. An artist perforce has to depend
on words, but this is merely his method of expression:
what he is speaking of here is, in fact, unimaginable. I
shall quote the whole poem, since it is so pertinent to the
present discussion:

Come, let us build a temple to oblivion
with seven veils, and an innermost
Holy of Holies of sheer oblivion.

And there oblivion dwells, and the silent soul
may sink into god at last, having passed the veils.

But any one who shall ascribe attributes to god or oblivion

let him be cast out, for blasphemy.
For God is deeper forgetting far than sleep
and all description is a blasphemy.[111]

The last stanza is a vital one. This oblivion has no
properties, no characteristics that we can see beforehand;
for if we can, then it is not oblivion. As a matter of fact,
the man who insists on attaching preconceived qualities
or symbols to this oblivion will never know its bliss, its
newness, even when he is finally dead; he would not be
ready to share in its wholeness. Lawrence calls such dead
persons the "Unhappy Dead," for, as he tells us, they are
"unready, unprepared, unwilling, unable / to continue on
the longest journey": they, even when dead, are unable to
dissociate themselves from the old. They persist in

seeking their old haunts with cold ghostly rage
old haunts, old habitats, old hearths,
old places of sweet life from which they are thrust out
and can but haunt in disembodied rage.[112]

It is obvious that Lawrence recognizes the continuation
of the Self after death, in some form or other. All religious
thinkers do; without this the unknown will cease to have
any importance. But the curiosity of the artist here is in
regard to the union of the soul with the unknown. There
is the suggestion offered that perhaps these angry dead
never had a full life when they were alive. A life of fullness ("an act of pure attention"; "a man in his wholeness
wholly attending"; living by intuition) leaves its immediate reward in the satiation of the moment and the individual who has led such a life is left with no after-thoughts

or longing for it, once the moment is over. But these—the "Unhappy Dead"—are the unfortunate fellows who did not bother to enjoy the fullness of the living moment. (See his poem "Two Ways of Living and Dying" in *More Pansies,* where he elaborates on this: "So self-willed, self-centred, self-conscious people die / the death of nothing-ness, worn-out machines, kaput! / . . . But when living people die in the ripeness of their time / terrible and strange the god lies on the bed, wistful, coldly wonder-ful / beyond us, now beyond, departing with that purity / that flickered forth in the best hours of life, / when the man was himself, so a god in his singleness, / and the woman was herself, never to be duplicated, a goddess there / gleaming her hour in life as she now gleams in death / and departing inviolate, nothing can lay hand on her, / she who at her best hours was herself, warm, flicker-ing, herself, therefore a goddess, / and who now draws slowly away, cold, the wistful goddess receding.") [113] Imaginatively, the poet asks the living to appease these angry dead, to give them the "best" of food and drink, so that they may have their fill and be done with it. But the point he reasserts is that only when they have done with the known, only then will they be ready for the unknown.

The song of death is a song of "soundless silence" and "pivotal oblivion," "oblivion where the soul at last is lost/ in utter peace." The most beautiful of Lawrence's poems on this theme is "The Ship of Death," where some of the lines might mislead one to conclude that Lawrence is in fact speaking there not of "oblivion" but of a known shore. The lines in question are:

> The flood subsides, and the body, like a worn sea-shell emerges strange and lovely,
> And the little ship wings home, faltering and lapsing on the pink flood,
> and the frail soul steps out, into the house again filling the heart with peace.[114]

Here we must take into account the limitations that the art of letters imposes on an artist, before we come to any conclusion about this stanza. Lawrence was an artist the medium of whose expression was language, and since language is always based on a remembered image, he could not have avoided employing words having a particular association. But because he makes use of a certain flower in a composition, or refers to a particular season, shade, or color, or includes such commonly known words as "home" or "house" in a poem, that in no way justifies the inference that the long journey of death, in Lawrence's view, was to end in a place like "a house, one's own house," or in anything else known to man. The myths of Odysseus and Osiris, or the legends of the Etruscan tombs, are artistic representations of the hope that something continues in the end, after death. Lawrence borrows the beauty of these ideas, the hope, but the substance of his thought is that whatever continues can never be compared to anything known. The only way man can at all visualize death is to accept the total negation of the known, and what emerges beyond (we do not know *what* it is) is the hereafter. Otherwise the hereafter will have no joy, no sublimity; it will have no newness.

It is a bit difficult to decide which one of the three versions of "The Ship of Death" that have survived is the final one, having Lawrence's approval for publication. We have only Richard Aldington's word that manuscript "A" appears to him to be more "pondered" than manuscript "B" of the two volumes of verse discovered after Lawrence's death.[115] But on closer analysis one observes that "The Ship of Death" in manuscript "B" is a maturer poem, since it fits in more closely with the rest of Lawrence's observations on the theme (Horace Gregory remarks that it is "the best" of the two versions).[116] And we see that the six lines of manuscript "A" cited above— lines that tend to create confusion—are missing in the manuscript "B" version. The hope of some kind of continuation is certainly there, but only the hope—nothing beyond that. The beauty of Lawrence's discernment, the force of his vision, his skill as an artist are all in one sweep thrown overboard if we do not accept that Death in its real image emerges not in the doubtful six lines of "The Ship of Death" but in the seventy-two poems contained in the whole volume, *Last Poems*, and more especially in the twenty-three or so poems dealing specifically with the subject of death.

This is how the manuscript "B" runs:

> Oh lovely last, last lapse of death, into pure oblivion
> at the end of the longest journey
> peace, complete peace!
> But can it be that also it is procreation?[117]

Even Richard Aldington admits that "The two books must also have been in progress simultaneously,"[118] and it is suggested by the present writer that the first version quoted is merely a more fanciful representation of the theme whose basic idea is contained in the second version —or in the other contemporary poems. If this does not seem conclusive enough, here are lines from Lawrence's own typescript of the poem (the third version), which again have no reference other than to "oblivion":

> Oblivion, the last wonder!
> When we have trusted ourselves entirely
> To the unknown, and are taken up
> Out of our little ships of death
> Into pure oblivion.[119]

And even if we go by manuscript "A," all the poems cited above appear *after* "The Ship of Death." Thus, even chronologically, those six lines were superseded by poems not even casually mentioning the idea of new birth as resurrection in a recognizable form. Death is the severance of all bonds with the recognizable, and it ever remains as such.

When one looks at the closeness of Lawrence's concepts to Vedantic thought, one hold's one's breath in wonder. It is not surprising that Sri Aurobindo said: "Lawrence was a Yogi who had missed his way and come into a European body to work out his difficulties."[120] (Yogi in India means a man who has realized his Self, not a routine practitioner of physical exercises, as people in the West like to believe.)   It is this affinity to the Indian thought that Sri Aurobindo's comment is suposed to convey. It is a great pity that Lawrence never read the Upanishads, otherwise he himself would have been struck by the similarity.   Whatever he knew of Hinduism was through second-hand, or rather third-hand sources—through Buddhism via Earl Brewster, or through sensational works like those of Madame Blavatsky and doubtful versions of the Tantras. But he missed the central books, the Scriptures. Nevertheless, it is even all the more complimentary to him that he should arrive at the same conclusions, working only through the sharpness of his own intelligence (as does J. Krishnamurti; for he too, he states, has not read the Upanishads).   For we see that the Upanishads give exactly the same metaphor for man's reach of the unknown as Lawrence through his own reasoning: the metaphor of Deep Sleep. In the waking stage, the mind is ever busy weaving its web of fantasies, but when one is asleep—in a *dreamless* sleep—the mind is silent. So the Upanishads say that the state of perfect stillness of the mind is reached by man in Deep Sleep alone; that if man can at all visualize the glory of the unmanifested, it would be the kind of image seen in the state mentioned earlier.

The issue is not left at that. The Upanishads pursue it to its logical doubts and offer answers or explain it further. For, surely, it is a paradoxical situation; how can one have an "image" when one is in a sleep without images? As we see, Indra, the pupil, has his doubt too. Prajapati is explaining to him the Self, the understanding of the Self, and tells him: "When a man being asleep, reposing, and at perfect rest, sees no dreams, that is the Self, this is the immortal, the fearless, this is Brahman."[121] And Indra rebels:

> He said: "Sir, in that way he does not know himself (his self) that he is I, nor does he know anything that exists. He is gone to utter annihilation. I see no good in this."

> "So it is indeed, Maghavat," replied Prajapati; "but I shall explain him (the true Self) further to you. . . ."[122]

The explanation is simple enough and is consistent with the main argument of the Upanishads, and once one sees the problem in that light, the paradox vanishes. For the deep sleep, or the *samadhi*, or the *mukati*, or salvation, of the Vedantic philosophy does not mean total extinction; it means only extinction of the known. The unknown is implicitly accepted. But every picture that mind may conjure up of it will be purely imaginary, and so is dismissed. Even in a sleep with dreams, the image is the result of the known. So, so far as human imagination can extend, the Hindus could think of dreamless sleep as the only available illustration where the mind would be altogether free of the ascertained, the recognized, the familiar image. And whatever ensues then—we don't know *what* it is—is God, *Brahman*, the Unknown.

Time and again references come up in the Vedas: "The Self cannot be gained by the Veda, nor by understanding, nor by much learning."[123] The breadth and the scope of this can only be imagined when the Vedas are set beside the books of other religions or of later Hinduism, where always the particular sacred book, or the particular prophet, is prescribed, in all circumstances, as the last word of our search. As J. Krishnamurti has remarked:

can there ever be any 'search' when we start with a fixed result in our mind? The moment we set out to see God as Christ, or God as Mohammad, or God as Buddha, or God as a Person, the search for God has defeated its purpose. Hence, deep sleep—the only conceivable state of non duality between the known and the unknown, the state in which the known is not, so to speak, excluded, but lost in the unknown.

This final all-embracing stage, the fourth stage, which incorporates the waking stage, the sleeping stage, and the dream sleep stage, is described in one of the shortest (it has only twelve verses), the most difficult, and to my mind one of the most important Upanishads, *Mandukya Upanishad,* as follows: "The Fourth stage (Turiya), the wise say, is not inwardly cognitive, nor outwardly cognitive, nor cognitive both-wise; neither is it an indefinite mass of cognition, nor collective cognition, nor non-cognition. It is unseen, unrelated, inconceivable, uninferable, unimaginable, indescribable. It is the essence of the one self-cognition common to all states of consciousness. All phenomena cease in it. It is peace, it is bliss, it is non-duality. This is the Self, and it is to be realized."[124] Since the writer of the Upanishad knows words can never help him to describe this stage, what he does is that he negates all the accepted expressions. But this is the "Whole," from which both the unknown and the known flow according to the Upanishads. Forms appear and disappear; but the whole continues for ever.

The value of these passages becomes obvious when we remember Lawrence's description of the unknown as "oblivion." No further comment is necessary; Lawrence's meaning should be clear by now beyond doubt. We conclude with a hymn from *The Plumed Serpent,* a novel which, though a poor work of art because of its foreign setting where Lawrence could not be at home, has a good deal of solid theory in it. The passage below is the beautiful long song in praise of oblivion and the life-forms thrown out from this oblivion and their return to the very same oblivion; the song where Ramon says: "As a man in deep sleep has no tomorrow, no yesterday, nor today, but only *is*, so is the limpid, far-reaching Snake of the eternal Cosmos, Now, and for ever Now."

"There is no Before and After, there is only Now," he said, speaking in a proud, but inward voice.

"The great Snake coils and uncoils the plasm of his folds, and stars appear, and worlds fade out. It is no more than the changing and easing of the plasm.

"*I always am*, says his sleep.

"As a man in a deep sleep knows not, but is, so is the Snake of the coiled cosmos, wearing its plasm.

"As a man in a deep sleep has no tomorrow, no yesterday, nor to-day, but only *is*, so is the limpid, far-reaching Snake of the eternal Cosmos, Now, and forever Now.

"Now, and only Now, and forever Now.

"But dreams arise and fade in the sleep of the Snake.

"And worlds arise as dreams, and are gone as dreams.

"And man is a dream in the sleep of the Snake.

"And only the sleep that is dreamless breathes *I Am!*

"In the dreamless Now, *I Am*.

"Dreams arise as they must arise, and man is a dream arisen.

"But the dreamless plasm of the Snake is the plasm of a man, of his body, his soul, and his spirit at one.

"And the perfect sleep of the Snake *I Am* is the plasm of a man, who is whole.

"When the plasm of the body, and the plasm of the soul, and the plasm of the spirit are at one, in the Snake *I Am*.

"I am Now.

"Was-not is a dream, and shall-be is a dream, like two separate, heavy feet.

"But Now, I Am.

"The trees put forth their leaves in their sleep, and flowering emerge out of dreams, into pure I Am.

"The birds forget the stress of their dreams, and sing aloud in the Now, I Am! I Am!

"For dreams have wings and feet, and journeys to take, and efforts to make.

"But the glimmering Snake of the Now is wingless and footless, and undivided, and perfectly coiled.

"It is thus the cat lies down, in the coil of Now, and the cow curves round her nose to her belly, lying down.

"In the feet of a dream the hare runs uphill. But when he pauses, the dream has passed, he has entered the timeless Now, and his eyes are the wide I Am.

"Only man dreams, dreams, and dreams, and changes from dream to dream, like a man who tosses on his bed.

"With his eyes and his mouth he dreams, with his hands and his feet, with phallos and heart and belly, with body and spirit and soul, in a tempest of dreams.

"And rushes from dream to dream, in the hope of the perfect dream.

"But I, I say to you, there is no dream that is perfect, for every dream has an ache and an urge, an urge and an ache.

"And nothing is perfect, save the dream pass out into the sleep, I Am.

"When the dream of the eyes is darkened, and encompassed with Now.

"And the dream of the mouth resounds in the last I Am.

"And the dream of the hands is a sleep like a bird on the sea, that sleeps and is lifted and shifted, and knows not.

"And the dreams of the feet and the toes touch the core of the world, where the Serpent sleeps.

"And the dream of the phallos reaches the great I Know Not.

"And the dream of the body is the stillness of a flower in the dark.

"And the dream of the soul is gone in the perfume of Now.

"And the dream of the spirit lapses, and lays down its head, and is still with the Morning Star.

"For each dream starts out of Now, and is accomplished in Now.

"In the core of the flower, the glimmering, wakeless Snake.

"And what falls away is a dream, and what accrues is a dream. There is always and only Now, Now and I Am."[125]

4. LIFE AND WONDER

In the course of this book a number of separate pieces

of the Laurentian aesthetic have been discussed, and it is
hoped that by now they will be seen to fit in appropriately
with each other. Tradition, the joy of being alive, sharing
in the living moment, sin, good and evil, love, sex, marriage, friendship, intuition, reason, alertness, passivity, religion, death in life, physical death, new birth, God, many
paths to God, no path to God, Self, are some of the aspects
of that aesthetic. In *The Boy in the Bush,* we read: "It
didn't matter *what* you did, so long as you were good inside
yourself."[126] The novel was not originally written by Lawrence, but the spirit of the novel as it stands—this emphasis
on being "good inside"—is his; and this particular sentence
is representative of a lot more. "Good" for Lawrence was
not the dictated right and wrong, the word of a command-
ment; it was anything an individual genuinely felt through
his intuition. In their depth, according to him, genuine
feelings are mostly creative, hence moral and binding. But
Lawrence would not limit these feelings to a particular
code or morality in advance. The good is not to be equated
with not-good; it is to be adjusted against spontaneity
(which, of course, is always moral!). Through its own
mysterious ways spontaneity strikes and whatever then follows is natural and hence good. As Leo R. Ward says in a
paper entitled "Common Ground on 'Good'":

> The important points are (a) we are and (b) we like
> to be. And it is not merely men who are and like to be, but
> animals also in their way, and plants in their way, and
> inorganic real beings also in their way. I hold that each of
> these in its way exhibits appetitus, horme, desire, by which
> appetitus, horme, desire I mean above all an inner demand,
> a thrust, a drive not imposed on the being, but native and
> integral to it; and the object basically of that demand-thrust
> is to be.[127]

It is this very urge that Lawrence's art tries to mirror. To
borrow from Mary Freeman, in Lawrence, "Each act is

to be measured, not by 'does it work,' but by 'does it further life?' "[128]

However, the onus of distinguishing between genuine feelings and spurious feelings, Lawrence kept saying, rested on the individual. In one of his critical essays, published in 1928, he wrote: "Sentimentalism is the working off on yourself of feelings you haven't really got. We all *want* to have certain feelings: feelings of love, of passionate sex, of kindliness, and so forth. Very few people really feel love, or sex passion, or kindliness, or anything else that goes at all deep. So the mass just fake these feelings inside themselves. Faked feelings! The world is all gummy with them."[129] We have his own answer to the query this may lead to: "And how? How? How shall we ever begin to educate ourselves in the feelings?" he asks. The reply is: "Not by laying down laws, or commandments, or axioms and postulates. Not even by making assertions that such and such is blessed. Not by words at all."[130] The only way an individual can learn what he really wants, and when he really wants it, is by coming to his own Self, by being himself.

Every time, any issue that we pose leads us to this end: the Self. It is a strange little spirit within us, a part of God, and it cannot be grasped by words. But it is not to be confused with the little self in us, the mentally created ideal we keep nursing all the time, that is, the ego, "the self that is begotten and born from the *idea* . . . a spurious, detestable product. This is man created from his own Logos. This is man born out of his own head. This is the self-conscious ego, the entity of fixed ideas and ideals, prancing and displaying itself like an actor."[131]

As an artist Lawrence had unlimited faith in the ability of the novel to portray the throbbing quick Self of life through its pages, as witness the number of essays he wrote on the subject (particularly "Morality and the Novel" and "Why the Novel Matters"). He felt that the one criterion of a great novelist was whether he could portray the gleam of life, the glory of the Self in his characters, or not. And so, if a man cannot hear the voice of the Self in him, let him go, he suggests, and read a "real" novel first: "If we can't hear the cries far down in our own forests of dark veins, we can look in the real novels, and there listen-in. Not listen to the didactic statements of the author, but to the low, calling cries of the characters, as they wander in the dark woods of their destiny."[132] That should help him. It is for each reader of his novels to assess how far his work lives up to that expectation. But this was the object he had in view. This was the aim of his art.

And the profundity, the wealth of his genius is seen in the recognition, the preference that he always gave to physical life over physical death. Even when he was himself dying, and even when apparently he was busy with the Death poems in his mind, the artist in him could still see that physical death, though unavoidable and though it led one to the unknown, could perhaps never allow him again the play of the imagination, the play of the craftsman, and as such was perhaps not as rich in colors as the living universe. As the man in *The Man Who Died* comprehends: "And the destiny of life seemed more fierce and compulsive to him even than the destiny of death. The doom of a death was a shadow compared to the raging destiny of life, the determined surge of life."[133] Compare this with the negligence and the dissolution of the ebb of life of the man in Lawrence's "The Man Who Loved Islands" and we can form some idea of how both life and death in their diverse ways had a strange pull for him and how he moved from one to the other in his stories. Lawrence the religious thinker clearly sees that death is a gateway to the unknown. In *Women in Love,* Ursula tells herself, "To die is to move on with the invisible. To die is also a joy, a joy of submitting to that which is greater than the known, namely, the pure unknown."[134] It is in this vein—"but better die than live mechanically a life that is a repetition of repetitions"—that the man in "The Man Who Loved Islands" goes and willingly embraces death; in this vein that the woman in "The Woman Who Rode Away" embraces extinction. But for Lawrence the artist, one need not have to physically die to have the joy of the unknown. The unknown is ever there in life itself; every new moment, in its newness, is nothing but a representation of it. One needs only the capacity to die to the past moments to enjoy the richness of the new.

We started this book with a chapter on Joy, the Delight of creation, and it is fitting that our study of Self should lead us to a similar joy. The art of Lawrence is the outcome of unreserved reverence for this wonder of life. He told Jessie Chambers once, "I think *wonder* is one of the finest words in our language";[135] he seems to have been captivated by the sense of magic implied by it, the sense of strangeness. At the end of his career, in "Hymns in a Man's Life," we find him writing:

When all comes to all, the most precious element in life is wonder. Love is a great emotion, and power is power. But both love and power are based on wonder. Love without wonder is a sensational affair, and power without wonder is mere force and compulsion. The one universal element in consciousness which is fundamental to life is the element of wonder. You cannot help feeling it in a bean as it starts to grow and pulls itself out of its jacket. You cannot help feeling it in the glisten of the nucleus of the amoeba. You recognise it, willy-nilly, in an ant busily tugging at a straw; in a rook, as it walks the frosty grass. They all have their own obstinate will. But also they all live with a sense of wonder. Plant consciousness, insect consciousness, fish consciousness, animal consciousness, all are related by one permanent element, which we may call the religious element inherent in all life, even in a flea: the sense of wonder. That is our sixth sense. And it is the *natural* religious sense.[136] (Lawrence's emphasis)

And between his beginning and his end, it was wonder
again that really attracted him: wonder of a new-born
baby, wonder of a new-born day, wonder of a new-born
Self.

> Creation is a great flood, forever flowing, in lovely and
> terrible waves. In everything, the shimmer of creation, and
> never the finality of the created. Never the distinction be-
> tween God and God's creation, or between Spirit and Matter.
> Everything, everything is the wonderful shimmer of creation,
> it may be a deadly shimmer like lightning or the anger in the
> little eyes of the bear, it may be the beautiful shimmer of
> the moving deer, or the pine-boughs softly swaying under
> snow. Creation contains the unspeakably terrifying enemy,
> the unspeakably lovely friend, as the maiden who brings us
> our food in dead of winter, by her passion of tender wist-
> fulness. Yet even this tender wistfulness is the fearful danger
> of the wild creatures, deer and bear and buffalo, which find
> their death in it.
> There is, in our sense of the word, no God. But all is
> godly. There is no Great Mind directing the universe. Yet
> the mystery of creation, the wonder and fascination of cre-
> ation shimmers in every leaf and stone, in every thorn and
> bud, in the fangs of the rattle-snake, and in the soft eyes of
> a fawn. Things utterly opposite are still pure wonder of
> creation, the yell of the mountain-lion, and the breeze in
> the aspen leaves. The Apache warrior in his war-paint, shriek-
> ing the war-cry and cutting the throats of old women, still
> he is part of the mystery of creation. He is godly as the
> growing corn. And the mystery of creation makes us sharpen
> the knives and point the arrows in utmost determination
> against him. It must be so. It is part of the wonder. And to
> every part of the wonder we must answer in kind.[137]

It must be noticed that wonder utterly excludes curiosity. The mind will miss its astounding swell if it is preoccupied. Most of all, it will immediately vanish if we try
to see the created world through a man-made pattern. Nature is red in tooth and claw, and, knowing the expression,
we still wish to believe in this-must-be and that-must-not-

be. There is an inborn urge in every created being, natural to the nature of that being; in the fulfillment of that urge, however repugnant it may be to our man-made moral sensibility, it is the wonder of creation that is fulfilled; it is the Self in that particular type of life *being* itself, being the *is* in itself. Lawrence found this is-ness in the Mexicans, as is evident in one of his essays on them, just quoted from. And he found the same is-ness in the ancient Etruscans, as revealed in their tombs:

> So all creatures are potential in their own way, a myriad manifold consciousness storming with contradictions and oppositions that are eternal, beyond all mental reconciliation. We can know the living world only symbolically. Yet every consciousness, the rage of the lion, and the venom of the snake, *is*, and therefore is divine. All emerges out of the unbroken circle with its nucleus, the germ, the One, the god, if you like to call it so. And man, with his soul and his personality, emerges in eternal connection with all the rest. The blood-stream is one, and unbroken, yet storming with oppositions and contradictions.[138] (Lawrence's emphasis).

And he would have liked to see the same is-ness accepted and acknowledged all over the world.

5

The Fourth Dimension of Existence

The title for these concluding remarks is borrowed from D. H. Lawrence; the expression "the fourth dimension of existence" combines the three aspects of Lawrence that we have been discussing. He makes use of it repeatedly in some of the essays included in his volume *Reflections on the Death of a Porcupine*. Reference to two of them, "Aristocracy" and "Blessed are the Powerful," was made above in the opening chapter. The import of all of them is the same: the glory of the man who has his being in tune with the unknown. Such a man, according to Lawrence, while living in the spatial universe of length, breadth, and height, is yet above it. He lives in the "fourth" dimension, the creative universe.

Here, according to Lawrence, is "the inexorable law of life":

1. Any creature that attains to its own fullness of being, its own *living* self, becomes unique, a non-pareil. It has its place in the fourth dimension, the heaven of existence, and there it is perfect, it is beyond comparison.

2. At the same time, every creature exists in time and space. And in time and space it exists relatively to all other existence, and can never be absolved. Its existence impinges on other existences, and is itself impinged upon. And in the struggle for existence, if an effort on the part of any one type or species or order of life, can finally destroy the other species then the destroyer is of a more vital cycle of existence than the one destroyed. (When speaking of existence we always

259

speak in types, species, not individuals. Species exist. But even an individual dandelion has *being*.)

3. The force which we call *vitality*, and which is the determining factor in the struggle for existence, is, however, derived also from the fourth dimension. That is to say, the ultimate source of all vitality is in that other dimension, or region, where the dandelion blooms, and which men have called heaven, and which now they call the fourth dimension: which is only a way of saying that it is not to be reckoned in terms of space and time.

4. The primary way, in our existence, to get vitality, is to absorb it from living creatures lower than ourselves. It is thus transformed into a new and higher creation. (There are many ways of absorbing: devouring food is one way, love is often another. The best way is a pure relationship, which includes the *being* on each side, and which allows the transfer to take place in a living flow, enhancing the life in both beings.)

5. No creature is fully itself till it is, like the dandelion, opened in the bloom of pure relationship to the sun, the entire living cosmos.[1]

The fourth dimension thus is a state in which, according to Lawrence, a person is completely himself, one with the nature of his being, and is at the same time open to a living relationship with everything else in the universe. It is a state which, as brought out in the preceding chapters of this work, signifies a total acceptance of life in all its forms. An individual who keeps himself open to the wonder of existence and who acknowledges the beauty of the physical world, gives implicit recognition to the power of the unknown from which the known ever springs. Lawrence writes, however, "Only the matter suddenly enters the fourth dimension."[2] The idea, as may be obvious by now, is that this state, of "fourth" dimension, of *being*, cannot be achieved by effort. For the living moment is unpredictable and hence it cannot be faced through pre-

conceived notions; it can only be lived. Basically, Lawrence inveighs against jargon—whether the jargon of science, or art, or religion—because jargon takes man away
from the living reality; it reduces the individual to a mere
machine, a robot, with fixed and automatic reactions to the
multifarious challenges of life. As V. de Sola Pinto so
aptly puts it, "Lawrence is the prophet of the free soul,
the unique individual as opposed to the mass."[3] To quote
Pinto again: "his is a creed of the salvation of the individual soul: the dignity of man saved by divine grace without the intervention of priest and Church."[4]

Thus, even in Lawrence's criticism of Christianity, what
really emerges is not a condemnation of the Christian
ethics but of the Christian dogma. In effect, it is condemnation of the mechanized manner in which most religions of the world are practiced. Phrases and words are
torn from their context, are divested of their true, living
meaning, and are used in an inane, lifeless way by clergy
and layman. As Lawrence comments in one of his reviews:

It all depends what you make of the word God. To most
of us today it is a fetish-word, dead, yet useful for invocation.
It is not a question of Jesus. It is a question of God, Almighty
God. We have to square ourselves with the very words. And
to do so, we must rid them of their maddening moral import,
and give them back—Almighty God—the old vital meaning:
strength and glory and honour and might and beauty and
wisdom. These are the continual attributes of Almighty
God, in the far past. And the same today, the god who enters
us and imbues us with his strength and glory and might and
honour and beauty and wisdom, this is a god we are eager
to worship. And this is the god of the craftsman who makes
things well, so that the presence of the god enters into the
thing made. The workman making a pair of shoes with
happy absorption in skill is imbued with the god of strength
and honour and beauty, undeniable. Happy, intense absorption in any work, which is to be brought as near to perfection
as possible, this is a state of being with God, and the men
who have not known it have missed life itself.[5]

E. M. W. Tillyard in *Some Mythical Elements in English Literature* relates Lawrence to the eighteenth-century myth of "retirement" from life, from the busy world, in order to contemplate the beauty of the divine. He comments: "The classic example of the same process is D. H. Lawrence, whose life from one side could be called a series of unsuccessful attempts to find the right place to retire to for the exercise of the particular forms of religion he came to profess."[6] Lawrence undoubtedly had a desire to found a colony, but it was not any particular form of religion that he wished to practice there. He felt that the present mechanized society left no scope for the freedom of the soul, and so the best way open to man was to get away from it and begin again. But for Lawrence the religion of eternal life was life itself. Even the humblest of occupations, as the passage cited above from him shows, had for him the touch of the divine in it. For, when a man is completely absorbed in the fulfillment of the living moment, physically as well as mentally, he is reflecting the great glory of God in himself. In that complete absorption —whether with the work in hand, or with play, or with physical and spiritual fulfillment—the individual transcends the barriers of time and space, barriers of the spatial universe, and enters the "fourth" dimension of existence, a heaven of peace, or what the Hindus call *shantih*. Delight of creation, love and marriage, and self-realization are therefore all dependent in Lawrence on the individual living in that "other" mode of existence, the creative mode. For while living in the fourth dimension, the individual becomes a veritable God himself, a part of the Infinite. Nothing else can then equal him in his own distinct beauty and magnificence and joy. He becomes singular in the power that he derives from such an existence. He becomes unique.

Before closing I propose to place here two more ex-

tracts, one from one of Lawrence's essays and the other
from *Apocalypse,* which show how much of a serious artist
Lawrence was, and how much he believed in the beauty of
the material that his art handled.

I quote first from the essay, "Why the Novel Matters":

Nothing is important but life. And for myself, I can
absolutely see life nowhere but in the living. Life with a
capital L is only man alive. Even a cabbage in the rain is
cabbage alive. All things that are alive are amazing. And
all things that are dead are subsidiary to the living. Better
a live dog than a dead lion. But better a live lion than a live
dog. *C'est la vie!*

It seems impossible to get a saint, or a philosopher, or a
scientist, to stick to this simple truth. They are all, in a
sense, renegades. The saint wishes to offer himself up as
spiritual food for the multitude. Even Francis of Assisi
turns himself into a sort of angel-cake, of which any one
may take a slice. But an angel-cake is rather less than man
alive. And poor St. Francis might well apologize to his body,
when he is dying: "Oh, pardon me, my body, the wrong I
did you through the years!" It was no wafer, for others to
eat.

The philosopher, on the other hand, because he can think,
decides that nothing but thoughts matter. It is as if a rabbit,
because he can make little pills, should decide that nothing
but little pills matter. As for the scientist, he has absolutely
no use for me so long as I am man alive. To the scientist,
I am dead. He puts under the microscope a bit of dead of
me, and calls it me. He takes me to pieces, and says first one
piece, and then another piece, is me. My heart, my liver,
my stomach have all been scientifically me, according to the
scientist; and nowadays I am either a brain, or nerves, or
glands, or something more up-to-date in the tissue line.

Now I absolutely flatly deny that I am a soul, or a body,
or a mind, or an intelligence, or a brain, or a nervous system,
or a bunch of glands, or any of the rest of these bits of me.
The whole is greater than the part. And therefore, I, who
am man alive, am greater than my soul, or spirit, or body,
or mind, or consciousness, or anything else that is merely a
part of me. I am a man, and alive. I am man alive, and as
long as I can, I intend to go on being man alive.

For this reason I am a novelist. And being a novelist, I consider myself superior to the saint, the scientist, the philosopher, and the poet, who are all great masters of different bits of man alive, but never get the whole hog.[7]

It is a notable piece in defence of the novelist as the *supreme* artist. The emphasis, it should be noticed, is on "wholeness." Not that Lawrence decries or disowns the individual components—soul, mind, and the rest; he simply says no one of them is as important as the living man. It is the cry of the artist against "excess" in life, in favor of the type of character that Lawrence creates in *The Man Who Died*.

And now I quote from *Apocalypse*:

What man most passionately wants is his living wholeness and his living unison, not his own isolate salvation of his "soul." Man wants his physical fulfilment first and foremost, since now, once and once only, he is in the flesh and potent. For man, the vast marvel is to be alive. For man, as for flower and beast and bird, the supreme triumph is to be most vividly, most perfectly alive. Whatever the unborn and the dead may know, they cannot know the beauty, the marvel of being alive in the flesh. The dead may look after the afterwards. But the magnificent here and now of life in the flesh is ours, and ours alone, and ours only for a time. We ought to dance with rapture that we should be alive and in the flesh, and part of the living, incarnate cosmos. I am part of the sun as my eye is part of me. That I am part of the earth my feet know perfectly, and my blood is part of the sea. My soul knows that I am part of the human race, my soul is an organic part of the great human soul, as my spirit is part of my nation. In my own self, I am part of my family. There is nothing of me that is alone and absolute except in my mind, and we shall find that the mind has no existence by itself, it is only the glitter of the sun on the surface of the waters. So that my individualism is really an illusion, I am part of the great whole, and I can never escape. But I can deny my connections, break them, and become a fragment. Then I am wretched.

What we want is to destroy our false, inorganic connections . . . and re-establish the living organic connections with the cosmos, the sun and earth, with mankind and nation and family. Start with the sun, and the rest will slowly, slowly happen.[8]

Does all this sound hysterical? We go back to R. P. Blackmur (see Chapter 4) and his misinterpretation and misrepresentation of Lawrence. As Richard Ellmann says of Blackmur's remarks: "But surely this was not what Lawrence meant. He was distinguishing the archetypal self, purged of everyday accidents, from the self-consciousness of an inhibited young man bound by a particular space and time."[9] If it was the word "demon" or "ghost" in Lawrence that startled R. P. Blackmur, he should have understood that it could be an essential word in the vocabulary of an artist to signify the creative spirit in himself. Criticizing Blackmur's conclusions, Pinto states in "Poet without a Mask": "This seems to me to be a travesty of Lawrence's meaning. By the 'demon' Lawrence certainly did not mean a mere 'outburst of personal feeling.' He meant what he calls in the Foreword to *Fantasia of the Unconscious* 'pure passionate experience,' or experience at a deeper level than the personal."[10] In a lecture now published, "Theory and Function of *Duende*," the Spanish poet Lorca states that no art can ever emerge unless the artist is moved by *duende*—a ghost, a demon inside him—first. He quotes another well-known Spanish artist as telling a singer, "You have voice, you have style, but you will never be a success because you have no duende." One of the important paragraphs in his lecture is: "Thus the *duende* is a power and not a behaviour, it is a struggle and not a concept. I have heard an old guitarist master say: 'The *duende* is not in the throat; the *duende* surges up from the soles of the feet.' Which means that it is not a matter of ability, but of real live form; of blood; of ancient culture; of creative action."[11]

Lawrence was one of the most sensible of men and a most versatile genius in that his mind saw life in pliability, not in rigid "consistency." Pliability is the very law of nature. "Start with the sun," he says; start with anything; it does not matter. What does matter is contemplation without curiosity about the result; not "becoming" but "being"; openness to the divine, living in the fourth dimension; intuition ("an act of pure attention"; "a man in his wholeness wholly attending").

> Every real discovery made, every serious and significant decision ever reached, was reached and made by divination. The soul stirs, and makes an act of pure attention, and that is a discovery.[12]

Lawrence was a great admirer of Herman Melville's *Moby Dick*, particularly of the might and the glory of the big whale described there. In the best of his own passages the image of Moby-Dick surfacing comes to my mind, huge and vital and uproariously naughty, lashing the waters with his big powerful tail, blowing mountain-high spouts of jets into the air, and constantly rolling, constantly turning, now here, now there, often angry, often silent, but agile as ever, resplendent as ever, carrying his shining hump with ease and pride and gushing forth, ever gushing forth, in sheer delight, sheer joy, sheer power of being alive. Lawrence was a Moby-Dick himself. So is his work.

Appendix

Lawrence and *Lady Chatterley's Lover:*
the Chronicle of "Battered Warriors"
(Reprinted from *Quest*, No. 27, Oct/Dec 1960) *

Probably no writer has ever been condemned more on
hearsay than D. H. Lawrence. Till the other day the novel
with which his name is generally associated was not available in English bookshops in its complete and unmuti-
lated form. Several of his other important books, like the
posthumously published volume of essays entitled *Phoenix*
and his philosophical documents called *Psychoanalysis
and the Unconscious* and *Fantasia of the Unconscious,*
have long been out of print.** And yet, there are men who
believe that D. H. Lawrence is a "horribly obscene" author. Somehow a myth has grown about his lewdness,
and such people find it thrilling to keep the illusion alive.
After all, they have heard of their supremely good and
great writers but of none supremely evil, and the name of
so-widely-spoken-about Lawrence, therefore, satisfies a
deep romantic longing in their mind. It will perhaps be
years before such a public can allow the man, whom a
capable critic like Leavis has called "the greatest creative
writer in English of our time," his due. But let us hope
that with the publication in England of the unexpurgated
edition of *Lady Chatterley's Lover* (thirty years after the
death of the author), people will be willing to give up
some of their superstitions about him. For if they read the

---

* This article was published before the Lady Chatterley Trial took
place in London in the winter of 1960.
** All reprinted since.

267

book carefully, they will find that Lawrence is neither vulgar nor obscene, only a little more honest and a little more outspoken than most writers.

The first feeling that comes when one has read the complete *Lady Chatterley's Lover* is that of dismay and disappointment. For compared with Lawrence's best novels it appears to be a poor and sadly inferior work—inferior in characterization, inferior in plot, and inferior in achievement. Not only that, it looks on the face of it a glaringly unethical book. It is the story of a woman who leaves her husband at a time when he desperately needs her help (he is a cripple), and goes away with another man. From what we see, Clifford Chatterley is a good husband to Constance Chatterley in every accepted sense of the term. He tends to her needs with particular care and is fond of her. Unfortunately he cannot give her any sex life, but this is not because of disease or impotence: it is because of an accident, a wound he suffered during the war. In the circumstances one would expect a wife to give him love and devotion and comfort. Accidents are a normal feature of human life, and if, because of one of them, a party to a marriage is physically incapacitated, all the codes of ethics presume that the other party will do everything possible to alleviate his suffering. But Constance behaves ignobly; she first deceives her husband with another man and then separates from him to marry a gamekeeper with whom she thinks she is in love.

This is, however, not the whole truth, and we must take a deeper and more sympathetic account of Lawrence's mind to see what he meant to do in this book.

It may sound a little new to those who have not read much of Lawrence, but he was, in his own right, perhaps the greatest seer of this century. For the main theme of all his works, from *The White Peacock* down to *Lady Chatterley's Lover,* is not "sex" but "self." There is no other writer of our day who has emphasized so much, repeatedly, the need of a thorough spiritual basis for every action of our day-to-day existence. T. S. Eliot has accused him of heresy, but as V de S. Pinto has pointed out in *D. H. Lawrence: Prophet of the Midlands,* he had more of the living tradition in him than Eliot himself. In fact his heresy amounts to nothing more than asserting that, though Christian culture (Eliot's antonym for heresy) is great, reality is not essentially limited to *one* type of faith or to one type of teaching alone. He goes further, and believes that all these "faiths" are in a way an impediment to understanding reality, for the approach of the intellect is essentially limited. Almost like the Vedantins, he time and again says that the infinite—God, self, reality, whatever one may call it—can never be comprehended in its entirety by the finite, that is, the mind. In his own words, "all law, all knowledge holds good for that which already exists in the created world. But there is no law, no knowledge of the unknown which is to take place" (*Phoenix*). So knowledge of any one type, be it Christian knowledge or any other, only limits the scope of reality, which, if it is to have the name of reality at all, must perforce be of a nature surpassing the boundaries of man-made definitions.

This is a very profound conclusion and it shows the depth of Lawrence's understanding. Apart from Wordsworth, few English writers display such a wide and magnificent range of feelings, and we know that Wordsworth was promptly rebuked by his contemporaries for what they thought of as pantheistic utterances. Having established for himself that reality has to be envisaged in a shape and manner that can be all-comprehensive and universal, Lawrence sets about finding *some* common factor in life to which men and women of all races, indeed living creatures of every kind, may be paying obedience from a natural inclination, without any compulsion or binding or fear created by the intellect (in the last resort, even our devotion to an anthropomorphic form of religion is

mostly the result of fear: fear of the hereafter). Here he
parts company with Wordsworth, and where Wordsworth,
in spite of his remarkable vision and power, still sees the
life of the "spirit" as something distinct and apart from
the life of the "body," in Lawrence the two become one.
("Why do you persist in separating soul and body? I can't
tell, in myself, or in anybody, one from the other." D. H.
Lawrence in a letter to Mrs. Rachel Annand Taylor.)
Since the infinite can never be known as infinite, Lawrence says that man must look for it in its manifestations
as the finite. This obviously includes a reverence for every
created being, for every created thing, but most of all it
means a reverence for the constant and recurrent drama
of creation in which every created being is busy. Birds,
beasts, animals; plants, trees; man: generations rise, reproduce, and then perish. And this endless dance is going
on around us everywhere, all the time, so fascinating that
we are compelled to join in it by a natural hunger and
urge of the body.

Lawrence thereby comes to the alarming but apparently true conclusion that the only common agent that
can satisfy all the requirements of universality is sex. He
sees in sex a divine gift, a divine power; power that never
exhausts itself and is a source of constant perpetuation of
life. And so, Lawrence argues, before a man can have any
realization of the deeper mysteries of life, he must first
have a full and thorough realization of this divine gift in
man. It may be borne in mind that under no condition
is sex mentioned by him as the end of life. For him the
end is deeper, much deeper; it is the realization of self.
But a man cannot realize his "self" until he has bathed
in all the glories of the created world, *including* the sexual glory. Here is a beauty of the universe that can be
intuitively felt by all of us. It requires no other qualifica-
tions except honesty and personal integrity. And when
one has realized this power, the way is open for one to go

further, for in healthy sex we have gone the nearest to the creator and may go still nearer. To quote from him, "God, Almighty God, is the father, and in fatherhood man draws nearest to him. In the act of love, in the act of begetting, Man is with God and of God. Such is the Law" (*Phoenix*).

For Lawrence the created world, the world of males and females and the desire between them, is a symbol of divine joy. We are "hollow men," not because we have lost contact with the spirit (the intellectualized version of the spirit as offered by organized religions and T. S. Eliot), but because we have lost contact with the body, the healthy body with its healthy needs. It is a process that started many generations back, when man began formulating his knowledge into neatly outlined "theories," and is still continuing. The present civilization, Lawrence would say, is thus suffering from a sort of emotional neurosis, as the result of constant inhibitions and suppressions to which men have subjected their natural instincts, preferring to live by acquired habits. And of all the acquired habits, none has done more harm to us than orthodox theology, which insists on making a sharp distinction between the spirit and the body, saying that the one is clean and the other unclean, implying thereby that if we follow one of these we have to give up the other, implying further thereby that no one should dream of entering the world of the spirit without surrendering the world of the body. There is a willful conditioning of the mind in such an approach, a deliberate superimposition of evil on a simple, elementary process of nature; for it leaves no way out for man except to regard the body as evil or as synonymous with sin. As is clear, this amounts to an allegation of inherent contradiction in the design of the universe; that is to say that the laws by which this design lives and flourishes are morally unsound. Lawrence, on the other hand, rebels against this basically unwholesome outlook and looks upon the human body as a sacred temple, where to every man and every woman, reality is being constantly revealed, every day, every moment, provided we pay to the body, the temple, its rightful homage. "When the two clasp hands, a moment, male and female, clasp hands and are one, the poppy, the gay poppy flies into flower again; and when the two fling their arms about each other, the moonlight runs and clashes against the shadow; and when the two toss back their hair, all the larks break out singing; and when they kiss on the mouth, a lovely human utterance is heard again—and so it is" (*Phoenix*).

Thus healthy sex is Lawrence's road to sanity and self-knowledge. Not for a moment does he refer to it in an irreverent tone. His friends testify to what a puritan and scrupulously moral man he was in life, and how anything said or done in a vulgar manner used to shock him. Though he eloped with a married woman, his view was that he was going to *marry* her and not have an affair with her. Frieda Lawrence records in *Not I, But the Wind* that when she was still living with her former husband, she once invited Lawrence to spend a night with her when her husband was away from home, and Lawrence refused, saying that that would be immoral as she was not yet his wife. Subsequently, when they were married, all his life he remained faithful to her and though he came to know a number of women, there is no evidence of his having had any sexual relation with any of them. The whole point of Lawrence is missed if we do not see that when Lawrence talks of sex, he means not the variety of sexual experience, but the intensity of the experience, the intensity between two persons devoted to each other for a lifetime.

Thus he concerns himself almost exclusively with people who are either already married or are going to marry; it is a treatment of sex within the confines of the family. In the best of his stories, the man or the woman is faithful to a particular partner—at least, that is the idea—and within the sphere of that exclusively limited and select emotional field he ranges his discussions. In contrast, most of the modern novelists treat sex as a game of musical chairs: constant change, new partners, the sooner the better. And even within the sphere of the family that he explores, the emphasis is on normal sex; in spite of what Richard Aldington says, there is hardly any instance of sexual perversion, violence, or morbidity dwelt on at length anywhere, in the whole range of his creative writing.

This was the man who has been painted as a sexual maniac by people half acquainted with his work. His novels, poems, short stories, plays, and essays are nothing but a long hymn to the beauty of the created world and to the process of creation. It was in this vein that he wrote his masterpieces, *The Rainbow*, the finest novel of marriage in the whole history of English literature, and *Women in Love*. And it was in this vein that he wrote *Lady Chatterley's Lover*.

But as already stated, *Lady Chatterley's Lover* is, comparatively, a poor work of art, and it is a great irony of fate that Lawrence should be remembered primarily by a book that is not his best. First, as mentioned before, there is a major weakness in the very conception of the plot, in the sense that Sir Clifford Chatterley is the victim of an accident and, as such, his inability to give sexual life to Constance Chatterley is not because of any bodily sickness that would justify Constance leaving him. Second, we see that the story and the characters do not develop as naturally as in Lawrence's other books. We become increasingly conscious of it as we proceed with the novel. Practically everything appears to be prejudged, as if the novelist were arguing from a fixed point of view. This is particularly obvious in his treatment of Clifford Chatterley, where he sees to it that in whatever dramatic situation he places Clifford, whether it is an argument with his sister-in-law, a discussion with his wife, or an encounter with his gamekeeper—notice the Chair incident in the garden—he comes out badly and humiliated. Finally, Lawrence uses in this novel expressions that are, by themselves, normally considered improper and unbecoming.

We must not ignore the fact, however, that when Lawrence wrote *Lady Chatterley's Lover*, he was a dying man. For years he had been persecuted by ununderstanding critics and cruel officials, and slowly he had grown very, very bitter about it. He knew he had not much longer to live and this was perhaps his only chance of hitting back at his adversaries. It was partly in this mood of retaliation that the book was planned and, as his letters of this period show, he was looking forward to shocking the world with what he was writing ("Frankly a phallic novel," "a bomb," "a flood of urge," etc.). This does not indicate lack of seriousness of purpose, or any sacrifice of principles in his effort to shock. On the other hand, the novel was to be a complete proclamation of what Lawrence believed. But it was to be so in as outspoken and frank a language as possible. "It's what the world would call very improper. But you know it's not really improper—I always labour at the same thing, to make the sex relation valid and precious, instead of shameful. And this novel is the furthest I have gone" (*Letters*). This explains the "prejudged" nature of the story, to which I have referred above. Lawrence deliberately meant it to be a didactic book. It is the sort of work that the French call *engagé*—a polemical work; Lawrence wrote it to prove a certain point. And it was in this zeal, in his desire to go "the furthest," that he employed words and expressions that he, as a great artist, could surely have avoided and yet achieved his objective.

For, in spite of what Lawrence's defenders may say, in the heat of the debate Lawrence overstepped his mark and went too far. Certain words connected with the functions and organs of sex are not commonly used in written English and a frequent reference to them appears objectionable and undesirable. In the privacy of their love and passion, a man and a woman may use any expression they find mutually satisfying, and probably they do. But Lawrence's professed aim was to rehabilitate these words in the everyday language. Now, language is subject to change. Perhaps there was a time when public usage of these words had an innocence about it, but in the course of the last few hundred years it has come to acquire a meaning associated with impropriety. A time may come again when the old innocence returns. But for that we have to start with the deed and not with the word; a mere chanting of these words at a greater speed will not usher in the change. Once our actions acquire the tenderness Lawrence has in mind, the language may evolve toward what he is aiming at. But as it is, one recoils from such open references. We may as well admit that there is no reasonable argument possible in favor of Lawrence on this ground. Even the plea of artistic necessity cannot be justifiably offered. Lawrence does not resort to this type of language in *The Rainbow*, for instance, and he makes his meaning as clear there—even clearer—as in *Lady Chatterley's Lover*.

But, as is obvious, this is a matter of terminology, and terminology and words alone do not make a word obscene; it is the intention behind them that really matters. And it is here that Lawrence has been wronged so badly: judged by the motive of the artist and the purpose of the whole book, *Lady Chatterley's Lover* is, by any standard, *not* an obscene book. After all, there is a lot of sex, several taboo words and expressions, even in the Bible. There is a lot of sex in the *Mahabharata*. And yet it would be folly to regard the Bible or the *Mahabharata* as obscene. Considered anew, we find *Lady Chatterley's Lover* a serious and moral novel (moral in pertaining to right and wrong conduct), and barring the drawbacks listed above, based on the general pattern of the Laurentian approach to life. "A delicate and tender phallic novel," Lawrence calls it, and he is right; dealing with sex, for that is the way to ultimate fulfillment, but with "phallic consciousness," not with "cerebral sex-consciousness" (Lawrence's words). It deals ultimately with the impact of science and industry and regimented intellect on man, for it is these allied factors which determine whether sex in our homes is going to be of one kind or the other. It is improper in places, but not dirty. And it is honest.

It is the profound misfortune of Constance Chatterley that she cannot experience the benefit of this phallic reality of which Lawrence talks so religiously. (The term "phallic" with Lawrence does not refer to the sexual moments of life alone but to the whole span of our existence, where the vision is that of relaxation, repose and rest as contrasted with tension and excitement.) Her world with her husband is a world of tension. I have earlier noted the somewhat disturbing fact that she leaves a crippled husband and therefore shirks her duty. To be fair to her (and to Lawrence), the fact is that only after a long life with Clifford does she realize that she is slowly drying up into nothingness and contemplates separation from him. She is a dutiful wife to him and the first half of the work describes in detail the care with which she looks after Clifford. Slowly, however, the emptiness of her own life, the void in which she is living, grows and almost stifles her.

Wragby was there, the servants . . . but spectral, not really existing. Connie went for walks in the park, and in the woods that joined the park, and enjoyed the solitude and the mystery, kicked the brown leaves of autumn, and picked the primroses of spring. But it was all a dream; or rather it was like the simulacrum of reality. The oak-leaves were to her like oak-leaves seen ruffling in a mirror; she herself was a figure somebody had read about, picking primroses that were only shadows or memories, or words— no substance to her or anything . . . no touch, no contact!

This feeling of nothingness keeps mounting in her:

Poor Connie! As the years drew on it was the fear of nothingness in her life that affected her. Clifford's mental life and hers gradually began to feel like nothingness. Their marriage, their integrated life based on a habit of intimacy, that he talked about: there were days when it all became utterly blank and nothing. It was words, just so many words. The only reality was nothingness, and over it a hypocrisy of words.

And again:

Nothingness! To accept the great nothingness of life seemed to be the one end of living. All the many busy and important little things that make up the grand sum-total of nothingness!

And finally, almost inevitably:

A sense of rebellion smouldered in Connie. What was the good of it all? What was the good of her sacrifice, her devoting her life to Clifford? What was she serving, after all? A cold spirit of vanity, that had no warm human contacts.

This gradual change is admirably conveyed to the reader, intermingled with pertinent comments by Lawrence himself. One cannot help feeling for Constance Chatterley in her loneliness, particularly in the long scene where she undresses herself in her room and looks at her naked body: the hanging drooping ruin in every line of her, in every curve, in every muscle.

It made her feel immensely depressed and hopeless. What

hope was there? She was old, old at twenty-seven, with no
gleam and sparkle in the flesh. Old through neglect and
denial, yes denial.

Here is the hunger of the body, to which Lawrence had
referred in the sequence of poems, *Look! We Have Come
Through!* ("Yet there it is, the hunger which comes upon
us, / which we must learn to satisfy with pure, real satisfaction; / or perish, there is no alternative.") It is not a
random, perfunctory sexual contact that this young, ripe-
like-corn-but-rotting woman requires (this explains her
dissatisfaction at her relationship with Michaelis, her husband's friend). It is the day-in-and-day-out replenishing,
the permanent living within the confines of a healthy,
phallic atmosphere that is her longing. Because of this
denial she is losing her hold on herself; she is not par-
taking of the ecstasies of the self; she is entering a spiritual
death.

And so, with the true ritual of sex lacking, her marriage
to Clifford comes to an end. Mellors—who in his life is an
equally battered human being—is only an excuse, a form
of incentive, who hurries the process. If it had not been
he, there would have been someone else like him, sooner
or later. For this is an unnatural living together of two
persons and it cannot go on.

But it is time we saw *Lady Chatterley's Lover* in its true
perspective. Its impish title has trailed the weary name of
Lawrence far too long ("D. H. Lawrence, author of *Lady
Chatterley's Lover*"—that is how people refer to him).
It is true that the book offers a searching analysis of the
ills of the human psyche. But it stands to the best of
Lawrence—*The Rainbow* and *Women in Love*—in the
same relation, if one may use a comparison, as Tolstoy's
Resurrection (another polemical novel) stands in relation to *War and Peace* and *Anna Karenina;* and we may
remember this while assessing his greatness as an artist.

Nevertheless, a complete study of the book (not a study in patches) leaves a distinct impression of the author's forthright honesty, sound sense of judgment, and moral intelligence. For that alone, it deserves serious consideration. In *Apropos of Lady Chatterley's Lover,* Lawrence later said that the impotence of Sir Clifford was symbolic: it signified the physical and spiritual death of modern man, living in contact not with the soil but with the machine. Treated symbolically, Mellors represents this man from the soil, and in his victory over Clifford and his success with Constance, the novel thus is, in the last resort, a study of the triumph of nature over anti-nature, life over anti-life.

Notes

NOTES TO CHAPTER 1

1. AH, p. 350.
2. MDL, p. 18.
3. EB, p. 175.
4. EB, p. 86.
5. V, X, cxxix, 1–8.
6. V, I, i, 8–9.
7. V, I, 1, 1–4.
8. V, I, cxiii, 2, 17.
9. V, VII, xlix, 1–2.
10. V, X, cxxvii, 1–2.
11. V, X, clxviii, 3–4.
12. DHL.12, pp. 230–31. ("Aristocracy")
13. DHL.12, p. 151. ("Blessed Are the Powerful")
14. DHL.12, p. 151. (*Ibid.*)
15. DHL.12, p. 152. (*Ibid.*)
16. MH, p. 13.
17. U.1, II, 6.
18. U.1, II, 8.
19. DHL.12, p. 238. ("Aristocracy")
20. DHL.15, p. 116. ("The Risen Lord")
21. SR.1, p. 352.
22. EB, p. 112.
23. DHL.15, p. 113. ("The Risen Lord")
24. A.1, p. 64.
25. A.1, p. 66.
26. DHL.21, p. 696. ("Life")

NOTES TO CHAPTER 2

1. CW, p. 162.
2. NU.1, p. 2.
3. TSE.1, p. 14. ("Tradition and Individual Talent")
4. TSE.4, p. 121.
5. TSE.3, p. 27.
6. VSP.1, p. 5.

7. VSP.1, p. 9.
8. TSE.1, p. 14.
9. TSE.5, p. 5. ("To whom I owe the leaping delight. . . .")
10. SR.2, p. 44.
11. DHL.17, p. 2.
12. BR.1, p. 50.
13. BR.1, p. 51.
14. BR.1, p. 63.
15. DHL.21, p. 768. ("Introduction to Pictures")
16. DHL.21, p. 765. (*Ibid.*)
17. FC, p. 28.
18. NPW, p. 34.
19. DK, p. 276.
20. Z, p. 130.
21. Z, p. 147.
22. Z, p. 155.
23. Z, p. 136.
24. VL, p. 108.
25. VL, p. 109.
26. FC, p. 55
27. SS, p. 33.
28. U.3, 1.
29. DHL.21, p. 724. ("On Being Religious")
30. DHL.8, p. 16.
31. DHL.8, p. 16.
32. U.4, I, iv, 3.
33. U.4, I, iv, 4.
34. KMA, p. 63.
35. KMA, p. 63.
36. KMA, p. 65.
37. WH, n.p.
38. DHL.21, p. 745. ("The Duc de Lauzun")
39. EB, p. 225.
40. DHL.12, p. 90. ("The Crown")
41. A.1, p. 88.
42. A.1, p. 87.
43. DHL.9, p. 25. ("Benjamin Franklin")
44. DHL.9, p. 118. ("Dana's *Two Years Before the Mast*")
45. DHL.9, p. 12. ("The Spirit of Place")
46. DHL.1, p. 379.
47. DHL.1, p. 428.
48. DHL.1, p. 237.
49. GH, p. 32.

50. GH, p. 33.
51. DHL.1, p. 318.
52. DHL.1, p. 327.
53. DHL.1, p. 329.
54. DHL.1, p. 290.
55. DHL.1, p. 387.
56. DHL.1, p. 380.
57. DHL.1, p. 405.
58. DHL.1, p. 494.
59. DHL.21, p. 25. ("Pan in America")
60. DHL.21, p. 26. (*Ibid.*)
61. A.1, p. 90.
62. A.1, p. 90.
63. DHL.9, p. 31. ("Hector St. John de Crèvecoeur")
64. DHL.9, p. 31. (*Ibid.*)
65. DHL.21, p. 219. ("Introduction to the American edition of *New Poems*")
66. DHL.21, p. 7. ("Adolf")
67. DHL.21, p. 16. ("Rex")
68. AL, p. 23.
69. AL, p. 24.
70. DHL.2, p. 9.
71. DHL.2, p. 9.
72. AL, p. 23.
73. AL, p. 22.
74. DHL.21, p. 167. ("Women are so Cocksure")
75. AL, p. 24.
76. AL, p. 25.
77. EB, p. 254.
78. EB, pp. 254–55.
79. AL, p. 25.
80. EN, p. 22.
81. EN, p. 276.
82. NU.2, p. 5.
83. NU.3, n.p.
84. KM, p. 57.
85. DHL.8, p. 24.
86. DHL.8, p. 24.
87. DHL.1, p. 445.
88. DHL.20, p. 944. ("The Lovely Lady")
89. DHL.20, p. 946. (*Ibid.*)
90. WRO, p. 212.
91. DHL.20, p. 955. ("The Lovely Lady")

92. RAT, letter No. 2, n.p.
93. RAT, letter No. 7, n.p.
94. EB, p. 295.
95. DHL.21, p. 794. ("The Flying Fish")
96. DHL.21, p. 795. (*Ibid.*)

NOTES TO CHAPTER 3

1. DHL.16, p. 47.
2. DHL.16, p. 48.
3. DHL.21, p. 193. ("We Need One Another")
4. DHL.21, p. 194. (*Ibid.*)
5. DHL.16, p. 10.
6. CC.1, p. 24.
7. CC.1, p. 27.
8. CC.1, p. 73.
9. GV, p. 171.
10. DHL.21, p. 515. ("Study of Thomas Hardy")
11. MDL, p. 69.
12. CC.1, p. 9.
13. DHL.16, p. 31.
14. DHL.24, p. 201. ("Chastity")
15. DHL.12, p. 122. ("The Novel")
16. DHL.12, p. 122. (*Ibid.*)
17. DHL.21, p. 191. ("We Need One Another")
18. AH, p. 677.
19. DHL.21, p. 531. ("Morality and the Novel")
20. DHL.12, p. 163. (" . . . Love was Once a Little Boy")
21. DHL.21, p. 153. ("Love")
22. DHL.21, p. 156. (*Ibid.*)
23. DHL.16, p. 22.
24. DHL.16, p. 22.
25. DHL.7, p. 309.
26. EV, p. 44.
27. DHL.20, p. 417. ("The Ladybird")
28. DHL.10, p. 281.
29. DHL.7, p. 309.
30. DHL.13, p. 354.
31. JMM.1, p. 84.
32. DHL.12, p. 184. (" . . . Love was Once a Little Boy")
33. JMM.4, p. 28.
34. FT, p. 98.
35. DHL.12, p. 115. ("The Novel")
36. DHL.21, p. 162. ("Making Love to Music")

37. DHL.4, p. 134.
38. DHL.23, p. 257. ("Manifesto")
39. WR, p. 22. ("England," by J. Isaacs)
40. SRH, p. 254. ("Protestant Orientation in Contemporary Poetry," by Amos N. Wilder.)
41. EW, p. 200. ("Sex")
42. DHL.15, p. 102. ("The State of Funk")
43. DHL.17, p. 155.
44. DHL.16, p. 13.
45. DHL.15, p. 99. ("The State of Funk")
46. DHL.16, p. 11.
47. DHL.20, pp. 686–88. ("St. Mawr")
48. RG, p. 157.
49. FT, p. vii. ("Foreword," by T. S. Eliot)
50. FRL, p. 309.
51. DHL.21, p. 531. ("Morality and the Novel")
52. EV, p. 39.
53. DHL.10, p. 188.
54. DHL.21, p. 153. ("Love")
55. DHL.10, p. 188.
56. DHL.10, p. 190.
57. DHL.10, p. 192.
58. DHL.10, p. 194.
59. SB, p. 226.
60. SB, p. 228.
61. SB, p. 233.
62. DHL.18, p. 25.
63. DHL.18, p. 28.
64. DHL.10, p. 146.
65. DHL.10, p. 196.
66. DHL.8, p. 174.
67. JAD, p. 9.
68. DHL.16, pp. 40–42.
69. MRA, p. 34.
70. KMM, p. 38. ("Our Social Heritage," by K. V. Rangaswami Aiyanger)
71. AH, p. 41.
72. FL, p. 22.
73. AH, p. 688.
74. EN, p. 683.
75. DHL.2, p. 318.
76. DHL.2, p. 149.
77. ET, p. 201.

78. DHL.2, p. 285.
79. DHL.2, p. 284.
80. DHL.2, p. 365.
81. SSK, p. 72.
82. DHL.22, p. 546.
83. DHL.22, p. 546.
84. FL, p. 25.
85. DHL.4, p. 158.
86. FL, p. 141.
87. FRL, pp. 96–97.
88. DHL.21, p. 218. ("Introduction to the American edition of *New Poems*")
89. DMH, p. 102.
90. FL, p. 16.
91. MS, p. 50.
92. FRL, p. 111.
93. DHL.3, p. 270.
94. DHL.4, p. 15.
95. DHL.3, p. 22.
96. DHL.3, p. 95.
97. DHL.21, p. 325. ("Review of *A Second Contemporary Verse Anthology*")
98. DHL.3, p. 98.
99. DHL.3, pp. 99–100.
100. DHL.3, p. 102.
101. DHL.8, p. 82.
102. DHL.4, p. 337.
103. DHL.4, p. 21.
104. DHL.4, p. 46.
105. DHL.3, p. 47.
106. DHL.3, p. 49.
107. DHL.3, p. 51.
108. DHL.3, p. 243.
109. DHL.3, p. 54.
110. DHL.3, p. 72.
111. DHL.3, p. 73.
112. DHL.3, p. 84.
113. DHL.3, p. 47.
114. DHL.3, p. 85.
115. DHL.3, p. 85.
116. DHL.3, p. 116.
117. DHL.3, p. 125.
118. DHL.3, p. 241.

119. MSP, p. 98.
120. MSP, p. 98.
121. DHL.4, p. 262.
122. DHL.4, p. 263.
123. DHL.4, p. 507.
124. DHL.8, p. 97.
125. DHL.8, p. 98.
126. DHL.4, p. 507.
127. DHL.3, p. 92.
128. DHL.3, p. 93.
129. DHL.4, p. 330.
130. DHL.4, p. 331.
131. DHL.4, p. 320.
132. U.4, IV, iii, 21.
133. DHL.7, p. 151.
134. DHL.5, p. ix.
135. DHL.7, pp. 154–55.
136. EV, p. 23.
137. EB, p. 276.
138. DHL.20, p. 519. ("The Captain's Doll")
139. DK, p. 284.
140. DHL.7, p. 136.
141. DHL.8, p. 123.
142. DHL.8, p. 123.
143. DHL.8, p. 123.
144. DHL.8, p. 124.
145. MRA, p. 26.
146. MRA, p. 10.
147. AH, p. 299.

NOTES TO CHAPTER 4

1. BR.2, p. 107.
2. TSE.2, p. 59.
3. DHL.9, p. 12. ("The Spirit of Place")
4. LV, p. 81. ("D. H. Lawrence and the Concept of Potentiality")
5. DHL.9, p. 13. ("The Spirit of Place")
6. DHL.9, p. 76. ("Edgar Allan Poe")
7. RPB.2, p. 16.
8. DHL.6, p. 118.
9. DHL.8, p. 120.
10. AH, p. xi.
11. AH, p. xiv.
12. JK.2, p. 14. ("Foreword," by Aldous Huxley)

13. JK.2, p. 17. (*Ibid.*)
14. JK.1, p. 50.
15. JK.3, p. 96.
16. JK.5, p. 6.
17. DHL.7, p. 303.
18. DHL.7, p. 307.
19. JK.4, p. 67.
20. JK.4, p. 67.
21. DHL.21, p. 202. ("The Real Thing")
22. DHL.21, p. 670. ("The Reality of Peace")
23. DHL.21, p. 714. ("Democracy")
24. RPB.1, p. 286 ("D. H. Lawrence and Expressive Form")
25. AH, p. 286.
26. A.1, p. 843.
27. JK.3, p. 68.
28. JK.3, p. 69.
29. KS, p. 98. ("New Light on Temptation, Sin, and Flesh in the New Testament," by Karl G. Kuhn)
30. MB, pp. 290–91.
31. DHL.4, p. 326.
32. DHL.7, p. 305.
33. DHL.21, p. 220. ("Introduction to the American edition of *New Poems*")
34. EWS, Chs. II and VI. ("Biological Goals" and "God")
35. DHL.12, p. 132. ("Him with His Tail in His Mouth")
36. SSK, p. 207.
37. M, p. 91.
38. M, p. 91.
39. JMM.2, p. xiv.
40. M, p. 95.
41. JK.2, p. 129.
42. DHL.13, p. 188.
43. DHL.21, p. 736. ("Thinking about Oneself")
44. SSK, p. 249.
45. NU.4, n.p.
46. DHL.19, p. 90.
47. RR, p. 37.
48. EB, p. 174.
49. EB, p. 174.
50. DHL.15, p. 98. ("The State of Funk")
51. AL, pp. 72–73.
52. DHL.4, p. 158.
53. AH, p. 404.

54. AH, p. 409.
55. AH, p. 426.
56. AH, p. 344.
57. AH, p. 347.
58. AH, p. 361.
59. AH, p. 366.
60. AH, p. 367.
61. AH, p. 371.
62. FRL, p. 173.
63. FRL, p. 174.
64. GH, p. 246.
65. JMM.3, p. 59.
66. DHL.17, p. 75.
67. SR.1, p. 344.
68. DHL.13, p. 283.
69. DHL.21, p. 729. ("On Being Religious")
70. DHL.13, p. 190.
71. DHL.13, p. 209.
72. DHL.13, p. 360.
73. G, IV, 7.
74. U.4, III, ix, 1–2.
75. DHL.2, p. 256.
76. DHL.21, p. 146. ("New Mexico")
77. DHL.20, p. 1105. ("The Man Who Died")
78. DHL.18, p. 98.
79. DHL.25, p. 111. ("Thought")
80. DHL.18, p. 98.
81. CC.2, p. 198.
82. DHL.20, p. 1113. ("The Man Who Died")
83. DHL.20, p. 1113. (Ibid.)
84. DHL.25, p. 112. ("Conceit")
85. DHL.20, p. 1123. ("The Man Who Died")
86. DHL.20, p. 1125. (Ibid.)
87. DHL.20, p. 1135. (Ibid.)
88. DHL.20, p. 1138. (Ibid.)
89. DHL.4, p. 158.
90. DHL.4, p. 158.
91. DHL.20, p. 1138. ("The Man Who Died")
92. DHL.25, p. 132. ("Bodiless God")
93. DHL.25, p. 132. ("The Body of God")
94. DHL.25, p. 143. ("Pax")
95. RA, p. 75.
96. DHL.25, p. 153. ("Anaxagoras")

97. DHL.21, p. 682. ("The Reality of Peace")
98. DHL.4, p. 193.
99. DHL.2, p. 422.
100. DHL.2, p. 423.
101. DHL.3, p. 235.
102. DHL.15, p. 212. ("On Human Destiny")
103. DHL.15, p. 215. (*Ibid.*)
104. DHL.4, p. 55.
105. DHL.4, p. 196.
106. DHL.4, p. 504.
107. DHL.4, p. 505.
108. DHL.4, p. 505.
109. DHL.11, p. 312.
110. DHL.25, p. 172. ("Sleep and Waking")
111. DHL.25, p. 173. ("Tabernacle")
112. DHL.25, p. 169. ("Beware the Unhappy Dead!")
113. DHL.25, p. 114. ("Two Ways of Living and Dying")
114. DHL.25, p. 166. ("The Ship of Death")
115. DHL.25, p. xxxvi. ("Introduction to *Last Poems*," by Richard Aldington)
116. HG, p. 117.
117. DHL.25, p. 181. ("Ship of Death")
118. DHL.25, p. xxxvii. ("Introduction to *Last Poems*," by Richard Aldington)
119. DHL.25, p. 181. ("The Ship of Death")
120. A.2, p. 315.
121. U.5, VIII, xi, 1.
122. U.5, VIII, ix, 2–3.
123. U.6, I, ii, 23.
124. U.3, 7.
125. DHL.13, pp. 188–89.
126. DHL.11, p. 6.
127. LW, p. 345.
128. MF, p. 240.
129. DHL.21, p. 545. ("John Galsworthy")
130. DHL.21, p. 759. ("The Novel and the Feelings")
131. DHL.21, p. 711. ("Democracy")
132. DHL.21, p. 759. ("The Novel and the Feelings")
133. DHL.20, p. 1106. ("The Man Who Died")
134. DHL.4, p. 200.
135. ET, p. 105
136. DHL.15, p. 158. ("Hymns in a Man's Life")
137. DHL.14, pp. 112–14.

138. DHL.18, p. 122.

NOTES TO CHAPTER 5

1. DHL.12, p. 210. ("Reflections on the Death of a Porcupine")
2. DHL.12, p. 211. (*Ibid.*)
3. VSP.1, p. 17.
4. VSP.1, p. 23.
5. DHL.21, p. 396. ("Review of *Art Nonsense and Other Essays* by Eric Gill")
6. EMWT, p. 73.
7. DHL.21, p. 534. ("Why the Novel Matters")
8. DHL.17, pp. 222–24.
9. RE, p. 385.
10. VSP.2, p. 5.
11. L, p. 127.
12. DHL.18, p. 98.

Explanation of Symbols
Used in Notes

A.1 *The Life Divine*, by Sri Aurobindo (New York: Greystone Press, 1949).

A.2 *Letters of Sri Aurobindo*, Third Series (Bombay: Sri Aurobindo Circle, 1949).

AH *The Letters of D. H. Lawrence*, edited and with an introduction by Aldous Huxley (London: Heinemann, 1932).

AL *Early Life of D. H. Lawrence*, together with hitherto unpublished letters and articles, by Ada Lawrence and G. Stuart Gelder (London: Martin Secker, 1932).

BR.1 *D. H. Lawrence's Letters to Bertrand Russell*, edited by Harry T. Moore (New York: Gotham Book Mart, 1948).

BR.2 *Portraits from Memory*, and Other Essays, by Bertrand Russell, (First published, 1956. This edition: Readers Union. London: Allen & Unwin, 1958).

CC.1 *The Savage Pilgrimage: a narrative of D. H. Lawrence*, by Catherine Carswell (London: Chatto & Windus, 1932).

CC.2 *Lying Awake*, An Unfinished Autobiography and Other Posthumous Papers, by Catherine Carswell, edited and with an introduction by John Carswell (London: Secker & Warburg, 1950).

CW "Existential Criticism," by Colin Wilson (*Chicago Review* 12, no.2, Summer 1959).

DHL.1 *The White Peacock*, by D. H. Lawrence (London: Heinemann, 1911).

DHL.2 *Sons and Lovers*, by D. H. Lawrence (London: Duckworth, 1913).

DHL.3 *The Rainbow*, by D. H. Lawrence (London: Methuen, 1915).

DHL.4 *Women in Love*, by D. H. Lawrence (First published, 1920. This edition: London: Martin Secker, 1921).

DHL.5 *Women in Love*, by D. H. Lawrence, with a foreword by the author (New York: Modern Library edition, 1920).

DHL.6 *Psychoanalysis and the Unconscious*, by D. H. Lawrence (New York: Thomas Seltzer, 1921).

DHL.7 *Aaron's Rod*, by D. H. Lawrence (London: Martin Secker, 1922).

DHL.8 *Fantasia of the Unconscious*, by D. H. Lawrence (First published, 1922. This edition: London: Martin Secker, New Adelphi Library, 1931).

DHL.9   *Studies in Classic American Literature,* by D. H. Lawrence (First published, 1923. This edition: London: Heinemann, 1924).

DHL.10 *Kangaroo,* by D. H. Lawrence (London: Martin Secker, 1923).

DHL.11 *The Boy in the Bush,* by D. H. Lawrence and M. L. Skinner (London: Martin Secker, 1924).

DHL.12 *Reflections on the Death of a Porcupine,* and Other Essays, by D. H. Lawrence (First published, 1925. This edition: London: Martin Secker, New Adelphi Library, 1934).

DHL.13 *The Plumed Serpent* (Quetzalcoatl), by D. H. Lawrence (London: Martin Secker, 1926).

DHL.14 *Mornings in Mexico,* by D. H. Lawrence (London: Martin Secker, 1927).

DHL.15 *Assorted Articles,* by D. H. Lawrence (London: Martin Secker, 1930).

DHL.16 *Apropos of Lady Chatterley's Lover,* being an essay extended from "My Skirmish with Jolly Roger," by D. H. Lawrence (London: Mandrake Press, 1930).

DHL.17 *Apocalypse,* by D. H. Lawrence, with an introduction by Richard Aldington (First published, 1931. This edition: London: Martin Secker, 1932).

DHL.18 *Etruscan Places,* by D. H. Lawrence (London: Martin Secker, 1932).

DHL.19 *The Plays of D. H. Lawrence* (London: Martin Secker, 1933).

DHL.20 *The Tales of D. H. Lawrence* (London: Martin Secker, 1934).

DHL.21 *Phoenix,* The Posthumous Papers of D. H. Lawrence, edited with an introduction by Edward D. McDonald (London: Heinemann, 1936).

DHL.22 *The Married Man,* by D. H. Lawrence (*The Virginia Quarterly Review* 16, no. 4, Autumn 1940).

DHL.23 *The Complete Poems of D. H. Lawrence,* Vol. I (London: Heinemann, 1957).

DHL.24 *The Complete Poems of D. H. Lawrence,* Vol. II (London: Heinemann, 1957).

DHL.25 *The Complete Poems of D. H. Lawrence,* Vol. III (London: Heinemann, 1957).

DK   *Three Traditions of Moral Thought,* by Dorothea Krook (Cambridge: University Press, 1959).

DMH   *Some Studies in the Modern Novel,* by Dorothy M. Hoare (London: Chatto & Windus, 1938).

EB   *D. H. Lawrence, Reminiscences and Correspondence,* by Earl and Achsah Brewster (London: Martin Secker, 1934).

EMWT *Some Mythical Elements in English Literature,* being the Clark
      Lectures 1959–60, by E. M. W. Tillyard (London: Chatto &
      Windus, 1961) .

EN   *D. H. Lawrence: A Composite Biography,* Vol. III, 1929–1930,
      gathered, arranged, and edited by Edward Nehls (Madison:
      The University of Wisconsin Press, 1959) .

ET   *D. H. Lawrence, A Personal Record,* by "E.T." (London: Cape,
      1935) .

EV   *D. H. Lawrence, The Failure and the Triumph of Art,* by Eliseo
      Vivas (Evanston: Northwestern University Press, 1960) .

EW   *A Piece of My Mind, Reflections at Sixty,* by Edmund Wilson
      (New York: Farrar, Straus & Cudahy, 1956) .

EWS   *The Biology of the Spirit,* by Edmund W. Sinnott (London:
      Gollancz, 1956) .

FC   *D. H. Lawrence and the Body Mystical,* by Frederick Carter
      (London: Denis Archer, 1932) .

FL   *Not I, But the Wind . . . ,* by Frieda Lawrence (London:
      Heinemann, 1935) .

FRL   *D. H. Lawrence, Novelist,* by F. R. Leavis (London: Chatto &
      Windus, 1955) .

FT   *D. H. Lawrence and Human Existence,* by Father William
      Tiverton, with a foreword by T. S. Eliot (London: Rockliff,
      1951) .

G   *Bhagavadgita.*

GH   *The Dark Sun,* by Graham Hough (London: Duckworth, 1957) .

GV   *Morals and Man,* by Gerald Vann, O. P. (First published, as
      Morals Makyth Man, 1937. This edition: revised and with addi-
      tions: London: Fontana Books, 1960) .

HG   *Pilgrim of the Apocalypse,* A Critical Study of D. H. Lawrence,
      by Horace Gregory (London: Martin Secker, 1934) .

JAD   *Priapic Divinities and Phallic Rites,* by J. A. Dulaure (Paris:
      Isidore Liseux, 1890) .

JK.1 *Authentic Reports of Talks given by J. Krishnamurti,* Being the
      substance of the Discussions at Sarobia and the report of eight
      Talks at the Oak Grove, Ojai, during 1940, revised by J. Krish-
      namurti (Ojai, California: Krishnamurti Writings Inc., n.d.)

JK.2 *The First and Last Freedom,* by J. Krishnamurti, with a
      foreword by Aldous Huxley (London: Gollancz, 1954) .

JK.3 *Commentaries on Living,* From the Notebooks of J. Krish-
      namurti, edited by D. Rajagopal (London: Gollancz, 1957).

JK.4 *Commentaries on Living,* Second Series, From the Notebooks
      of J. Krishnamurti, edited by D. Rajagopal (London: Gollancz,
      1959) .

JK.5   *A Conversation with J. Krishnamurti,* by C. L. Nahal (New Delhi: Arya Book Depot, 1965).

JMM.1   *Reminiscences of D. H. Lawrence,* by John Middleton Murry (London: Cape, 1933).

JMM.2   *D. H. Lawrence: Son of Woman,* with a new introduction, by John Middleton Murry (London: Cape, 1954).

JMM.3   "The Living Dead—I: D. H. Lawrence," by John Middleton Murry (*The London Magazine* 3, no. 5, May 1956).

JMM.4   *Love, Freedom and Society,* by John Middleton Murry (London: Cape, 1957).

KM   *Love against Hate,* by Karl Menninger, with the collaboration of Jeanetta L. Menninger (London: Allen & Unwin, 1942).

KMA   "D. H. Lawrence and Blanche Jennings," by Kenneth and Miriam Allott (*A Review of English Literature* 1, no. 3, July 1960).

KMM   *Indian Inheritance,* Vol. III, Science and Society, edited by K. M. Munshi and N. Chandrasekhara Aiyer (Bombay: Bharatiya Vidya Bhavan, 1956).

KS   *The Scrolls and the New Testament,* edited by Krister Stendahl (London: SCM Press, 1958).

L   *Lorca,* introduced and edited by J. L. Gili (London: Penguin Books, 1960).

LV   *A Philosophy of Potentiality,* by Leon Vivante (London: Routledge & Kegan Paul, 1955).

LW   "Common Ground on 'Good'," by Leo R. Ward (*Papers of the Michigan Academy of Science, Arts and Letters,* Vol. XXXIV 1948. Michigan: University of Michigan Press, 1950).

M   *An Introduction to Metaphysics,* by Martin Heidegger, translated by Ralph Manheim (New Haven: Yale University Press, 1959).

MB   *More Light on the Dead Sea Scrolls,* by Millar Burrows (London: Secker & Warburg, 1958).

MDL   *Lorenzo in Taos,* by Mabel Dodge Luhan (New York: Alfred Knopf, 1932).

MH   *The Essentials of Indian Philosophy,* by M. Hiriyanna (London: Allen & Unwin, 1949).

MF   *D. H. Lawrence—A Basic Study of His Ideas,* by Mary Freeman (Gainesville: University of Florida Press, 1955).

MRA   *Kama Kala,* Some Notes on the Philosophic Basis of Hindu Erotic Sculpture, by Mulk Raj Anand (Geneva: Nagel Publishers, 1958).

MS   "I Will Send Address: New Letters of D. H. Lawrence," by Mark Schorer (*The London Magazine* 3, no. 2, February 1956).

MSP   *The Love Ethic of D. H. Lawrence,* by Mark Spilka (First published 1955. This edition: London: Dennis Dobson, 1958).

NPW   *The Ideas of the Fall and of Original Sin*, by N. P. Williams (London: Longman, 1929).

NU.1   The Statement of T. S. Eliot for the Lady Chatterley Trial, prepared but not delivered. Copy corrected by Eliot in his autograph in the Lawrence Collection, University Library, Nottingham.

NU.2   "That Women know Best," by D. H. Lawrence. Unpublished Essay. Original in University Library, University of California, Microfilm Copy in the Manuscripts Department, University Library, Nottingham.

NU.3   Letter from Frieda Lawrence to Prof. V. de Sola Pinto, dated January 30, 1953. Original in the Manuscripts Department, University Library, Nottingham.

NU.4   Unpublished letter from D. H. Lawrence to Miss E. Tietjens, dated July 27, 1917. Original in Newberry Library, Chicago, U.S.A. Copy in the Manuscripts Department, University Library, Nottingham.

RA   *Portrait of a Genius, But* . . . , The Life of D. H. Lawrence, 1885–1930, by Richard Aldington (London: Heinemann, 1950).

RAT   *Eight Letters by D. H. Lawrence to Rachel Annand Taylor*, with a Foreword by Majl Ewing (California: Pasadena, 1956).

RE   "Lawrence and his Demon," by Richard Ellman (*New Mexico Quarterly* 22, Winter 1952).

RG   *The Crowning Privilege*, by Robert Graves (First published, 1955. This edition: London: Penguin Books, 1959).

RPB.1   *Language as Gesture*, by R. P. Blackmur (London: Allen & Unwin, 1954).

RPB.2   *Anni Mirabiles*, 1921–1925, Reason in the Madness of Letters, by R. P. Blackmur (Washington: The Library of Congress, 1956).

RR   *Brave Men*, A Study of D. H. Lawrence and Simone Weil, by Richard Rees (London: Gollancz, 1958).

SB   *The Second Sex*, by Simone de Beauvoir, translated and edited by H. M. Parshley (London: Cape, 1953).

SR.1   *Eastern Religions and Western Thought*, by S. Radhakrishnan (London: Oxford University Press, 1939).

SR.2   *East and West*, Some Reflections, by S. Radhakrishnan (London: Allen & Unwin, 1955).

SRH   *Spiritual Problems in Contemporary Literature*, edited by Stanley R. Hopper (First published, 1952. This edition: New York: Harper Torchbooks, 1957).

SS   *Aitareyopanisad*, edited with notes, by Swami Sharvananda (Madras: Sri Ramakrishna Math, 1944).

SSK   *Koteliansky Papers*, Letters by D. H. Lawrence to S. S. Koteliansky, Vol. I (London: British Museum, Manuscript No. 48,966).

TSE.1   *Selected Essays*, by T. S. Eliot (London: Faber and Faber, 1932).

TSE.2   *After Strange Gods*, A Primer of Modern Heresy, by T. S. Eliot (London: Faber and Faber, 1934).

TSE.3   *The Classics and the Man of Letters*, by T. S. Eliot (London: Oxford University Press, 1942).

TSE.4   *Notes towards the Definition of Culture*, by T. S. Eliot (London: Faber and Faber, 1948).

TSE.5   *The Elder Statesman*, by T. S. Eliot (London: Faber and Faber, 1959).

U.1   *Taittiriya Upanishad.*

U.2   *Mundaka Upanishad.*

U.3   *Mandukya Upanishad.*

U.4   *Brhadaranyaka Upanishad.*

U.5   *Chhandogya Upanishad.*

U.6   *Katha Upanishad.*

V   *Rig Veda.*

VL   *The Mystical Theology of the Eastern Church*, by Vladimir Lossky (First published in Paris, 1944. English translation: London: James Clark & Co., 1957).

VSP.1   *D. H. Lawrence, Prophet of the Midlands*, by V. de S. Pinto (Nottingham: Sands & Son, 1951).

VSP.2   "Poet without a Mask," by V. de S. Pinto (*The Critical Quarterly*, Spring 1961).

WH   Manuscript Notes of William Hopkin (Mrs. O. L. Hopkin, 165 Nottingham Road, Eastwood, England).

WR   *Contemporary Movements in European Literature*, edited by William Rose and J. Isaacs (London: Routledge and Sons, 1928).

WRO   *A Bibliography of D. H. Lawrence*, by Warren Roberts (London: Rupert Hart-Davis, 1963).

Z   *The Zohar*, Vol. I, translated by Harry Sperling and Maurice Simon, with an introduction by Dr. J. Abelson (London: Soncino Press, 1949).

Indexes

2 INDEX OF
D. H. LAWRENCE'S VIEWS

Dead, The, 239 ("they cling on to the living")

Death, 167–68, 169 ("shan't have any need to despair"), 215, 228, 237–38, 247 ("pure oblivion"), 255 ("a joy of submitting to that which is greater than the known"). *See also* Oblivion, Sleep

Divinity, 266

Duality, 230

Ego, 100, 187, 264 ("My individualism is really an illusion")

Eternity, 202

Etruscans, 123 ("ease, naturalness")

Faked Feelings, 254 ("The world is all gummy with them")

Fate, 160, 173, 175 ("These promptings"), 207. *See also* Providence

"Father," 228–29

Father-quick, 86 ("the most intrinsic quick of all")

Fidelity, 96 ("something more important than love!")

First Cause, 53 ("is just unknowable")

Flux, 75 ("tell me of nothing changeless or eternal"), 76 ("mutation in blossom"). *See also* Change

Fourth Dimension, 260 ("not to be reckoned in terms of space and time")

Frazer, James, 44 ("have been reading")

Free love, 139, 157

Goals, 100 ("the realm of calm delight"), 197 ("Gaols, they are"), 203 ("All goals become graves")

God, 105 ("your soul inside is your only god-head"), 196 ("the very words rivet us down"), 197 ("no God outside you"), 219, 220 ("we shall never know!"), 222, 223 ("without an intermediary or mediator"), 235 ("no god/apart from poppies and the flying fish"), 241 ("My idea of Him is my own"), 244 ("deeper forgetting far than sleep"), 256, 257 ("no Great Mind directing the universe"), 261 ("depends what you make of the word"); as mystery, 171 ("never seeking in the least to define what He was"); as Person, 59, 211 ("but not a personal God"); as physical fulfillment, 165

Good and evil, 57 ("resistance to the life principle"), 58 ("Both exist")

Gothic, 123

Greeks, 123

Harvesting, 72 ("summer's splendid monuments of wheat and grass")

Heaven, 260 ("the fourth dimension")

Holy Ghost, 105 ("Tree of Life"), 190 ("which we may not deny"), 221

Hope, 229

Human Destiny, 241 ("the light of human God-knowledge")

Immortality, 58 ("undaunted suffering and undaunted enjoyment, both")

Indian civilization: Ajanta frescoes, 183 ("I loved them"), 184 ("no Will to Power here"); Gandhi's Ashram, 209 ("He is right"); Gandhi spinning-wheel, 209 ("is transmitting life to others"); Hindus, 19 ("horribly decadent"), 179; Hindus and Fate, 179 ("the Hindus were right"); Hindu thought, 20 ("That seems to me the true psychology"); Om, 52 ("a noise and a shape"), 53 "All I say is Om!"); Shiva, 32 ("have always worshipped Shiva"); Tagore, 19 ("this wretched